110 Strategies
for Success in
College and Life

by

Joan H. Rollins, Ph.D.
and Mary Zahm, Ph.D.

Bloomington, IN Milton Keynes, UK
authorHOUSE

AuthorHouse™
1663 Liberty Drive, Suite 200
Bloomington, IN 47403
www.authorhouse.com
Phone: 1-800-839-8640

AuthorHouse™ UK Ltd.
500 Avebury Boulevard
Central Milton Keynes, MK9 2BE
www.authorhouse.co.uk
Phone: 08001974150

The case examples used to illustrate success strategies in this book are authentic. However, the names of the people mentioned in them and identifying details have been changed to protect their privacy.

First published by AuthorHouse 2/6/2006

ISBN: 1-4184-4634-3

Library of Congress Control Number: 2004092562

Printed in the United States of America
Bloomington, Indiana

This book is printed on acid-free paper.

Acknowledgments

We want to express our sincere gratitude to our wonderful friends, family members, colleagues, and students who generously gave us permission to write about their life experiences and to include their pictures.

We want to thank Dr. Lorraine B. Dennis, Professor Emerita of Roger Williams University, for reviewing and commenting on drafts of our manuscript and Kenneth A. Zahm for his technical assistance in preparing the manuscript for publication.

We also want to thank Bristol Community College for giving us permission to use the cover photo.

This book is dedicated to our students who inspired us to write it.

About the Book

Many colleges and universities use high Scholastic Aptitude Test (SAT) scores as a criterion for college entrance. Yet, *Joan H. Rollins, Ph.D.* and *Mary Zahm, Ph.D.*, have found that high Scholastic Aptitude Test (SAT) scores alone do not guarantee high Grade Point Averages (GPA) and college graduation. They have also seen many students who have low SAT scores successfully complete college by using the holistic strategies outlined in this book.

This book presents 110 strategies for success in college and in life that are derived from psychological research that has been published in scholarly journals and books. First and foremost, the authors were inspired to write this book to provide students with proven strategies that can increase their effectiveness and efficiency as learners, test takers, and writers. The book shows students how to gain self-insight, identify and achieve goals, think critically, make decisions, prioritize in order to make the most of their precious resources of time and money, and utilize their strengths and remediate their weaknesses. In each chapter, you will read about students who successfully used the strategies outlined to achieve balanced lives as well as honors in their college careers. Since learning does not take place in a vacuum, students are provided with the "rules of the game" for navigating through the regulations common to most colleges and universities.

110 Strategies for Success in College and Life is a must read for the entering freshmen, whether coming right out of high school or after a hiatus due to years working and/or taking care of a family. It is especially appropriate for minority and first generation college students who may have fewer mentors to help them along the college path. Ideally, the beginning college student would read this book during the summer before starting college or during the freshman year of college to learn how to get the most benefit from his or her college experience right from the start and would refer to relevant parts of it throughout college.

Primarily, this book teaches you to become *proactive*. A proactive person is one who intentionally and consciously plans and acts in advance to effectively deal with an expected difficulty or anticipated life challenge, rather than passively reacting to the behaviors of other people and to life events. A proactive, successful person is one who has the self-insight, information processing, critical thinking, self-management, and social skills needed to make self-affirming decisions. A proactive, successful person also has the ability to control his or her own behaviors, moods, and environment in order to reduce stress and increase his or her pleasure and life satisfaction.

How can a proactive, successful person know in advance what difficulties she or he might encounter in college or what actions will be effective to achieve success? Many people experience common problems and challenges in college. Researchers, including us, have experimentally studied many of these problems and challenges and have identified certain beliefs, attitudes, habits, strategies, and techniques that enable people to achieve their optimal level of academic success. The empirically derived success strategies and recommendations in each chapter of this book are based on the results of the most recent, relevant psychological and educational research. Therefore, the authors know that you can achieve success in college by learning and following them.

Overview of Contents

Chapter One is designed to prepare students for college both motivationally and in terms of learning the "rules" of college so that they will have smoother sailing the whole way. It helps point the way for minority and non-traditional students to seek the resources available to them and reminds all students of the value of meeting with their advisor to help chart their course. It advises students to follow the operating procedures of the college or university. These include following the code of conduct of the college, learning your degree requirements, and not disappearing, but instead officially withdrawing from a class you decide to drop.

Chapter Two reveals to students that research has shown that time management may be a better predictor of their grade point average than their SAT scores. It provides students with step-by-step instructions in how to structure their time by prioritizing according to their values, and breaking down their goals into specific sub-goals. Students are instructed to have a flexible plan, avoid procrastination by rewarding themselves after a study session, and take advantage of their most productive times by tapping into their circadian rhythm.

Chapter Three focuses on the benefits of students learning about themselves and developing positive self-esteem, self-efficacy, and emotional intelligence during their college career. It explains the latest research on personality theory and includes some self-administered personality tests in order to help students gain self-insight and select a college major. Students are encouraged to choose life roles that enable them to express their authentic personality and suit their desired lifestyle.

Chapter Four cuts through the confusion in the literature on learning styles. It encourages students to identify their own learning style and to even analyze that of their professor in order to be able to work more effectively. Further, students are shown the experimental research that indicates which learning styles lead to more efficient processing of information.

Chapter Five is probably the key chapter in the book because it provides students with the experimental research findings on learning and memory and shows them how to apply this research by integrating it into their own study habits. It describes the importance of self-regulation, self-efficacy, surface and deep learning, mastery and performance learning, chunking and mnemonic devices, repetition, and meta-cognitive strategies for achieving exam success.

Chapter Six focuses on active learning. Students are warned not to be passive vessels waiting to be filled with knowledge, but to play an active role in their own learning. They are instructed to carefully read their syllabus and follow it, attend class, ask questions, and organize notes. They are taught how to write with the "Hamburger" method of essay construction, how to revise their writing, how to plan their search for information for a term paper, and how to overcome test anxiety and learn to take tests successfully.

Chapter Seven focuses on strategies to help students learn to be critical and creative thinkers as well as effective decision-makers and problem solvers. They are warned about the pitfalls of common systematic mental biases or distortions in thinking that researchers have identified such as anchoring, sunk costs, negative stereotypes, and self-handicapping. Students are encouraged to learn to brainstorm, gather and evaluate evidence, and to rely on logical reasoning processes when making judgments in order to make effective decisions that better facilitate goal achievement. This chapter also teaches students how to develop proactive coping strategies for dealing with anticipated life challenges and stress.

Chapter Eight focuses on strategies for exploring, setting, and achieving personally meaningful life goals. It informs students about research demonstrating the need for setting goals based on their highest life priorities and directing their time, energy, and money toward achieving them. It provides self-assessment tools for identifying their highest priority educational, career and personal life goals and outlines strategies for making these goals manageable, believable, and achievable.

Chapter Nine warns students that a college diploma is not enough to guarantee that they will get a high paying professional job after graduation. It informs them of skills and experiences researchers have identified that are valued by employers such as computer literacy, information management skills, leadership skills, and job related work experience. It explains how students can develop these skills and gain these experiences through taking selected courses, holding college leadership positions, and participating in service-learning or internships in order to become more marketable to employers. It discusses the value of building a mentoring network and outlines practical strategies for demonstrating proof of these skills and experiences to potential employers by constructing a resume and a job portfolio.

Table of Contents

CHAPTER SIX ATTEND CLASS, READ AND WRITE EFFECTIVELY, OVERCOME TEST ANXIETY, AND ACE YOUR EXAMS 109

CHAPTER SEVEN IMPROVE YOUR CREATIVITY, CRITICAL THINKING, AND DECISION MAKING SKILLS 137

Illustrations

Figures

Tables

Chapter One
Learn the Rules of the Game in College

Most college and university admissions offices select college freshmen based on their high school Grade Point Averages (GPAs) and standardized test scores such as the Scholastic Aptitude Test (SAT), which measure intellectual achievement and cognitive (mental) factors including math and verbal academic potential. So, one might expect that the students who had high school GPAs and SAT scores that were adequate to get them accepted into a college would have no trouble being successful and earning their college degree. Nevertheless, many students who begin college fail to graduate.

The low and decreasing validity of the Scholastic Aptitude Test (SAT) has been documented particularly for an increasingly heterogeneous college population. "College enrollment increased 62% for students of color between 1988 and 1998...." (American Psychological Association, 2003, p. 379). In a nationally representative sample (N = 10,080), SAT scores were found to "overpredict" grades of males, Asians, Hispanics and Blacks, and "underpredict" grades for females and Whites (Lynn & Mau, 2001). Overpredicting means that students do not do as well as expected based on their SAT scores, whereas underpredicting means that students get better grades than would be expected based on their SAT scores. In a sample of Mexican-American students, SAT scores did not predict either completion of college or grades (Gandara & Lopez, 1998). At the University of Hawaii, among students graduating from Hawaiian secondary schools, SAT scores had a low and decreasing validity. Although students graduating from Hawaiian high schools had higher SAT scores than the national average, their college grades were lower than the national average (Wainer, Saka, & Donoghue, 1993).

More recent graduation rates for students at "four-year" baccalaureate colleges and universities across the United States reveal that low graduation rate is an increasing problem. Only 51% of college students graduated from baccalaureate institutions within five years of initial enrollment. When comparing graduation rates of public and private colleges and universities, a difference was found. Fewer students at public universities had graduated within five years than at private universities (41.2% and 55.5%, respectively) (ACT, Inc., 2002). Graduation rates for students attending community colleges are also low. Only 56% of students attending two-year community colleges in the 1995–1996 academic year graduated within three years (Higher Education and National Affairs American Council on Education (HENA), 2002). The drop out rate is costly in terms of personal lives, the college's spending financial aid and other resources on students who do not graduate, and society's loss of benefit from a trained citizenry. Why do students who have adequate high school GPAs and SAT scores at the time of acceptance into college drop out? A body of research has been emerging in recent years reporting certain psychological factors or cognitive skills and behavior patterns not measured by intelligence tests to be correlated with Grade Point Average (GPA) of college students. We call these psychological, cognitive, and behavioral skills that are found to be associated with success in college, "strategies." They include managing one's time effectively, using one's mental abilities efficiently, and having emotional self-regulation skills. The purpose of this book is to describe these strategies that have been derived from research in psychology and education that have been demonstrated to improve college student performance.

If you desire to become a successful college student, we know that you can do it. The first step toward achieving your goal of success in college is to learn effective coping strategies for building on your personal strengths and minimizing the adverse impact of your limitations. Additionally, you will achieve success by your continual efforts to develop your unique talents and to reach your full potential over the course of your college career and your life. Another important step toward achieving success in college is to develop your basic academic skills such as reading, writing, public speaking, and mathematics, which are required for success in general education college courses and in many careers.

Don't be too concerned at this point if you do not know how to assess your skills, talents, or your personal strengths and limitations. We help you assess how prepared you feel you are for the rigors of college work and offer guidance about how you can ensure your success in college. Read on! In *110 Strategies for Success in College and Life* we tell you how to acquire the skills you need and how to use them.

Discover the Potential Benefits of Your College Education

Congratulations on your decision to pursue a college degree! You have made a life changing decision that will positively influence your life as well as the lives of your family members. What are some of the major benefits that you expect to attain from your college experience? How do your answers compare to those of other college freshmen?

Researchers have found that students entering college may have very different expectations about how their college experience will benefit them. Since 1965, researchers at the University of California at Los Angeles (UCLA), in association with the American Council on Education, have asked entering college freshmen to indicate the reasons they enrolled in college. The results of the survey conducted in the fall of 2000 suggest that many students enroll in college primarily to increase their standard of living. Approximately three-fourths of the students reported that they are going to college "to be able to get a better job" and "to be able to make more money." Slightly fewer (62 percent) of the students reported that they enrolled in college "to gain a general education and appreciation of ideas" (Sax, Astin, Korn, & Mahoney, 2000). Were the reasons you had for enrolling in college similar to or different from those of the freshmen sampled by UCLA?

As you begin college, you may not be aware of all of the potential benefits of your college education. What are some additional benefits, which you may not have thought of, that you can expect to attain from your college education if you apply yourself to your fullest potential?

First and foremost, you are positioning yourself to be successful in college and life by becoming a lifelong learner. You will learn basic academic skills such as how to think critically, learn effectively, and express yourself clearly as well as the subject material being presented. Possessing these skills and knowledge will enable you to become a leader in your family, career, and community as well as a positive role model for others. People will seek your advice and will respect your educated opinions and judgments.

A second important benefit of having a college education is that it will increase the quality of your intellectual life. As you master your required general education college courses—such as those in philosophy, psychology, sociology, science, history, literature, music, and art—you will gain a deeper understanding and appreciation of your own cultural heritage as well as that of others in our global village. You will be exposed to novel ideas and experiences and will be challenged to develop your own philosophy of life or system of values by which you will live.

A third important benefit of having a college education is that it will increase the quality of your work life and your career opportunities. You will have more freedom in making career decisions than a high school graduate. Once you master advanced specialized courses in your college major or selected field of academic study for a specific degree program, you will have gained the required expertise to pursue a career in your chosen field or to go on for further professional education.

A fourth important benefit of having a college education is that it will increase the quality of your life and your income. In general, men and women who graduate from two- and four-year college programs earn higher salaries.

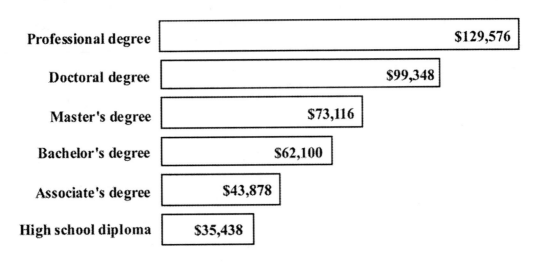

Figure 1.
Mean Total Money Earnings in 2003 for
Full-Time Workers 25 Years or Older

Source: U.S. Census Bureau, Current Population Survey, 2004 Annual Social and Economic
Supplement, as reported by the U.S. Census Bureau (2004). Retrieved July 16, 2005, from
http://pubdb3.census.gov/macro/032004/perinc/new03_010.htm

As the data from the U.S. Census Bureau (2004) in the Figure above reveal, a degree can make quite a difference in one's average annual earnings and the average earnings one can expect over one's working life. For example, the average (mean) annual earnings of full-time American workers 25 years or older who are high school graduates ($35,438) was $26,662 less than the average earnings for workers with bachelor's degrees ($62,100). If we multiply this wage gap by 40 years of employment, we can estimate that the high school graduate would earn approximately $1.1 million dollars less than the college graduate over his or her working life. These data clearly show that by earning a bachelor's degree you will have a positive impact on your financial future.

Focus on Your "Vision for Your Success" and Have a Step by Step Plan to Stay on Course

Success in college will not happen by luck or by accident. It facilitates your academic achievement to have life goals, which are the purposes toward which your efforts are directed or the objectives you intend to accomplish. You also need a life plan, a detailed outline of the steps that you must complete to achieve your goals. Your plan not only helps you remain mentally focused on the steps you need to complete, but also is a visual tool that enables you to chart your progress toward achieving your goals. However, many entering freshmen are explorers who do not know what they hope to accomplish in college. Rather, they hope to discover areas of knowledge that they love to study and find meaningful work in a related field. If you are an explorer, the best way to start defining your life goals is to focus your attention on creating your future life vision depicting what you and your life will be like when you graduate from college.

Start to define your vision for your success by reflecting about how you and your life will be different when you graduate from college and record your answers in a success journal or notebook for future reference. Develop the habit of updating or refining your future life vision any time during your college career and your life. Understanding and visualizing the key components of your future life will provide an incentive that motivates or impels you to take action and work to turn your vision into your reality. In later chapters we provide success recommendations to help you develop a step-by-step plan for achieving the success goals implied in your vision for your future.

In a diary study investigating the uses of visualization as a cognitive tool for effective living (Kosslyn, Seger, Pani, & Hillger, 1990), people reported using visualization techniques for such diverse activities as problem solving (e.g., forming cognitive maps for navigation purposes), mental practice (e.g., forming an image of a swimming stroke), memory improvement (e.g., trying to remember a name by forming an image of someone's face), and emotional or motivational inducement (e.g., using imagery to induce a relaxed state under stress). Likewise, you can use meditation, creative visualization, and reflection techniques to plan your future life vision, privately rehearse and refine new behaviors associated with achieving all of your desired goals before performing them in public, and generate creative solutions for the roadblocks you encounter in your life.

When you use meditation, creative visualization, and reflection together regularly, you will be better able to create a clear, integrated, and self-affirming life vision and identify the college, relationship, career, and personal goals that will lead you to living it. It is important that you achieve a clear, integrated, and self-affirming future life vision before attempting to implement any of your future life plans. Doing so will help you avoid the problems that people typically experience when they impulsively make a desired life change, such as taking a job they don't like because it has a high salary or making a geographic move for a new job, without first assessing how it will impact other aspects of their personal and professional lives. Using meditation, creative visualization, and reflection regularly to reevaluate your future life vision will also help you to anticipate, identify, proactively prepare for, and be in a position to meet life challenges and to capitalize upon new opportunities in our fast-paced and changing world. Once you can picture your future life vision and goals clearly in your mind, you will be able to start turning the future life of your dreams into your reality. Creating your future life vision, however, does not guarantee change. It must be followed by choice and decision making about your goals, making plans for achieving your goals, and execution of your plans.

Do not be concerned if you think that you do not know how to meditate or use creative visualization techniques. There is really no right or wrong way to meditate. It is more important for you to develop a reflective style that feels natural to you and to make sure you meditate on a daily basis than it is to follow a particular ritual. Most of us practice some form of meditation and creative visualization when we daydream. You probably already do know how to use these techniques, but are not consciously aware of the exact steps you use in the process. Use meditation and visualization techniques to begin to create a vision of your future by following the steps outlined below. Then you can modify them to suit yourself. You will learn to become proficient in using these techniques as you practice them.

- To begin creating a vision of your future life, get into a relaxed, meditative state. You can either lie down or sit in a comfortable position with your back straight and your feet touching the floor.

- Starting with your feet and moving upward, tense and relax every part of your body, in turn, while breathing deeply. Quiet your mind to achieve a mental state in which you can think clearly about your future life vision. Many people find that the easiest way to quiet their mind is to focus on their breathing. As stray thoughts enter your mind during meditation sessions, gently release them (by mentally putting them in an imaginary bubble and letting them float away with your breath as you exhale, for example) and return your attention to your breathing. If you recall hurtful things that happened in your past, say a short prayer or affirmation indicating that you now release the person who has hurt you from punishment by you without condoning their behavior. Refocus your attention on your future life.

- Next, imagine yourself living the part of your future life upon which you are currently focusing your attention. You may find it helpful to pretend that you are watching a movie of yourself, the star of your life, enacting your future life movie script when using creative visualization (Zahm, 1996). You can visualize yourself achieving one of your important life goals or enacting a particular role in your future life script and reflect on the result of achieving it. Doing so will help you verify that achieving your goal will really enable you to live the future life you desire.

- As you identify areas in the imaginary preview footage that do not seem to suit you, mentally stop the movie and edit the film until the scene truly captures the essence of your future life dreams. Continue to preview and edit the important scenes in your future life movie again and again until they seem perfectly comfortable and very real to you.

- During subsequent meditation and creative visualization sessions, mentally picture and evaluate each essential area of your future life movie, in turn, in order to create a clear, coherent, and self-affirming future life vision. Try to make the vision as vivid as possible by using as many senses as you can. If you are imagining that you are walking at the beach, for example, hear the ocean waves and the seagulls, feel the damp sand under your feet, and smell the salt air.

- You can also use visualization and reflection to privately rehearse and fine tune new behaviors mentally—including interactions with members of your family, a professor, or a boss—before performing them in real life situations. Privately rehearsing and evaluating different possible scenarios for upcoming situations in which you will be interacting with others will also help you determine the outcomes with which you would feel most comfortable. Gaining insight about what you want to happen will help you chose your actions in real life situations.

- After each creative visualization session, reflect on it, and capture the new ideas and insights you gain about your future life vision in your success journal. This information will be very useful to you when you are defining your detailed professional and personal life goals.

- If desired, you can put pictures and text that remind you of your future life vision in your success journal or create a collage depicting them to help you visualize the life of your dreams more clearly.

You can also use experiential exercises during your meditation and creative visualization sessions to help you gain self-insight about your talents and interests that you might like to use in your future life career. For example, imagine that you are very old (over 90). Pretend that you are watching a movie of yourself sharing the highlights of your career achievements with your family and friends. As they ask you what work role you perceive to be the most significant one of your lifetime, what will you say? Will you say that it was achieving a career role, such as becoming a doctor, politician, lawyer, teacher, writer, dancer, or athlete? Then, ask yourself if you desire to perform that career role at some point during your life. If yes, ask yourself when you might like to do that and what small step you could do right now to start planning to turn that future life dream into your reality. Record in your success journal insights gained about your future life career goal while performing these experiential exercises for future reference.

Maybe you have low self-efficacy concerning a college major for which you are suited that was formerly a nontraditional gender role stereotyped "masculine" or "feminine" area. You may think that a specific career might be inappropriate for you to pursue because you have not challenged your old beliefs. Perhaps you might have deficits or low self-efficacy in areas such as writing or mathematics because you had unrewarding experiences in these areas in high school but you can learn to master these skills in college. Keep an open mind as you explore new areas of interest in college. You may discover new talents that you may not realize you have. If you have developed a habit of restricting your major and career options in the past, try to expand your vision of your future life by imagining yourself satisfactorily performing some type of work that you feel you would truly find challenging and would love doing during your meditation and visualization sessions.

Determine How Prepared You Believe You Are to Succeed in College

Researchers are finding that many entering freshmen, especially community college and continuing education students, have some basic academic skill areas in which they possess great or moderate strength and others in which they have some areas of weakness. According to Wes Habley, director of the ACT, Inc. Office for the Enhancement of Educational Practices:

> About two-thirds of high school graduates now go directly to higher education, but some of them aren't prepared—whether academically, financially or socially—to succeed. Unless they're offered and take advantage of course-placement recommendations and participate in developmental courses and other support services, they can quickly find themselves in over their heads. (ACT, Inc., 2001).

Based on these research reports about the under-preparedness of students and declining graduation rates, we encourage students to honestly assess their own skills. If you are like most entering students, you probably have some basic academic skill areas in which you could use some tutoring and others in which you might only require some fine-tuning.

If you feel that you may have deficits in your basic academic skills that will make it difficult for you to be successful in entry-level college courses, be proactive and advocate for yourself to make sure you get the support you need to be successful in college. Ask your academic advisor assigned by the college if you need to take developmental courses or ask your professors about the availability of free tutoring services. Once you identify any skill deficits, you can overcome them and be successful in college, as many students have done. The story of 24-year-old Madeline, a community college student, is a good example.

After one of her early general psychology classes, Madeline told her professor that she feared that she might have a difficult time achieving an "A" in her course. She explained that she never graduated from high school and thought she might have deficits in her basic academic skills and general education. Madeline said that she "had blown high school off because she didn't see the value of it" and asked advice about getting extra help with the class work. Madeline had dropped out of high school and was now a single mother working at a low paying job. She said that she was starting college after earning her high school equivalency certificate. Madeline emphasized that she intended to succeed in college because she didn't want her son to see her working for a fast-food restaurant all her life. She wanted to earn a college degree so that she could have a higher paying and more satisfying career and, thereby, improve their lives. Madeline received the tutoring help she needed and earned her "A" in the general psychology course. She went on to earn an Associate's degree.

Decide if You Will Attend College on a Full-Time or Part-Time Basis

If you are just starting college, you may be surprised to learn that each course you take will probably require approximately three hours of class attendance per week and three to six hours of preparation and homework to earn an excellent grade, depending on the course requirements. Do you have enough time to devote to full-time studies or is attending part-time more appropriate for you at this time? Do you have other work and family responsibilities that will limit your time for school? How can you make a decision?

First, check with the financial aid officer on your campus who can tell you about any grants, scholarships, or other sources of financial assistance that you are eligible to receive to help pay for your college expenses. You might be eligible to receive money for tuition, books, or room and board if you live on campus. If you are eligible, you can work fewer hours and focus more of your time on your schoolwork.

Assess the available time you have for taking college courses and doing homework assignments. Take only the classes for which you realistically have time to perform well. Don't make the same mistake that Sophia, a community college student, made. Sophia insisted on enrolling in six courses against the advice of her academic advisor even though she was a single parent with several minor children, was working outside the home part-time, and was an international student still learning English. Needless to say, Sophia only completed a few of her courses with passing grades and ended up on academic probation. It is a smarter strategy for students with time constraints to attend college part-time and perform well in each class rather than to try to rush through a full load of courses and end with a low college Grade Point Average (GPA).

We all know many busy people who manage to balance a wide array of activities and perform each one of them very well. Jack, a college student featured in the Success Profile in this chapter, is one such busy person who has a passion for learning about and working with computers. He balances his academic and paid work obligations exceptionally well. If you focus on your goals and manage your work and study time efficiently, like Jack, you will find that you can succeed in college as well as meet your family and work obligations.

Success Profile—Jack

Jack is a 24-year-old junior and computer science major at a four-year college. When Jack was five years old, his mother was taking an introductory computer science course at the local community college. Jack became fascinated watching her write a simple computer program as a homework assignment. Because of his interest, his mother bought him some computer games such as PAC Man™ and learning programs such as Math Busters™. Jack loved playing on the computer. Jack did well in elementary school and high school, earning a Regents diploma in upstate New York where he lived. Following high school he enrolled in a community college, attending full time while also working 20 hours per week, first at a pizza restaurant, then on campus as a tutor for computer science courses and at the campus video store. Jack graduated in two years, receiving an A.S. (Associate of Science) degree in math and science. He returned to the community college the following fall, completing a second associate's degree in computer science.

After receiving his two associate's degrees, Jack got a full-time job as a software engineer in a big company where he worked for ten months. During that time he met a girlfriend who wanted to move to Rhode Island to be closer to her father. He quit his job and moved to Rhode Island where he got a job for a computer applications developer. After working there for 13 months, the company restructured and laid-off a number of people, including Jack. Last summer his girlfriend, who was very homesick, went back to her family in New York. Jack decided to stay in Rhode Island because of the availability of many cultural activities such as concerts in the area. Jack enrolled as a full-time college student majoring in computer science. On campus, Jack works 20 hours per week as a computer trouble-shooter for faculty and staff as part of the Information Services. Although he lives off campus, Jack arrives on campus by 8 a.m. every morning and spends the day in classes, studying, and working. Jack's guidelines for being a successful student are:

- Develop self-discipline.
- Go to every class.
- Take notes in every class.
- Review the previous week's notes every weekend.
- When a test is coming up review all the notes.
- Begin a term paper on the day it is assigned.
- Complete a project at least a week before it is due.
- Don't be afraid to help other students, you learn by teaching.
- Organize a study group of students from your class, and ask each other questions, and take turns teaching each other.

Jack plans to go on for a master's degree in computer science after graduation.

Seek Advice about
College Courses You Should Take

Are you wondering which college courses you should take, when you should take them, and how many you can successfully handle at once? Does the college catalog look like a confusing array of options? Don't worry, you do not have to figure it out all by yourself. Entering students are assigned an academic advisor who will help them select appropriate courses and decide on a tentative plan of study that fits into their life schedule.

Most professors at our colleges have had student advisees who never made an appointment to see their advisor during their entire college career. Some students wait to see their advisor for the first time when they are placed on probation for having a failing Grade Point Average (GPA) and they are required to schedule a meeting. Don't let that happen to you. Make an appointment with your advisor at least once a semester and more often, if needed, to get the guidance and support you need to be successful.

In order to benefit from your meeting with your advisor, be prepared. Bring a copy of your high school transcript and any previous college transcripts with you, if possible, so that your advisor can see what courses you have already taken and which ones you still need to take in order to complete your requirements. What should you be prepared to discuss? How can your advisor help you? Ask him or her any questions you have about the general education requirements at your college and the specific requirements for your college major if you have already decided on one. Make sure you have a file on your computer or a notebook in which you keep track of your progress in meeting these requirements, so that at any point in time you can see what courses you have completed and still need to complete in order to graduate.

Discuss with your advisor any deficits or conditions that might impede your ability to be successful in college so that he or she can help you create a well-balanced academic plan that makes sense for you. These deficits or conditions might include deficits in your basic academic skills, work and family responsibilities that will limit the time you have for college work, and physical or learning disabilities. For example, if you are a slow reader or have limited time to devote to reading, you will not want to take too many courses with a very heavy reading load in one semester. Likewise, if you feel that you may have to struggle in your math course, leave plenty of time for homework assignments. Discuss your interests, preferred programs of study, and areas of special expertise with your advisor so that she or he can help you select suitable courses as well as a tentative plan of study for your college career. Your tentative plan will act as a guide suggesting when to take sequences of courses as well as courses that are only offered in the fall or spring semesters or in alternate years. Many students who do not visit their advisors regularly do not graduate on time because they are unaware of the schedule for the classes they need for graduation. You can always consult with your advisor and revise your plan later when you get a better idea of the college major you desire to choose.

Photo courtesy of Bristol Community College.

Participate in a Learning Community

Research conducted for over 25 years by Alexander Astin (1993) has consistently found that students who were involved on campus (students who were full-time, participated in campus clubs and organizations, lived on campus, worked on campus, and had more frequent interactions with faculty and others) were more likely to graduate from college than others. Colleges and universities are beginning to discover the value of structuring learning communities for first-year students, of establishing peer mentoring, peer tutoring, and reciprocal teaching programs for improving the students' satisfaction, achievement, and retention.

Learning communities, in which students who live in the same college residences and also take the same classes, are being established at a number of colleges and universities. At a large Midwestern university, 626 first-year students completed questionnaires about their college experiences (Pike, 1999). Students in the formal residential learning communities had gains in learning and intellectual development in comparison with residents in traditional college residences. Students in the residential learning communities also had significantly higher levels of involvement, interaction, and integration within the university.

At the Fourteenth International Conference on The First-Year Experience that was held in conjunction with the Fifth Pacific Rim First Year in Higher Education Conference in Honolulu,

Hawaii in 2001, papers and presentations by faculty and staff from colleges and universities in different places in the world reported that one of the factors contributing to first-year student success was the social integration of students into the school. For example, Susan Bens and Jana Danielson (2001) of the University of Saskatchewan presented a summary of their first-year experience program that included having "peer coaches," upperclassmen who lead seminars, and learning about the academic and campus environment. First-year students, who had been randomly selected to participate in the program, were not only more satisfied with their interactions with upper year students and professors but also had higher grades than the control group.

Linda was part of a living and learning community for nursing students during her freshman year at Northeastern University in Boston. She found that it worked very well because all of the students living in the residence had the same heavy course load and schedule, so they were all serious about studying for exams at the same time. The student nurses also formed small study groups to help one another, shared resources such as computer equipment and information, and formed close friendships. As an upper-class student, Linda shared off-campus housing with a few of these student nurses. Linda graduated with honors, as did many of the other students in her original learning community. She was offered and accepted a job at a hospital in which she had been trained as a student.

Colleges, universities, and community colleges also have learning communities for commuter students. These learning communities involve linked classes in which the professors teaching the classes link them together with a common theme and shared assignments. Students are encouraged to join study groups and form friendships with their peers and professors. Learning communities for commuter students are taught at Bristol Community College and many students have benefited from participating in them. For example, a general psychology course was linked with an English writing course, with a learning community theme of the impact of the media on our lives. This learning community worked well because students shared assignments for both classes. Students were learning how to conduct a psychological literature review on an aspect of how the media impacts our lives in the psychology course and learning how to write a formal report of it in the English course. The shared assignments of these learning communities decrease the students' workload without reducing their opportunities for learning or the course requirements. Participate in learning communities if they are offered at your college in order to streamline your workload and gain more opportunities for interaction with peers who share your interests and your professors.

Know Your Degree Requirements.
Document Your Progress

Most two- and four-year college programs require the beginning student like you to take general education courses, in which you will master basic academic skills needed for success in your professional life as well as the general knowledge needed to become an educated citizen of the world. For example, general education programs typically include required or elective options such as courses in:

- Literature;

- Mathematics;
- Science (e.g., astronomy, biology, environmental science);
- Social sciences (e.g., history, geography);
- Behavioral sciences (e.g., psychology, sociology); and
- Humanities (e.g., philosophy, art, music).

When you select a college major and gain acceptance into a specific program, you must take the required courses in the major field and may also have to take specific courses in other departments. To earn a college degree, you must complete all the requirements for your major, as of the day you were accepted into the program, and complete the number of credit hours your college or university requires for graduation with an acceptable GPA. If you complete the requirements for graduation in a two-year community college degree program (at Bristol Community College it is 60 credit hours), you will earn an Associate's Degree. If you complete the requirements for graduation at a four-year college or university degree program (at Rhode Island College it is 120 credit hours), you will earn a Bachelor's Degree. The same process applies to post-Baccalaureate graduate programs from which one can earn a Master's or Doctor's Degree, with the additional requirements of a comprehensive examination and a thesis in most master's programs and all doctoral programs.

As you can probably see, it is very important that you become familiar with the requirements for your particular degree program of study as of the day you were accepted into it and make sure you complete all of the degree requirements. Don't rely on your advisor or anyone else to keep track of your progress. Every year professors hear stories from disappointed students who thought they were ready to graduate but found, to their dismay, that they need to take one or more additional courses. For example, Byron, a community college student, said that his former academic advisor told him that he could substitute an elective for an Education Program requirement, but his new advisor would not accept the switch because he didn't have a signed statement to that effect from his former advisor. Consequently, Byron had to spend valuable time during his last semester filing and defending appeals to the Program Coordinator (faculty or staff person in charge of the administration of a specific college degree program) and the Academic Dean (administrator in charge of all the college's degree programs). Since he didn't have written proof to document the approved change, Byron had to take the required course during the summer and received his degree in August instead of May.

A surprising number of students accumulate many more credits than they need for graduation (some with as many as 145 or 150 credits when typically only 120 credits are needed for graduation from a 4-year college), but they still lack either the courses in their selected college major or general education requirements that they need for graduation. Some of these students have never met with an advisor. We would advise them to ask the college's Records Office to give them an "audit," a list of courses they must complete in order to graduate, then to take only those courses. Many would be able to get promotions or better jobs with their degree. Then they can return to take courses that interest them for personal development and life enrichment.

Avoid disappointment at graduation time by taking responsibility for knowing your degree requirements outlined in the catalog the year you were accepted into the program and making sure you fulfill them. If your advisor, or the department chair, gives you a variance in your degree program, make sure that the appropriate forms are completed and signed by the advisor or department chair and filed with the records office (also called Registrar's office at some schools).

Understand and Follow Your College's Code of Conduct

When registering for college, students are given a college catalog containing both descriptions of the programs of study offered and a student handbook containing the code of conduct that all students must follow in order to remain enrolled. Be sure to read the student handbook section outlining the code of conduct and make sure you understand and follow the rules of the college at all times. These rules of conduct, which help maintain civility on campus and in the surrounding community, concern topics such as:

- attendance policies and regulations (e.g., maximum number of missed classes allowed);
- plagiarism of written work (i.e., not citing sources in essays and research papers);
- cheating on tests;
- hate crimes, such as rude and derogatory comments and discriminatory actions towards members of minority groups;
- if, when, and where one can use alcoholic beverages on campus;
- sale or use of illegal drugs on campus;
- fighting on or off campus;
- use of obscene language;
- sexual assault;
- sexual harassment; and
- stalking.

College is not like grade 13 of high school. No one may inform you of the college's rules or remind you of the need to follow them. Even if no one points out the rules of your college to you, you are still bound to abide by them as well as the laws of the local community. Amazing as it may seem, there have been newspaper reports of students who were expelled from college for violating local community laws and/or college regulations. For example, three nationally known members of a popular basketball team attending a private college in our area were recently expelled for participating in a fight at a local bar ("Three Providence players are expelled for fighting," 2000). At another prominent university, a student was suspended for lying to a professor about why he was absent from class (Arenson, 2000).

Don't let your wonderful dreams of success in college disintegrate into thin air by being expelled or suspended from college for violating either the rules of conduct of your college or the local laws of the community. If you feel that your personal rights are being violated, report the situation to your campus police or in the case of sexual harassment, to the Affirmative Action Officer immediately.

Don't Fade into the Sunset;
Get Help or Officially Withdraw

Many college students get into trouble because they either do not understand or forget to abide by the class attendance rules and regulations of their college and their professors. For example, we have noticed that some students just stop coming to a class after they receive a disappointing grade on their first test and simply fade into the sunset in hopes of avoiding failure. When they get their grades at the end of the semester, they are shocked to see that they received an "F" because they never officially withdrew from the course.

If a student stops coming to class and doesn't officially withdraw from the course, many colleges require the professor to assign a grade of "F" to the student's permanent record. Some colleges allow the student to appeal the "F" grade, but it is much easier to officially withdraw from a class than to get involved in the time consuming and frustrating petition process. In contrast, some colleges require that a student be dropped from the course by the professor after a certain number of cuts (three or six) which may include coming to class late. Other colleges require the professor to keep the student enrolled until either he or she officially withdraws or the semester ends. Some colleges allow the professor to determine his or her attendance and drop policies. Students who are dropped from classes might also find that their health insurance is dropped since they are no longer enrolled full-time.

Be on the safe side. Come to class a few minutes ahead of time so that you are present when attendance is taken. Understand and follow the attendance and grading policies of your college and each of your professors. If you are having problems attending classes or completing assignments, contact your professor or advisor and ask for help or advice. Don't be like Denise who didn't visit her advisor until she flunked out.

Denise had flunked out of at the end of spring semester. She said that she had been put on academic probation at the end of first semester because she had failed her courses. Denise said she failed because she had "mono" (mononucleosis). Denise enrolled in four courses for spring semester because she was feeling better. She continued to have health problems, however, and was unable some days to get out of bed. She failed all of her courses.

Denise had a letter from her doctor describing her health problems. Her advisor asked her if she had spoken to any of her professors about the health problems she was having. She said "No". Her advisor said that she should have spoken with her professors, shown them a letter from her doctor, and asked them if she could have a grade of Incomplete in the courses.

Under the rules of her college, Denise could have until the end of the following semester to make up the Incomplete grade, and up to the discretion of the professor even longer, if the student has a legitimate reason. Her advisor said that she believed that most if not all of her professors would have given Denise Incomplete grades and she would not have flunked out of college. Her advisor told Denise that all was not lost, however, and that she could still take courses at the college as a non-matriculated student. She could take one or two courses a semester. If at the end of 18 credits she had a C or better average, she could reapply to be a degree candidate.

If you are having health or personal problems that prevent you from attending class or doing the assignments, speak to your professors about it. If you can't come in person, call or e-mail your professor. Most professors have voice mail and e-mail so that you can leave a message and your home phone number and they will contact you. Explain that you are having health problems. Offer to bring in a note from your doctor. Ask if you can have a longer time to complete your work. Make sure you understand the exact procedure for requesting the Incomplete, the date by which your work must be completed, and exactly what you need to do to complete the course requirements.

Read your college catalog and student handbook. Make sure that you understand the requirements for completing your specific college program as well as the civility, attendance, and grading policies of the college.

Are You a Minority or First Generation College Student? If So, Be Successful through Finding Mentors, Focusing on Your Goals, and Using College Resources

If you are a minority student (a student who is also a member of a recognized minority group such as African-American, American-Indian, Mexican-American/Hispanic) or if your parents did not attend college, you may need to seek encouragement and institutional support to ensure your success in college. Why?

In American society some young people from minority groups such as African American and Hispanic still face many problems—urban decay, racism, poor schools, lack of economic opportunities, teenage pregnancy, drugs and violence—are some of the most prevalent. Their parents may not have had an opportunity to attend college and, therefore, may not know how to help them to succeed. Having been the beneficiaries of White privilege, we don't presume to have the answers for Black or Hispanic youth. But, we can look to research focusing on the insights of those who have had to face discrimination in achieving educational success for strategies to recommend.

For example, advice gleaned from in depth interviews with 15 successful African-American women university students can be summarized in the following statements (Lorentz, Maton, & Greene, 2001).

> Everybody has the potential to be successful. Just find somebody that's going to push you. Find somebody that cares about how you do academically, socially, everything. And, if your parents can't give it to you, find somebody that will. (p. 4).

> Think of the immediate steps to get to your goal, and think of the long term steps. Focus on that long-term goal versus what is happening here now. Persevere, you may be struggling here now, but stay focused on your long-term goal, and you will eventually reach it. There may be a party now, it may be rough now, but just stick with it. Work hard for it, and you will eventually achieve your long term goal. (p. 4).

When questioned about the lack of success of some of their peers, these successful African American women students cited reasons such as

> ...letting other things such as popularity distract one from goals, getting pregnant and having to raise a child, not keeping up with schoolwork because of a dating relationship, and lack of effort, motivation and purpose. (p. 4).

A qualitative study of high-achieving African American males reported on the importance of parental-determined academic engagement, both discipline and nurturance in the home, and community connectedness. The results of this study suggests that these family and formal community influences could counteract some of the negative influences of neighborhood peers, poor schools, and society (Maton, Hrabowski, & Grief, 1998).

The research summarized above suggests that some students from minority groups thrive with encouragement and support from parents and mentors. Do minority students and their parents value education? Do parents of minority students encourage them to excel in school? A survey of a diverse sample of high school students in nine different high schools found that African American and Hispanic students and their parents are just as likely to value education as other students and parents (Steinberg, Dornbusch, & Brown, 1992). "Yet on average, African-American and Hispanic youth devote less time to homework, perceive their parents as having lower performance standards, and are less likely to believe that academic success comes from working hard" (p. 726).

What strategies are most useful for helping at-risk minority college students succeed? Researchers have found that the best predictor of college GPA for the at-risk students was willingness to seek assistance from tutors or reading teachers (Nelson, 1994). We encourage *all* students who have reading difficulty or are struggling with writing or a specific course to seek help from the tutoring or writing centers at their college or university for that purpose. If English is not your first language, get information about your college's English as Second Language (ESL) Program and join it.

Photo courtesy of Bristol Community College.

Both academically at-risk and high-ability African-American and Mexican- American/ Hispanic undergraduates who were successful in their college programs were also found to be more receptive to career counseling than unsuccessful students were (Nelson, 1994). We encourage *all* students to find a career counselor or mentor who is willing to encourage and advise them about possible paths to follow for achieving their educational and career goals. The results of the research summarized in this section imply that it is particularly important for minority students, who are more likely to be first generation college students, to find a mentor to encourage and advise them. Many colleges have a Mentoring Program specifically designed for providing support and advice to students who are members of a minority group or for first generation college students. Look in your college's catalog to see if there is one on your college campus. If there is one, join it to make sure you get the support and encouragement and skills training you need to be successful and to have an opportunity to make friends with other students. If there is not a program, seek out someone on campus such as your advisor or a favorite professor who seems willing and able to act as a mentor for you.

Are You a Slightly Older Student?
If So, Investigate the Programs at Your College
Designed to Help You

Are you a non-traditional aged student preparing to enroll in college or have you recently done so? Today, there is a growing diversity among students in age, gender, social class, ethnicity, and previous educational and life experiences as well as physical and intellectual abilities in many private and public colleges and universities. During the past several decades, there have been a growing number of college students in the United States over 25 years of age. Many of them attend part-time (National Center for Education Statistics (NCES), 1998). The majority of these older students are striving to balance college work with demanding family and/or work roles.

Why are so many adults attending college? The increased numbers of adult students entering higher education in the United States can be attributed, in part, to cultural changes, including: changing family and work roles; rapid technological growth resulting in more job opportunities requiring advanced education; desire for personal growth; and increased leisure (Entwistle, 1983). Some people already in the workforce seek retraining for different careers or new roles in current careers. For others, college is a dream delayed until children have entered school, or preparation for a new or different career necessitated by divorce, disability, or death of a spouse (Waskal & Owens, 1991).

How are colleges meeting the needs of adult learners? Many two-year community colleges and four-year colleges and universities have designed certificate programs to help people gain proficiency in specific job related skills, such as computer networking, multimedia design, culinary arts, child care, or medical records management without having to pursue a college degree. These programs are designed to attract adult learners who desire to gain new work skills or update their present skills. Some of these students are already working in their field and may or may not have a college degree, whereas others are not currently working and may never have attended college previously. Many community colleges, colleges, and universities have also instituted open admissions policies for continuing education students, which means that no specific high school GPA or test scores are required for admission. Now adults, who may not have graduated from high school in good standing, can enroll in several general education courses and prove that they can perform well in college by doing so. Some community colleges have even instituted a forgiveness policy. This forgiveness policy allows adults who dropped or flunked out of college in the past to return and prove that they are now more mature students. If successful, their earlier failing grades are purged from their college GPA and they can continue to work toward their college degree with a "clean slate."

How are colleges changing to meet the educational needs of adult learners with deficits in basic academic skills? Since many entering traditional aged and adult students do not possess all of the requisite skills to ensure success in college, many continuing education programs at community colleges, colleges, and universities are now providing developmental academic programs that help under prepared students gain the required background for college level courses. Many colleges also provide free tutoring services to help under prepared learners of all ages acquire the basic academic skills needed to become successful performers in college. Help is usually available for improving writing, test taking, study, and computer skills in tutoring centers or computer labs. At many colleges, free tutoring is also available for specific courses.

How well do older adult students fare in college? Some entering adult students are well prepared for success in college and may already have earned a degree. Others may not possess all of the requisite basic academic skills and general education background to ensure their success in college. Compared to their under prepared traditional counterparts, however, many older learners have better self-management skills as well as more life experiences that they can use to write about or help them relate to and interpret their course material. Consequently, they often perform very well.

Earn Course Credit for Relevant Educational or Life Experiences

Some college and continuing education programs allow students to earn course credits for their previous educational achievements and life experiences. For example, students in transition to college directly from high school may take advanced placement tests, if they have successfully completed advanced placement courses in high school. If they score at or above the level required by their particular college, they are allowed to enroll in more advanced courses in that area.

Continuing education students may also be awarded college credit for previous education, such as training in practical or registered nursing. Another way students have earned college credit is by passing a test, such as the College Entrance Level Examination Program (CLEP). CLEP exams, which are given in place of taking specific courses, are constructed by the College Board in Princeton, New Jersey and administered at the student's college or university or one in the area. By gaining college credit for educational experiences and by passing some CLEP exams, some students are able to start college as a junior. Another advantage of taking CLEP exams is that the cost for taking the exam is usually much less than that of taking a college course. CLEP exams do not count in a student's GPA because they are taken on a pass/fail basis, but the credits count toward graduation. Before you take a CLEP exam, however, check with the appropriate office at your college or university to find out how many, if any, CLEP credits will be accepted, which CLEP exams will be accepted, and which courses they replace.

In a growing number of colleges, students can earn college credit by preparing an academic portfolio. An academic portfolio documents how one's previous life or work experiences allowed him or her to gain proficiency in the basic academic skills that would have been gained in specific college courses for which credit is being sought. With this option, students enroll in a special course in which they are instructed about how to prepare their portfolio in order to be successful in getting the desired course credits at their college or university.

These are all good ways for beginning continuing education students with proficiency in basic academic skills or specific knowledge and skill areas to get a head start toward completing their degree. Not only does this save time, but it also can save a student a considerable amount of money.

Ask your college program advisor to give you more information about the specific options your college offers for students to get college credits for knowledge and life experiences. As with college entrance tests, you can pay to take review courses for many tests you may be asked to take throughout your college career and you can get books containing practice test that will help you prepare for many of these tests at most general book stores.

Success Recommendations

This section contains a summary of the main points in this chapter to help you reflect on and recall what you have learned.

- **Discover How You Expect College to Benefit You.** As you begin your college career, think about the major benefits that you anticipate gaining from your college experiences. Then think about the many other potential benefits discussed that you may not have thought about before.

- **Create "Your Vision for Your Success."** Think and write about your future self and future life as you desire them to be when you graduate from college. Be as specific as possible at this early point in your college career. Doing so will help you visualize your dreams and goals more clearly and you will be more motivated to make your future life vision your reality.

- **Assess Your Basic Academic Skills. Get Needed Tutoring Help.** Consider whether you have the requisite skills you need to successfully complete specific courses before selecting them. If you are not sure how to proceed, ask your advisor or a professor who teaches a specific course that interests you to help you decide.

- **Determine How Much Time You Have for College Courses and Homework.** Identify the days and amounts of time that you have available for attending college courses and completing homework assignments. Use your answers as a guide when deciding whether to attend full- or part-time and when selecting your courses.

- **Seek Advice before Selecting Courses.** Make an appointment with the advisor assigned to you to introduce yourself and to ask how you can best prepare for selecting your program of study and courses. Develop the habit of consulting with your advisor and asking for advice about which college courses you should take, how many at a time, and in what order.

- **Participate in a Learning Community.** Join a learning community consisting of linked courses with the same students enrolled in them if these are offered at your college. Doing so will help you to streamline your workload and gain more opportunities for interaction and support from peers and professors.

- **Know Your Degree Requirements.** Document Your Progress. Become familiar with the requirements for your particular degree program of study as of the day you were accepted into it and make sure you complete all of the degree requirements. Take responsibility for documenting your progress and keeping track of any variances approved by your advisor.

- **Understand and Follow the Code of Attendance and Conduct.** Review the policies for student attendance and conduct or civility in your college catalog and student handbook. Make sure that you understand and follow all of the rules of attendance and conduct detailed in it as well as the local laws of the community in which your college is located. Nothing will sabotage your success in college as much as being suspended or expelled from school for conduct violations.

- **Don't Fade Into the Sunset.** If you want to drop a class for any reason, speak with your professor about it. Then, make sure you officially withdraw from the class so that you are not assigned a failing grade for it. If you are a full-time student, first check with the financial aid officer on your campus to make sure that dropping the course won't jeopardize any financial aid you may be receiving or your health insurance. Also check with the financial office to see if you are eligible for a rebate if it is early enough in the semester.

- **If You are a Minority or a First Generation College Student, Be Successful through Finding Mentors, Goal Setting, Hard Work, and Using Institutional Resources.** If you are a member of a minority group or a first generation college student, be sure to get the help and support you need from your college. Seek assistance from reading teachers or subject area and writing tutors whenever you feel you need to do so. Find out where to get the help you need. Get involved in college groups and activities so that you have a chance to meet people and develop a feeling of connection with your professors and classmates.

- **If You are a Slightly Older Student, Investigate Programs at Your College Designed to Help You.** Most community colleges, colleges, and universities have special programs designed to enable non-traditional and continuing education college students to achieve their educational goals and earn a college degree. Investigate the programs at your college and take advantage of the ones you need.

- **Seek Advice about Getting College Credit for Life Experiences.** If you feel that you have areas of strength in basic academic skills or work experiences for which you could get course credit, ask your academic advisor about the options and procedures for accomplishing that at your college.

Chapter Two
Manage Your Time, Energy, and Money Wisely

Perhaps the most important skill you can learn for college and life is mastering your time, energy, and resources effectively. To succeed in college, you must learn to organize your time into daily, weekly, and semester time blocks and use your energy to your best advantage. Money worries detract from college performance as does working at a meaningless job in order to pay credit card bills. How can one balance the multiple demands of college, work, family, and friends as well as have some time for solitude and rest? Psychological researchers have identified attitudes and skills that impact how we can balance it all at any given point in time. Success strategies and recommendations that can be gleaned from the results of their research that will help you identify and achieve your goals for college and in life are in this chapter.

Believe that You Can Succeed through Your Own Efforts and by Using the Appropriate Study Skills to Gain Mastery in Your Course Material

Since recent research that was cited in Chapter One has revealed that having a high IQ or high SAT scores are not sufficient for college achievement, what other psychological factors are also necessary? An important component of the Academic Self-Regulation Scale (See Chapter 5, Table 4) (Rollins Zahm, Merenda & Burkholder, 2002) which correlates with GPA is hard work. This finding was not surprising to us, in view of the work of Carol Dweck and others describing the differences in academic achievement between *Entity theorists* and *Incrementalists* (Hong, Chiu, Dweck, Lin, & Wan, 1999). Students who are Entity theorists believe that intelligence is a fixed trait and tend not to perform as well at academic tasks, particularly after negative feedback. In comparison students who are Incrementalists believe that high grades in school demonstrate hard work and tend to try harder after negative feedback. The Entity theorists think that if they were smart enough to perform a specific task it would be easy for them to do it. So they quit before accomplishing goals that are difficult. In contrast, students who are Incrementalists are willing to put in the amount of time and effort required because they believe they can accomplish their goals through hard work.

Dweck and Leggett (1988) suggested that Entity and Incremental theorists have different sources of self-esteem: Entity theorists derive self-esteem from proving that their ability level is adequate, whereas incremental theorists derive self-esteem from working hard and mastering challenging tasks. Do college students change their self-view as a result of their academic experience? What is the impact of holding the Entity or Incrementalist view on academic achievement and self-esteem?

The stability of college students' implicit self-theory and the impact of subscribing to the Entity or Incrementalist views on actual academic performance, academic behavioral response (helpless or mastery), and self-esteem were assessed in a longitudinal study reported by Robbins and Pals (2002). Academic ability, perceived performance, academic self-confidence, goal orientation (performance or learning), causal attributions for hypothetical and real academic achievement situations, and affective response to academic achievement were also assessed since previous research has found these factors to be moderators of the effects of implicit self-theories. The sample for this longitudinal study included 508 ethnically diverse undergraduate students (56% female) who entered the University of California at Berkeley in 1992. Six assessments were conducted over a four-year period every year from the first week of college through the fourth year of college.

Robbins and Pals (2002) reported that their findings were consistent with the predictions of the theory. Specifically, entity theorists show a maladaptive helpless-oriented response to academic challenge. They strive for academic success to prove they have high ability, yet they explain away their successes as due to luck, an uncontrollable factor. Incremental theorists, in contrast, show an adaptive mastery-oriented response, they strive to gain knowledge and they explain their academic performance in terms of internal, controllable factors such as effort and study skills. Incremental theorists believe that they can overcome any failure with hard work and better study strategies. Success is viewed as resulting from hard work rather than luck. Emotionally, entity theorists "...felt more distressed about their academic performance and were less likely to feel determined and inspired, despite performing as well as Incremental theorists. Finally, Entity theorists generally had lower self-esteem than Incremental theorists, and this disparity widened over four-years of college." (p. 329)

What are the implications of this research for you? First, the results of this research show that you will feel better about your chances of succeeding in an academic context if you hold the adaptive self-belief of the Incremental theorist and focus your attention on the process of learning the course material rather than on the performance outcome, your grade. They also show that you must truly believe that you are in control of your academic destiny and that you can succeed in college through your own efforts and by using study skills that are appropriate for the type of course material you are learning and for the type of exam you will take. We discuss how to choose appropriate study strategies for different types of course material and exams in Chapter Six. Second, the results of this research highlight the fact that your self-esteem will increase during your college years if you develop the Incrementalist orientation. You will also gain self-confidence and increase your self-efficacy for completing academic work as you improve your academic skills and successfully learn the required information to complete your entry-level courses.

Schedule Your Time

Research shows that effective time management is a better predictor of student grades than Scholastic Aptitude Test (SAT) scores (Pokay & Blumenfeld, 1990). In one study at the University of Georgia, ninety students completed a self-report questionnaire about their study habits, and four years later their cumulative grade point average (GPA) was obtained from university records (Britton & Tesser, 1991). Two time management components, *Time*

Attitudes and *Short-Range Planning* were significant predictors of students' GPA four years later. These measures were better predictors of GPA than were SAT scores.

Students who scored high on the *Time Attitudes* factor reported that they are able to spend more time studying by saying "No" when people ask them to engage in activities that would interfere with school work, and they give school work a higher priority than grooming. They stop unprofitable activities before wasting too much time on them and they have a greater sense of control over their time. This probably represents a sense of self-efficacy or judgments of one's ability with regard to time management.

According to Britton and Tesser (1991), the *Short-Range Planning* factor was the next best predictor of GPA. Students who score high on short-range planning organize their week and their day. They have a clear idea in advance of what they intend to accomplish during the next day. They write a set of goals, To-Do lists which reflect their priorities, and a schedule for doing the activities for each day. They set priorities that are reflected in their weekly and daily planning lists and honored in the implementation of their plans. One study of time management with 165 college students found that students who perceived that they had control of their time "reported significantly greater evaluations of their performance, greater work and life satisfaction, less role ambiguity, less role overload, and fewer job-induced and somatic tensions" (Hoff-Macan, Sahani, Dipboye, & Phillips, 1990, p. 760).

One approach that has shown success in helping students on academic probation to improve their grades is time management peer counseling, which is counseling conducted by students who have been trained to teach specific college management skills by members of the college's counseling center. A group of freshman on academic probation who were assigned to time-management peer counseling achieved the highest mean GPA of the groups studied at the end of the semester. They were followed by a "rap session" group, a group that was were contacted but did not participate in any intervention, and a group of high-risk students that was not contacted (Bost, 1984).

The results of this research indicate that effective time management is important for success in college. Therefore, we describe the steps for you to take to manage your time effectively in this chapter. Do you need immediate professional help in this area? If your answer is yes, the Counseling Centers at most colleges and universities have peer tutoring or workshops available for teaching time management skills. Check with your college's counseling center to find out if they, or another office on campus, offer some type of training in time management.

Success Profile—Shane

Shane is a tall, 21-year-old African American student who is entering his senior year of college. Shane moved from another state to live with an aunt and her family because he was having difficulty getting along with his father. After graduating from high school, where he was an A/B student, he took a year off to decide what he wanted to do. During that year he spent most of his time hanging out with his friends and around the house. After moving in with his aunt, he attended a community college for two years, graduating with an Associate's degree. Then he transferred to a four-year college, where he is an accounting major.

Shane works full-time, 8 a.m. to 5 p.m. five days per week, in customer service for a computer software company. He also works part-time for another company in customer service from 6 p.m. to 10 p.m. one night a week and on Sundays from 12 p.m. to 5 p.m. Despite these many hours at work Shane is a full-time student taking 12 credits per semester and, at the time of this interview, had a 3.15 grade point average. What is Shane's advice to other students juggling work and school? Shane says that he sets goals every semester in terms of how well he wants to do. As Shane goes into his senior year, he is setting the goal of making the Dean's list for fall semester. Shane said that he carefully plans his time. Because of work, he takes all of his classes in the evening. He said that he goes to every class and pays close attention in class, trying to relate the material covered to what is in the textbook. Although he doesn't always have time to read the text chapters before class, he reads the chapter summaries and skims the text. He studies all day on Saturdays and goes out on Friday and Saturday nights. Shane said it is important to stick to the schedule you have for yourself and to apply yourself.

Shane believes that it is important to hang out with others who share similar values and goals. All of his friends are in college. His girlfriend attends another college where she regularly makes the Dean's list. Shane also has long-term goals. He would like to become a financial analyst and work in that position long enough to save money to open his own business. He would like to open a club. Since he goes to clubs on his nights out, he believes he knows enough about the types of music and other aspects of a club that would make it successful.

Prioritize and Act on Multiple Goals According to Your Values

Do you frequently feel that there is not enough time for you to finish all of your work and have fun too? Slightly older college students who are full- or part-time workers and parents say that there is always too much to do and too little time in which to do it. They want to do it all and to excel at everything. Many say they feel guilty because they don't have much time to spend with their families. Running out of time is also a very common complaint among traditional aged students who find it hard to meet deadlines for assignments, keep up with part-time or full-time jobs, take care of themselves, and still have time for fun with friends.

In *7 Habits of Highly Effective People*, Stephen R. Covey (1989) explains that the most important aspect of effective time management is setting and acting upon goals that reflect one's personal priorities within the time available. He stresses that our personal priorities must be based on universal moral principles governing right action. Covey recommends that we stop responding to unscheduled unimportant emergencies, which he calls the *squeaky wheels* of life, such as habitual last minute requests for a ride during times when one has classes or work scheduled. Instead, he suggests that we develop a habit of focusing our attention and efforts on performing important tasks associated with life goals that help us develop our full potential and lead a balanced and happy life. Covey believes that focusing our attention on achieving our highest priority life goals will motivate us to identify and perform goal-related activities in the following five areas.

- *Prevent problems*—Activities might include taking developmental courses or getting tutoring help if needed, attending class, making sure your car is in good working order so you can get to college and work on time, not driving under the influence of alcohol, and saving money for emergencies.

- *Build satisfying close relationships* —Activities might include maintaining contact and spending quality time with family and friends and developing satisfying romantic relationships as well as communicating with classmates and professors.

- *Learn new skills*—Activities might include taking classes that will allow you to improve your basic skills such as writing, communicating, and using the computer.

- *Look for and act upon new opportunities for ourselves*—Activities might include asking about the availability of work on campus, forming a study group, and taking a leadership position in a college club or activity.

- *Find time for recreation and leisure*—These activities might include making time for activities such as playing sports, going to the theater, and exercising as well as periods of rest and solitude.

Psychological researchers have found that people who effectively manage their time prioritize their goals and schedule time for important life events, tasks, and activities (Covey, 1989; Lakein, 1973; Britton & Tesser, 1991). When you have multiple life goals, therefore, you should prioritize them in terms of the essential beliefs and core values you have chosen to guide you in your life. Prioritizing your goals is an important step in deciding which tasks and activities to schedule to perform at any given point in time (Hoff-Macan et al., 1990; Britton & Tesser, 1991). It is also an important step in monthly, weekly, and daily life planning because it helps you to determine the spacing of and optimal sequence for performing various tasks and activities.

This research on time and life management suggests that the first steps toward achieving success and living a well-balanced life are to identify and prioritize your most cherished values, based on universal moral principles, and the highest priority life goals associated with them, such as becoming an educated person and graduating from college. What are your important core values and highest priority life goals? How does what you do every day lead to achieving your goals? Do you have personal priorities that include goals and tasks in each of the five areas Covey specified? What are they? Take time to define your values, important goals, and activities that support achieving those goals and record them in your success journal for later reference.

Remember to review and revise your priorities and change your life goals as your life circumstances change. For example, you may have decided to attend college part-time because you are working long hours at a job and now find that you can attend college full-time after being awarded financial aid or winning a scholarship. You might be starting a demanding college program that you previously felt was not an option for you but now you have more time to devote to your studies.

Break Complex Tasks into
Manageable Specific Sub-Tasks

Psychological researchers have found that people who accomplish their goals are realistic in their expectations of how much they can accomplish in a given day, week, or semester and have a habit of scheduling time (Covey, 1989; Lakein, 1973; Britton & Tesser, 1991). For example, successful students do not enroll in more courses than they can successfully complete during one semester or work so many hours at a job that they can't complete their course assignments and earn good grades.

Researchers have also found that people who accomplish their goals proactively break large, complex goals and associated tasks into smaller more manageable specific and clearly defined chunks of work or sub-goals and objectives. They also determine the optimal sequence in which these clearly defined smaller chunks of work should be completed and set tentative, flexible deadlines for starting and accomplishing each one. Successful students prioritize their goals according to what is important to them and the due dates by which the work needs to be completed. They plan to accomplish high priority goals and associated tasks before low priority ones (Lakein, 1973; Kirschenbaum et al., 1982; Martin & Osborne, 1989; Britton & Tesser, 1991).

People who accomplish their high priority goals also have developed a habit of reviewing their schedule and their goals frequently to determine if they are using their time in the most effective manner. They continually ask, "What is the best use of my time right now" (Lakein, 1973). They are flexible enough to change their schedule if really needed to perform a newly identified higher priority task or to handle a crisis or emergency. If they find that they can not finish all of their scheduled tasks within the given period of time, they reschedule completion of some of the low-priority, non-essential tasks for some time in the near future. However, people who effectively manage their time do not make a habit of abandoning their schedule lightly or missing important work deadlines to focus on the *squeaky wheels* of life—those low priority tasks and activities that are trying to demand their attention. They take responsibility for controlling their own time by following their schedule in order to achieve their goals. They don't let others set their priorities for them (except in the case of their professors whose assignments have to be their priorities if they want to complete the course). Types of activities that create interference for students include friends coming by their dorm rooms to hang out during planned study time, or for commuting students, habitual last minute requests for transportation to school, work, or doctor's appointments from family members and friends.

Begin scheduling your time for each semester by identifying all of the complex goals you need to accomplish for each course. Once you identify your complex goals for the semester, break each one into smaller sub-goals or manageable chunks of work by defining long-, medium-, and short-term objectives (Locke & Latham, 1990). Then simplify each complex task you need to complete to accomplish that goal as you encounter it. For example, your major goal might be to earn a college degree and completing an economics paper is one of the complex tasks that you must accomplish on your path to achieving that goal. You could break down the goal of completing your paper into the following sub-goals: selecting a topic and preparing an outline; conducting your library research and assembling the reference section; typing a draft of your paper using a computer; and revising your final paper before the date on which it is due to be completed.

Make your progress toward achieving your goals and sub-goals measurable by setting realistic dates by which you can plan to accomplish each of your goals and sub-goals (Locke & Latham, 1990). In the example of completing the research paper discussed above, you might set tentative dates by which you will begin and complete sub-goals such as your library research, your reference section, and typing the paper. Finally, prioritize the order in which your sub-goals need to be completed in order to hand in the paper by the date on which it is due. Periodically, check to make sure that you are completing each of your sub-goals within your specified period of time. Revise the details concerning your plan if needed in order to achieve your goal. You would follow the same procedure for each one of your complex assignments and tasks. You will find that achieving each of your sub-goals will be self-reinforcing and will help you to remain highly motivated.

Follow Shane's lead and mange your time in order to achieve your goals. Create a schedule for each month of the semester that reflects your highest priority goals. Every Sunday check and update your monthly schedules and draw up a schedule of daily activities that support your highest priority goals for each day of the coming week. Schedule the times you will be studying, as well as other times when you will be in class, at work, and engaged in recreational activities such as attending a football game or spending an evening with your boyfriend or girlfriend, partner, or members of your family. Look ahead to see what important college or work deadlines you have for the following month and check to make sure you have scheduled the tasks you need to complete to meet them. Look at your daily schedule each evening before you go to bed, and prepare for the next day by packing the books, assignments, and supplies you'll need for the next day and choosing the clothes you'll wear. If you look at your schedule again each morning, you will know where you have to be and what you will be doing. You will no longer have to make the choice at 2 p.m., for example, when you get out of your last class if you should go to the library to study chemistry or hang out with your friends.

Coordinate your time management schedule with your romantic partner, friends, study partners, work colleagues, and members of your family, as needed, to ensure that your needs, desires, and goals and everyone else's are supported to the greatest possible extent. Ask family and friends to contact you about any favors they plan to ask of you in advance and explain when you have time available for this purpose. Learn to say "no" to the *squeaky wheels* and time wasters that continue to disregard your schedule and drain you of the precious time of your life.

Avoid "burn out" by taking care of yourself and making time for fun. One way to accomplish your health and academic goals and to still have time for your romantic partner and friends is to engage in academic, health and fitness, and other activities with important people in your life. Rather than exercise alone, engage in your daily exercise with a friend, family member or romantic partner. Whether you walk, jog, swim or play racquetball for exercise, make it a time to deepen your relationship with another person through participating in it together. For example, Wendy bought Yoga tapes and has a friend come over a few hours a week to practice Yoga postures with her, following along with the videotape. Be creative and think of ways that you can schedule in time to relax and take care of yourself while having fun with a friend.

Have a Flexible Plan and Reward Yourself for Doing Your Work

Should you reward yourself for performing your schoolwork on schedule? The answer is "Yes," according to a study conducted by Kirschenbaum, Malett, and Humphrey (1982) to determine how different types of planning, scheduling, and rewards for persistence and goal achievement in completing scheduled tasks impact college grades. The participants were 63 freshmen who were enrolled in an 11-week study improvement program during their second semester of college. The students were assigned to one of three types of groups:

- *Specific monthly schedule group*—was taught how to develop specific daily hour-by-hour study schedules, which outlined in detail what, when, and where they would accomplish each assignment.

- *Moderately specific monthly schedule and reward group*—was taught how to develop a moderately specific monthly schedule. They were instructed to identify what needs to be done in their courses over a four-week period and to note when they had time to complete their assignments. For example, a student might indicate that he or she had Monday, Wednesday, or Sunday of the upcoming week to read his or her chemistry assignment and complete the problems in Chapter Two. The students in the group developing the moderately specific monthly schedule were free to do the assignments any time they could during the available days. If they did nothing one day, they had to catch up on their work on the remaining two days. There was a weekly reward for completing all study assignments successfully.

- *No schedule group*—was not taught how to develop a schedule and was not rewarded. This third group, which consisted of students not enrolled in the program but having similar academic abilities as those in the two other groups, was used as a control group.

The research was clear in showing that different types of planning and scheduling did impact student's grades. In the one-year follow up study, it was found that students who used the more flexible moderately specific monthly planning schedule in combination with rewards to encourage themselves to persist in achieving their goals had significantly better performance in school work than did the students who used other methods. Kirschenbaum and his colleagues (1982) concluded that one reason that the more flexible schedule proved to be more successful is because students do not have to feel bad about themselves if they miss completing work for a day or two. There is still available time to make up the work. Students using moderately specific monthly plans felt more in control of their time. They felt that they controlled their schedule rather than having their schedule control them. The rewards also provided an incentive to stick with the moderately specific monthly plan.

This research finding implies that in order to achieve your important goals you should develop the habit of using a flexible, moderately specific monthly planning schedule to organize your weeks and your days. Remember to reward yourself for each of your achievements in college. Researchers have found that students who proactively manage their time well in advance and stick to a moderately flexible schedule with rewards meet their deadlines, get better grades, and have more time for fun.

Develop the habit of using a weekly activity schedule or planner in which to record relevant information from your monthly schedules for the semester. An electronic planner can save you time by enabling you to automatically create a weekly plan and daily "To Do" list from the information entered in the monthly planner. Students may also have access to a planner with the same time saving features on a college or course website. If you have an electronic planner or one provided for you by your college, use it to organize your time. If you do not have access to such devices, create your weekly schedule using your own weekly planner. Copy and review the information you entered in your monthly schedule and revise the information as you enter it into your weekly and daily planners. Update your monthly, weekly, and daily plans, as needed, to follow a moderately flexible plan. Add new appointments as they come along and reschedule tasks when necessary. Only reschedule high priority tasks for which you will still have time to meet your deadlines. Use your weekly planner to create your daily "To Do" list, which is an especially useful tool during hectic or stressful times during the semester.

Do Not Procrastinate, Save the Best for Last

Most people put off doing what they know they have to do but find difficult, or boring, or unpleasant, such as studying for an exam, and do other things such as watching television, or going out with friends. But if we save the best for last, we are more likely to do a better job on the task we have to do. A psychologist, David Premack, proposed the Premack Principle, which says that more preferred activities can serve as a reward for less preferred activities (as cited in Welsh, Bernstein & Luthans, 1992). If you arrange activities so that you engage in less preferred activities first, such as studying for an exam, and know that afterwards you will engage in something you enjoy, such as going to a basketball game with your friends, you will be more likely to get the studying done. You will also have greater enjoyment when at the game because you won't be worrying about doing the studying.

Industrial organizational psychologists have applied the Premack Principle to increasing productivity in organizations by giving employees the opportunity to perform more preferable tasks after performing less preferable tasks (Makin & Hoyle, 1993; Timberlake & Farmer-Dougan, 1991). Welsh, Bernstein and Luthans, (1992) applied this principle at a fast food restaurant. Performance of eight service workers were directly observed and rated during a seven-week period. Five of the employees were told that if the quality of their performance exceeded baseline at a targeted workstation, they would gain greater work time at a more preferred workstation. The results showed improvement of the performance of the service workers rewarded according to the Premack Principle, whereas there was no change in the performance of the workers who were not told their improved performance would allow them additional time at the preferred workstation.

So rather than procrastinating when you have studying to do, plan an enjoyable activity as a reward that will follow your getting your work done. When making out your schedule for the week plan to get the work done that has the greatest priority first. Then schedule a break during which you do something fun, rather than engaging in the enjoyable activity first. Because if you go out with your friends when you know you have an exam for which to study or a paper to write, you will be worrying about the work that has to get done, and won't enjoy yourself as much. You will also work more efficiently if you get the work done first, then go out and party.

Are you are a procrastinator? If yes, identify enjoyable activities you can schedule for yourself following successful completion of your homework assignments. If you find that you are having serious trouble getting your work done due to procrastination, seek help from a psychologist at your college's counseling center before this problem gets out of control. The psychologist can teach you specific methods that you can use to overcome your habit of procrastination and, thereby, meet your other deadlines and obligations.

Don't Try to be Perfect

While it is desirable to have a sense of control in one's life, the perfectionist is obsessive about trying to control every aspect of his or her life and of the lives of others. They are worriers who typically have a poor self-image and try to micromanage every detail of the situation. Is your way the only way to do things? Do you get upset if someone wants to do it another way? Perfectionists have unrealistically high standards. How would your life improve if you could release some control? Would you then be able to delegate some of the work you have been doing whether at home or at work and then have more time for doing school work and something you enjoy? Ironically perfectionism may lead to procrastination and the individual might not get anything done because he/she is too afraid that his/her efforts might be less than perfect.

Psychological researcher Carolyn Orange (1997) administered a Perfectionism Quiz to 109 gifted high school students who participated in an honors conference. The Perfectionism Quiz had 30 items defining a negative form of perfectionism, obsessive-compulsive behavior. The maximum possible score was 185, the maximum obtained score was 166, and the mean (average) score was 116. Ninety-seven participants (89%) scored in the highest categories, indicating that obsessive-compulsive patterns are a serious problem for them. An item analysis revealed that procrastination is a problem experienced by the gifted students who responded "almost always" to "I sometimes needlessly delay doing something I have to do."

Factor analysis extracted 9 factors that cumulatively explained 63% of the variance in the students' perfectionism scores. Of these, 6 factors were identified as possible dimensions of perfectionism in the psychological literature, including:

- Need for order
- Need for approval of others
- Obsessive, compulsive demands on self
- Anxiety and excessive worry

- Indecision

- Procrastination

This research suggests that some gifted people suffer from anxiety and excessive worry because they set unrealistically high standards for their own performance, which leads to procrastination. Thus, negative perfectionism can be an internal barrier that increases stress in your life and sabotages your success and happiness. Assess your personality and monitor your behaviors to determine if you typically exhibit the traits and behaviors associated with negative perfectionism. If you find that you are prone to negative perfectionism, you will need to learn how to set more realistic standards for your performance. Make an appointment with a psychologist or counselor at your college's counseling center who can help you learn to have more positive, self-affirming thoughts and more realistic standards of performance.

Learn to Structure Life on Campus

Debbie attended college at 17, the fall after graduating from high school, as many students do. She attended college in a different state from the one in which she lived, being away from home for the first time. Debbie always attended classes, but found the many distractions of college life irresistible, and as a result did not structure her study time very well. Debbie lived in what is called a corridor dorm. The bathroom was at the end of the corridor for all of the rooms on the floor. On the way down the hall, it was easy to stop and chat with the young women who always left their doors open. Although a very bright student, Debbie's performance was not what would have been expected by her SAT scores and her high school grades.

Research has shown positive psychological benefits of living in a suite style residence with a few rooms clustered around a bathroom and lounge as compared to living in a corridor style dorm. The students living in the suites had more control over the bedrooms and the common areas of the lounge and bathroom. Even though students had approximately the same amount of space and equal facilities in the two types of residences, students living in the corridor dorms were less satisfied. They felt crowded, felt less able to control their interactions with others, and felt a lack of privacy in the dormitory. Suite residents, developed deeper friendships with their suite mates, worked with one another more effectively, and were friendlier in their interactions with students in their classes and on campus (Baum & Davis, 1980; Baum, Harpin, & Valins, 1975; Baum & Valins, 1979).

This research would point to the fact that a student would be better able to control his/her study time and have more satisfying interactions when living in a suite style residence rather than a corridor style dormitory. It would be our recommendation to choose a suite style residence if you have a choice. What is the solution for corridor dorm residents? Debbie found that she was able to accomplish a lot more studying when she went to the library. It was quiet, with a lot fewer distractions than in the dorm. You will need to schedule your time to go to the library so that other distractions don't keep you from getting there. If you are a commuting student, schedule time to study in the library between classes.

Photo courtesy of Rhode Island College.

Can students living in dormitories perform as well academically or better than students living at home, in sororities or fraternities or in off-campus apartments? Blimling (1999) combined results from previous research into an overall statistical analysis based on the data from all of the published studies that sought to answer that question. The results of Blimling's analysis suggest that when past academic performance is taken into account, students living in on-campus residences do not do any better or worse than students living at home. Students living in dormitories get slightly better grades than fraternity or sorority residents do. Students living in dormitories also perform academically better than students living in off-campus apartments. All in all, whether you live at home, in an on-campus residence, in a sorority or a fraternity, or in an off-campus apartment is not the crucial determinant of whether you are a successful student. Far more important is how you structure your time, use learning strategies, and are conscientious about going to class, completing assignments on time, and studying on a regular basis.

Avoid Becoming Internet-Dependent

The Internet can be a double-edged sword for college students. On the one hand, it is a useful tool that allows students the ability to conduct research quickly and efficiently and to stay in touch with family members and friends economically via e-mail. Many colleges offer online virtual courses that do not require attendance in actual classes. The goal of most computer services centers at colleges and universities is to make it possible for all students to have ready access to the Internet from school or home, day and night. However, recent research conducted by Keith Anderson, a psychologist at Rensselaer Polytechnic Institute's (RPI's) counseling center, which was reported in *The Chronicle of Higher Education,* indicates that many college students spend far too much time on the Internet (as cited in Reisberg, 2000, p. A43). Anderson was inspired to conduct his research after meeting with an RPI student who was flunking out of college because he had become overly dependent on communicating via the Internet. This student admitted to Anderson that he was spending about 18 hours per day participating in an Internet "online community." How common is this problem of Internet overuse among college students?

In 1998–1999, Anderson surveyed 1,300 college students at seven schools in the United States and one in Northern Ireland. The participants were evenly divided between men and women and were in 18 different majors, including both liberal arts and the sciences. Of the 1,078 participants who said they use the Internet, Anderson found that about 10% overuse it and spend so much time participating in online activities that their grades, their health, and their social lives are affected. Of these 1,078 Internet users, 106 students (93 men and 13 women) met at least three of the seven criteria adapted from those used by professional psychologists and counselors to diagnose conditions such alcohol dependency in the *Diagnostic and Statistical Manual of Mental Disorders-IV (DSM-IV).*

These criteria include withdrawal from other activities, and inability to manage the amount of time engaged in Internet activities. Time spent on the Internet continually increases.

> The students who were classified as Internet-dependent spent an average of 229 minutes a day online for nonacademic reasons, compared with 73 minutes a day for other students. As many as 6 percent of the students spent an average of more than 400 minutes a day—almost seven hours—using the Internet" (p. A43).

Anderson found that male students enrolled in technical programs such as computer science, chemistry, physics, engineering, and math have a tendency to become more dependent on using the Internet than females with these majors or male and female students enrolled in other programs. These students who did become dependent on the Internet jeopardized their chances for success in college as well as their health by missing classes, skipping meals, isolating themselves from their friends and family, and failing to get enough sleep. Are you spending too much time on the Internet or playing computer games?

Be honest with yourself. If you suspect you may be Internet addicted, keep track of the time you spend on the Internet or playing computer games during this coming week. Note if this was free time or time that you had already scheduled for something else. If you find that you are having trouble limiting the time you spend on the Internet, seek help from a psychologist at your college's counseling center before your Internet dependency problem gets out of control. The psychologist can teach you specific methods that you can use to better control your time on the Internet and, thereby, meet your other deadlines and obligations. He or she can also help you to develop the skills needed to participate in quality face-to-face interactions with others. Do not isolate yourself from your family, friends, and peers. Do not limit your communication with others to e-mail. Plan quality time to interact with people face-to-face.

Exercise Daily

Good physical fitness, as defined by endurance and strength, can be greatly increased by exercise. Aerobic exercise, that stimulates and strengthens the heart and lungs, contributes substantially to improving physical health. The benefits of exercise for physical health are well known: increased cardiorespiratory efficiency, reduced risk of heart attack, lower body weight, maintenance of optimum blood pressure, improved cholesterol level, improved tolerance of stress, and even lower rates of certain forms of cancer (Taylor, 1999). Perhaps less well known are the psychological benefits of exercise. Exercise has been demonstrated to have a positive effect on psychological states, such as mood, self-esteem, and cognitive functioning (Brown, 1991).

Physical fitness has been found to buffer the effects of stressful life events. Fitness of 37 male and 73 female college students was measured by self-reports of engaging in exercise and objective measures of students' heart rates before, during, and after riding on an exercise bike. Students' frequency of illness was measured by a self-report checklist of illnesses they had experienced during the previous six months, by number of visits to the campus health services over a period of two semesters, and by three scales assessing psychological distress. Life stress was determined by the number and severity of negative events in the preceding 12-month period. "Life stress was strongly related to illness (health center visits) among subjects whose performance on the bicycle test indicated a relatively low level of physical fitness, but life stress had little ill effect among subjects whose fitness level was relatively high" (Brown, 1990, p. 560). Those who do little exercise and are out of shape are likely to succumb to illness when faced with negative life events, whereas those who exercise regularly and are in good physical condition are better able to withstand life stresses and stay well despite negative life events.

Exercise also significantly improves cognitive functioning. A statistical review (meta-analysis) of 134 studies of the impact of either acute or long-term exercise upon cognition obtained a small positive effect of exercise on mental performance (Etnier et al., 1997). In a cross-sectional study of 132 healthy individuals aged 24–76 years, Van Boxtel et al.

(1997) examined the effects of aerobic sports on participants' perceptions of their own health and their actual performance in selective cognitive tasks. The researchers found that participants who engaged more hours a week in aerobic sports not only felt healthier than the nonparticipants of the same age did but also performed better on tasks that reflect complex cognitive speed after correction for age, sex, and intelligence. The results of this research suggest that exercise, which also increases aerobic capacity, may be a way to slow down the effects of aging on complex cognitive tasks.

Aerobic exercise has shown large effects for the reduction of symptoms of depression and anxiety. A statistical review (meta-analysis) of 134 studies found large positive effects of exercise on the psychological state of those who had mild to moderate symptoms of anxiety and depression (Stich, 1995). Another review of studies of individuals with more severe clinical depression also found exercise to have large effects in reducing the depressed state. Among college students who were divided into four groups, aerobic exercise, cognitive group therapy, both treatments, or no treatment, aerobic exercise and/or cognitive group therapy were equally effective in reducing anxiety compared to no treatment (McEntee & Halgin, 1999). Exercise has even been shown to be effective in the treatment of panic disorder (Broocks et al., 1998). The therapeutic effect of exercise for patients with panic disorder was compared with drug treatment (clomipramine) and placebo. Outpatients (aged 18–50) suffering from panic disorder, with or without agoraphobia, were randomly assigned to a 10-week treatment of running, drug treatment, or placebo pills. Although the drug treatment improved anxiety symptoms significantly earlier and more effectively, the results also revealed that exercise alone, in comparison with placebo, was associated with significant clinical improvement of patients.

Weight training in a non-aerobic manner also has beneficial physical and psychological effects. Male law enforcement officers who participated in 16 weeks (three times per week) of weight training, as compared to officers who were not assigned to the exercise condition, demonstrated significant improvements in job satisfaction and decreases in hostility, depression, anxiety, and physical complaints (Norvell & Belles, 1999). One concern of this experiment was the high percentage of dropouts from the exercise condition (58%). The dropout group had significantly higher pretreatment scores on the psychological measures such as depression, anxiety, and hostility. Another important difference between those who completed the 16-week training and those who did not was whether they exercised alone (77% of the dropouts) or exercised with a partner (83% of the completers).

Exercise daily to safeguard your health and to increase your fitness so that you can better handle both daily hassles and major life stressors. Exercise can improve your mood, your health and your cognitive processes. Use the swimming pool and college fitness center. Consider walking for at least 20 minutes every day. If possible, walk outside and enjoy the stress relieving effect of being in nature. Have an exercise buddy. Exercising with a friend makes it much more likely that you will maintain your exercise regimen.

Photo courtesy of Rhode Island College.

Tune into Your Circadian Rhythms

Psychological research on sleep indicates that we all naturally have a 25-hour schedule (Mistlberger & Rusak, 1989). But, external stimuli in our environment such as day and night and the pressing demands in our sociocultural world (work, school, travel, leisure activities, etc.) cause us to modify our own biological clock's preference from a 25-hour schedule to a 24-hour schedule.

About 25% of people are "larks" who are early birds and love to get up early and get going, whereas 25% are "owls" who reach their peak of energy level later in the day or early evening (Anderson, Petros, Beckwith, Mitchell, & Fritz, 1991). If you are like most people, you will probably be more alert in the late morning than in the late afternoon. Women may also have monthly fluctuations that coincide with the ebb and flow of hormones during their menstrual cycle.

Do you know when your high and low energy periods of the day occur? To find out, observe yourself performing your routine activities and identify your own most and least productive periods of the day and night. If desired, you can also make notes about monthly fluctuations in your circadian rhythms. Once you determine your own circadian rhythms, plan to use some of your high energy and alertness periods for performing tasks related to achieving your most challenging educational goals. Remember to reserve other periods of high energy for spending quality leisure time doing mutually exciting activities with your loved ones in order to maintain your important relationships.

Avoid Credit Card Debt

When students enroll in college, they find that they receive many offers of credit cards. Credit card debt can be a land mine for students. It is so easy to pull out that little piece of plastic and buy that new sound system for your room, or clothes that have designer labels, or skip meals at the dining center to eat out. But the bills come due every month and if you only pay the minimum payment, you wind up paying high interest rates on most cards. If you skip payments, you ruin your credit rating. When you graduate, get a job, and want to buy a car or a home, you may find that banks and mortgage companies will at worst, turn you down, or at best, charge you a higher interest rate for the loan or mortgage. Credit card companies have in recent years actively targeted college students by offering pre-approved credit cards to students even when the student does not have a job. "Estimates indicate that some college students are heavily in debt: 14% have balances of $3,000 to $7,000 on their credit cards alone, and 10% owe amounts exceeding $7,000" (Vickers, 1999, as cited in Kidwell & Turrisi, 2000, p. 589). Nevertheless, most college students who have credit cards use them responsibly and only 41% carry a balance (Rose, 1998, as cited in Kidwell & Turrisi, 2000).

In a study conducted with 1,022 students at three public and private colleges, 735 of the students were found to have at least one personal credit card. There was an average of 2.6 cards per student with a range of from one to 18 credit cards (Pinto, Parente & Palmer). Women and juniors and seniors carried more credit cards than men and freshmen and sophomores. The more credit cards students had and the higher the balance on the credit cards, the more hours per week the student worked at a paid job. There was no difference between high and low academic performers and the number of credit cards the student carried or the balance on those cards, nor was there a difference in the number of hours worked per week in paid employment by low and high academic performers. Low performers, however, said they worked to pay off their credit card balances and agreed with the statement "If I was not working so many hours at my job, I would do better in school" (p. 54). Nevertheless, high academic performers were much more anxious about their credit card use than low performers. Credit card use thus had a detrimental impact on the psyches of both high and low academic performers in terms of either resenting having to work so many hours and not doing well in school, or because of worry caused by their credit card spending.

Using a debit card that allows you to spend money you have in your savings account is a wiser choice than a credit card. We would hope that if you do carry a credit card, you are able to pay off the balance every month. Student loans generally carry much lower interest rates than credit cards, and are preferable to credit cards to pay tuition, books, and living expenses.

Manage Your Money Wisely

Do you know where your money goes? Do you spend your money in a manner that will enable you to achieve your highest priority goals? The first step in financial management is to draw up a budget including all of your "fixed" expenses and discretionary income. You have made choices that led to your fixed expenses. For example, the tuition varies greatly at different colleges and universities. Although a relatively small city, Providence, Rhode Island boasts 6 Bachelor's degree granting colleges and universities. The tuition (fees are extra) for full-time undergraduate students at each of the colleges and universities for the 2005–2006 academic year are as follows: $27,510 at the Rhode Island School of Design; $30,672 at Brown University; $24,800 at Providence College; $19,200 at Johnson and Wales University; $5,348 (instate tuition) at The University of Rhode Island College of Continuing Education; and $4,676 at Rhode Island College (instate tuition—approximately 90% of the students there are in-state).

Many factors are a part of the decision to attend a particular college and university, the cost of tuition being only one. There are also many sources of scholarships that students should investigate. These scholarships are available from many fraternal organizations, such as the Elks, from ethnic or religious organizations, from foundations and community groups as well as from colleges and universities. A first step is a visit to your campus financial aid office. It will usually have on hand, lists of organizations that give scholarships, as well as the requirements for those scholarships offered by your own school.

A student enrolled at a state college last year had transferred from an Ivy League university because she said that the financial aid package the university had put together for her included large loans, and she did not want to go heavily into debt. She wanted to be a teacher and found that the state college had an excellent education program. You may be willing to trade coming out of college with large debts, however, for a prestigious Ivy League degree. Personal connections can be made at an Ivy League university that can serve later on to open doors in the corporate and professional world. The decision to attend a particular college or university is complex, and should be carefully thought through.

Colleges that offer a cooperative education program in which students spend alternate semesters working at jobs in their career field and taking college courses could be a good choice for you. This type of program enables students to earn money for college as well as to gain invaluable professional work experience. Students can also find out if they like working in a particular field or not, as well. Linda recently graduated from the cooperative education program in nursing at Northeastern University in Boston and landed a very good job at a hospital in which she did several semesters of her cooperative work experience.

Perhaps you would like to attend graduate school someday but think that you can't afford to do so. Something that many students do not realize is that it is easier to go to graduate school for free tuition than undergraduate school. Graduate schools offer research or teaching assistantships for most of their doctoral students that provide students with free tuition plus a salary. Students who have earned excellent records at state colleges, have then gone on to graduate school at more prestigious public and private universities such as Yale, UCLA and Harvard and been granted assistantships and not paid tuition and in addition received a stipend of several thousand dollars per year. Smaller colleges and universities that have Master's and Doctoral degree programs also have assistantships for graduate school, that provide free tuition and a stipend. Assistantships, however, are usually not available at professional schools such as medical, dental, veterinary, and law schools.

One student whom we shall call Terry had a 3.9 GPA, but when her professor asked if she were planning to go to graduate school she said that she could not afford it. The professor said that she could go to graduate school for free. All of the major Ph.D. granting universities, offer teaching or research assistantships to their graduate students. Terry is heading to a master's program next fall at a large state university. She applied for and received a graduate assistantship. She will get free tuition for 10 credits of coursework per semester (9 credits is considered full-time in graduate school) plus $8,000 as a teaching assistant. In addition, she received a block grant for $9,000.

Another financial trap many students get into is buying a more expensive car than they can afford. They then work 30 or 40 hours a week, while going to college, to pay for the car payments, gas, insurance, and upkeep of the automobile. Public transportation or car-pooling should be considered before putting a lot of money into an automobile. The fewer hours a student works while in college, the more time the student has to do well academically and to participate in enriching extracurricular activities such as writing for the newspaper, being on the debate team, acting in a theater production, taking part in student government, or volunteering with community organizations. Some work experience can also provide an opportunity to participate in a field the student might want to enter after graduation. For example, we encourage students who are considering going into clinical psychology or counseling to work part-time as part of the treatment team at a psychiatric hospital or other mental health agency. On the other hand, the time spent working in a fast food restaurant or holding a highway sign to direct cars around roadwork would better be spent studying or engaging in enriching campus activities. If you can obtain a paid job assisting a professor in your major field with research, that is a very good opportunity for learning and improving your likelihood of being accepted to graduate school.

Do you have trouble managing your money? If yes, identify your highest priority goals for which you need money and keep a record of how you are actually spending the money you have in support of those goals. Then assess areas in which you need to make changes in your spending habits in order to be successful in college. If you are spending so much money on clothes or a phone bill that you need to work extra hours to pay the bills and don't have time to study, you are jeopardizing your success in college. You need to stop spending money on frivolous items and spend more time doing your college work. Keep your mind focused on achieving your long-term goals and it will be easier to avoid impulsive spending. If you find that you cannot control your spending because you have a problem such as being addicted to shopping, seek help learning how to control your spending from a counselor at your college's counseling center.

Success Recommendations

This section contains a summary of the main points in this chapter to help you reflect on and recall what you have learned.

- **Plan to Work Hard, Meet Deadlines, and Succeed**. Understand that you have to be willing to put in the time and effort required to master academic skills, complete your assignments, and earn good grades. In order to meet your college work obligations, you need to act with integrity and behave in a responsible manner. You must develop self-confidence and a belief in your ability to succeed in college.

- **Schedule Your Time.** Do you possess the attitudes and skills you need to manage your time effectively? Assign schoolwork a high priority. Learn to say "No" when people ask you to engage in activities that would interfere with schoolwork. Gain a greater sense of control over your time by planning and organizing your semester, month, week, and day in advance and by completing your plans. If needed, seek time management counseling from your college's counseling center.

- **Identify Your Highest Priority Life Goals.** Identify your core values and highest priority life goals based on universal moral principles and your interests and aptitudes. Spend your time on activities that will enable you to achieve your goals.

- **Break Complex Tasks into Manageable Chunks of Work.** Change complex assignments into a clearly stated set of specific tasks. Then, define the sequence in which each task must be completed. Repeat these steps for breaking down each goal you have for this semester so that you can develop an accurate schedule to follow for successful completion of your academic work.

- **Reward Yourself for Completing Your Assignments.** When you are making up your plan of work for the week, plan time for work followed by some time for activities that you enjoy doing. Be sure to make the time to reward yourself so that you will continue to be highly motivated to achieve other goals and will avoid feeling "burned out." If you are having trouble managing your time, keep a detailed record of your time for one week to see where you are wasting valuable time.

- **Don't Procrastinate. Save the Best for Last.** Determine if you are in the habit of putting studying off until the last minute instead of doing it on a daily basis. Schedule your time so that you study some of each subject every day.

- **Don't Try to be Perfect.** Assess your personality to determine if you typically exhibit thoughts and behaviors associated with negative perfectionism. Examine the factors associated with perfectionism and think about whether you are a person who becomes so obsessed with perfection that you procrastinate to avoid failure. If you are, practice self-control and the excessive fears and worry associated with perfectionism. Seek help from your college's counseling center to learn how to replace negative thoughts with more realistic and self-affirming thoughts.

- **Structure Life on Campus.** If you are a young student away from home for the first time, choose a suite style residence if you have a choice. Develop the habit of studying in the library or another quiet place on campus. Schedule your time to go to study so that other distractions don't keep you from getting there.

- **Limit Time Spent on the Internet.** Avoid spending too much time on nonacademic activities on the Internet or playing computer games. If you find that you are having trouble limiting the time you spend on the Internet, seek help from your college's Counseling Center right away. Make sure you schedule quality time to interact with people face-to-face rather than exclusively online via e-mail or chat rooms.

- **Exercise.** You will improve both your mental and physical health by exercising. An added benefit of exercising is that your cognitive functioning also improves. If you exercise before studying, you will be able to understand and remember the material better.

- **Perform Your Most Important Tasks during Your High Energy Periods.** Plan to perform your most important tasks during your most productive periods of the day or evening when you have a lot of energy and can study effectively. You will be able to better focus on the material you are studying and learn it faster during times when you are alert.

- **Avoid Credit Card Debt**. College students are inundated with offers of credit cards. Don't get caught in the trap of spending freely and drowning in debt and then having to spend precious hours working to make the payments.

- **Manage Your Money Wisely.** Keep a record of your income and expenses. Compare tuition at various colleges and universities. Automobiles can be a poor investment. Keep your spending in line with your goals.

Chapter Three
Know Thyself

The purpose of this chapter is to provide you with research and exercises that help you to learn about yourself and develop positive self-esteem and self-efficacy for your college career. We also discuss personality theory and research and some self-administered personality tests in order to help you select a college major. You will feel a greater sense of well-being by choosing life roles that enable you to express your true personality. Do not try to copy other people. Choose roles that suit your desired lifestyle. Express your authentic personality in whatever role you are playing at the time. As William Shakespeare wrote:

> To thine own self be true, and it will follow as the night the
> day, thy canst not then be false to any man.

Develop High Self-Esteem in Personally Valued Areas

There is a treasure in life more important than silver and gold, that treasure is self-esteem—a person's evaluation of his/her self. Self-esteem refers to whether we value the qualities we have, whether we consider those qualities to be good or bad, and whether we like ourselves. An early social psychologist C. H. Cooley (1902) developed the concept of the "looking glass self" to indicate that people evaluate themselves based on how others perceive them. Modern social psychologists call this *reflected appraisal*. Fortunately, this is only one source of self-esteem.

According to Stanley Coopersmith (1967), who intensively studied the development of self-esteem in young boys in his classic studies, there are four main antecedents of self-esteem:

- *Success*—being able to competently do the tasks that one has to accomplish, which leads to favorable self-appraisals and acceptance by others.
- *Values*—being successful and not failing in the areas that the individual and his or her social group think are important.
- *Goals*—setting higher goals for oneself and believing in one's ability to achieve one's desired goals.
- *Defenses*—being able to eliminate or reinterpret stresses as well as to tolerate and minimize their consequences.

The results of Coopersmith's research suggest that success in an area of life may breed even more success. Success increases our self-esteem in the eyes of our significant others and ourselves, motivates us to aspire to achieve even more success in the future, and helps us develop the stamina and resilience to cope with stressors we encounter on our path to achieving related goals.

Does success in one area of life increase one's self-esteem in all other areas? Although most research uses a global measure of self-esteem, self-esteem is not one-dimensional. For example, you may consider yourself a good student and have a higher level of self-esteem in that area, but your body image may not measure up to the idealized media portrayal of women or men, and you may have a lower level of self-esteem in that area. It would impact on your global self-esteem depending on how important being a good student is to you, or how important having a model figure is. Self-esteem also changes over time depending upon what happens to us. For example, being fired from a job can lower one's self-esteem concerning the ability to succeed in a career, just as experiencing domestic violence or getting divorced can lower one's self-esteem concerning the ability to succeed in an intimate love relationship.

If you received negative messages indicating that you are inferior because of your gender, the socioeconomic status of your family, or minority group membership when you were younger, stop believing them. You do not have to continue to believe that you are inferior. Value yourself as a worthwhile human being and actively construct your own new self-concept, or mental picture of who you think you are, rather than passively accepting the reflected appraisal of others. Then, behave in terms of that new self-concept and you will come to believe it.

Self-esteem is often manipulated in laboratory experiments. By telling participants that they failed on a given task, researchers are able to experimentally lower self-esteem. Likewise, researchers are able to experimentally raise self-esteem by telling participants that they did particularly well on a task (Heatherton & Polivy, 1991). Although events in life such as flunking a course or being rejected by your romantic partner can temporarily lower self-esteem, some people are chronically low in self-esteem. Research consistently finds that a higher level of self-esteem is related to many positive psychological and behavioral characteristics whereas a lower level of self-esteem is related to negative ones.

People with a higher level of self-esteem are more accurate in judging their strengths and weaknesses, and generally have greater self-knowledge than individuals with a lower level of self-esteem (Baumgardner, 1990). Therefore, people with higher self-esteem set appropriate goals, and are able to make use of information about a task to determine the optimal level of persistence and personal effort that they will need to expend in order to successfully complete it (Sandelands, Brockner, & Glynn, 1988). A sense of self-certainty, the feeling that you know yourself, seems to be a factor leading to higher levels of self-esteem.

In contrast, a lower level of self-esteem is related to physical illness and depression, particularly among women, and difficulty in coping with stress (Baumeister, 1993). Lower self-esteem can set up a vicious cycle of failure. On an upcoming exam, a student with lower self-esteem expects to do poorly, which in turn leads to high anxiety. This high anxiety is likely to interfere with studying and to lead to failing the exam. Failing the exam further erodes self-esteem. Researchers have found that the teaching of academic skills to adolescents resulted in increased achievement and enhanced self-esteem (Bednar, Wells, & Peterson, 1995).

One implication of this research evidence is that it is important for you to value yourself and to believe that you are a worthy person. It is also important for you to develop competence and, thereby, higher self-esteem in areas of your life that you personally value because success will empower you to aspire to achieve even higher goals in those areas. Do you value yourself? What are the areas of your life in which you have higher or lower levels of self-esteem? What experiences contributed to your having higher or lower self-esteem in specific areas such as academic achievement, dating, and sports? In what skills do you need to develop more competence in order to achieve your desired success in college?

Bring Your Real Self Closer to Your Ideal Self

Humanistic psychologist and therapist Carl Rogers (1961) encouraged his clients to assess the gap between their real and ideal selves. He would ask his clients to rate themselves with a list of adjectives representing personal traits such as: logical, competent, honest, dishonest, feminine, masculine, passive, active. People are rated low in self-esteem if their ideal self-view is widely disparate from their real self-view on a cluster of adjectives representing a factor that they consider to be an important contributor to their self-concept (e.g., interpersonal skills, academic ability, athletic ability). If people give their real self a low rating (say, 1 or 2) on an academic trait such as being logical and give their ideal self a very high rating on the same trait (say, 8 or 9), they would be rated as having low self-esteem for that trait. Likewise, people are rated higher in self-esteem if their ideal self-view is rated very similar to their real self-view. In his Person-Centered Therapy sessions, Rogers focused on helping his clients break free from childhood conditioning that was hampering their personal growth during adulthood and to raise their self-esteem by closing the gap between their real and ideal selves. Following Rogers' humanistic lead, many contemporary psychologists, counselors, psychotherapists, and educators support the efforts of adults to overcome their self-limiting beliefs and self-sabotaging behaviors and to learn new ones that will enable them to go on to achieve their highest potential.

In order to become your best ideal self and create the future life you desire, you must believe that you have the capacity to grow and change and strive to become *self-actualized,* which means to become the best person that you can be. Select the 10 characteristics that best describe your ideal self and then rate your real and ideal selves on them. Your answers will show you the areas in which you have a gap between your real and ideal selves. How can you implement the desired changes?

You can create a scale for every characteristic you want to develop and rate yourself on a monthly basis to measure your progress toward becoming your ideal self. If you are seeing a therapist or counselor, this exercise can also help you to determine those areas that might be useful to focus on during your therapy sessions. Other strategies for helping you implement these and other changes to your present self and prepare yourself for success in college are in future sections of this book.

Develop a Complex Self-Concept

Who are you? How would you describe your present self? If someone were to ask you this question, how would you respond? Your response gives a good indication of your self-concept, which is an organized collection of beliefs about yourself. Your *social identity* is that part of your self-concept that is based upon your group memberships—such as your ethnic group, your family and church memberships, the school or college you attended, and your political party identification.

The self-concept acts as *a servomechanism* (self-correcting guidance system) by constantly regulating your behavior and influencing your goals. Cognitive aspects of the self are related to self-esteem. People with low self-esteem have less stable, less clearly defined, and less complex self-concepts (viewing the self as having fewer facets) than do people with high self-esteem (Campbell, 1990; Campbell, Chew, & Scratchley, 1991). This means that you can enhance your self-esteem by developing your interests and abilities and having multiple roles, such as student, employee or entrepreneur, wife or husband, mother or father, community volunteer, club member, golfer, church member, friend, and so on. Therefore, the most powerful way you can transform your present life into your desired future life is to expand your self-concept by active involvement in your campus community such as engaging in athletics, other extra-curricular activities, and work or volunteer activities in the community.

Cultivate the "Big Five" Positive Personality Characteristics

After years of measuring hundreds of personality characteristics and conducting complex statistical analyses of personality traits that people possess, psychologists have reached the conclusion that there are five basic ones (Digman, 1997). In addition to the positive pole, there is a negative pole for each of these "Big Five" fundamental trait dimensions or characteristics. These *"Big Five" traits* are:

- *Extraversion or Surgency*—The degree to which the individual is sociable, affectionate, fun loving, assertive, and leaderlike. The opposite side of this personality characteristic is introversion or the extent to which the person is reserved, retiring, quiet, sober, and withdrawn.

- *Agreeableness*—The extent to which individuals are sympathetic, trusting, cooperative, helpful, warm, friendly, and likable. Disagreeable people, on the other hand, are those who are irritable, unpleasant, ruthless, suspicious, uncooperative, and cold.

- *Conscientiousness*—Describes individuals who are hardworking, disciplined, persevering, responsible, dependable, organized, careful, and exhibit a need for achievement. People lacking in this characteristic are disorganized, careless, impulsive, irresponsible, undependable, and lazy.

- *Emotional Stability*—Describes individuals who have the ability to be calm, secure, self-confidant, self-satisfied, and steady. On the other hand, emotional instability characterizes someone who is neurotic, self-pitying, insecure, worried, anxious, and emotional.

- *Intellect or Openness to Experience*—Measures the extent to which a person is imaginative, cultured, broadminded, curious, likes variety, and is open to new experience. Someone who lacks this characteristic is concrete minded, practical, prefers a routine, is conforming, and has narrow interests.

The "Big Five" model of personality emphasizes the consistency of behavior across situations. In this view of personality, people are assumed to have personality traits that are highly stable in different situations, social roles, and time periods (McCrae & Costa, 1994). Humanistic approaches to personality have taken the perspective, on the other hand, that authenticity results from acting with a sense of choice and self-expression (Sheldon, Ryan, Rawsthorne, & Ilardi, 1997). According to the humanistic view, not all roles and situations are conducive to choiceful and authentic behavior. "Because felt authenticity is viewed as having dynamic impact on personality and behavior, people are expected to manifest different behavioral styles in different roles, that is, to be inconsistent in their traits" (Sheldon et al., 1997, p. 1381). Which view is valid?

Sheldon and his colleagues (1997) tested the validity of these two approaches to personality. In that study, the researchers asked college students to rate themselves on adjectives representing the "Big Five" traits in each of five psychosocial roles identified as being important to college students (student, employee, child, friend, and romantic partner). They also assessed cross-role variations in the "Big Five" traits and sense of authenticity felt across the five roles. Finally, they compared authenticity and consistency based measures of self-integration as a predictor of satisfaction and well-being.

Sheldon and his colleagues did find a systematic variation in the "Big Five" personality traits as the student moved from one role to another, which supports the humanistic position. "Specifically, participants reported being relatively most extroverted in the friend role, most neurotic in the student role, most conscientious in the employee role, most open to experience in the romantic partner role, and least agreeable in student and child roles" (Sheldon et al., 1997, p. 1390). However, there also was a great deal of cross role consistency, meaning that individuals carry the same basic personality traits as they move from one role and situation to another, as the "Big Five" theorists have suggested.

To what extent do the traits measured by the "Big Five" Factor Model of Personality predict perceptions of oneself and one's actual behavioral interactions with others on a daily basis? In a recent study, Barrett and Pietromonaco (1997) had undergraduate students complete personality scales and recorded and evaluated their interactions with others over a one-week period. These researchers found that:

- Individuals high in extraversion on the personality assessment interacted with more different partners, had more positive views of themselves and others in their daily interactions, and perceived themselves to have greater control of their interactions. Extroverts also reported more positive feelings on a daily basis.

- People high in agreeableness had higher self-esteem following low conflict interactions than did individuals lower in agreeableness.

- Participants high in neuroticism reported more self-disclosure during their social interactions and reported having less control than their interaction partners over their social interactions. Neuroticism was related to self-esteem only when there was conflict in the interaction, with neurotic individuals having less self-esteem after conflict.

- Individuals high in openness to experience reported greater intimacy in their interactions than those low in openness to experience.

- Individuals high in agreeableness showed the lowest self-esteem when their interactions were high in conflict in contrast to people low in agreeableness whose self-esteem was not negatively impacted by high conflict interactions.

- Individuals high in neuroticism and extraversion reported higher levels of positive emotions immediately following social interactions, whereas individuals high in neuroticism and low in extraversion had the most negative emotions following social interactions.

The results of research by Barrett and Pietromonaco (1997) suggest that the "Big Five" factor model of personality does have relevance to the emotions we experience in our daily interactions with others. These research results also suggest that if you want to describe someone's personality or predict their behavior, including your own, you could do so by querying and rating that person on each of the "Big Five" personality dimensions. Does the "Big Five" factor model apply to African-Americans as well as Caucasians? Research by Collins and Gleaves (1998), who studied African-American and Caucasian applicants for the position of security guard, found the five-factor model fit equally well for African-American and Caucasian applicants. How would you rate yourself on each of the "Big Five" personality dimensions?

For the Big Five personality factors (extraversion, agreeableness, conscientiousness, neuroticism, and openness to experience) only one, conscientiousness, has been found to be a positive predictor of academic achievement (Busato, Prins, Elshout, & Hamaker, 2000). This is consistent with the findings of our own research cited in Chapter Two that hard work and time management are keys to successful college achievement.

Select Life Roles that Enable You to Express Your True Self

Sheldon and his colleagues (1997) found that people felt more authentic in roles in which their "Big Five" traits were expressed, as noted above. Roles in which participants felt they had more choice and could be more expressive were the ones in which they felt they were more extroverted, agreeable, conscientious, open to experience, and non-neurotic. People reported feeling the greatest amount of well-being when they felt authentic across roles, had low conflict between roles, and rated themselves similarly in their different roles. The results of Sheldon's research suggest that you can develop the more positive "Big Five" personality characteristics by selecting flexible roles that allow you greater choice and expressiveness—in other words roles that are not rigid. Thus, it appears that we express our true selves when we feel comfortable enough in a role to allow our basic personality traits to shine through the specific demands of the role.

In order to be able to be true to yourself, you must first know yourself. Begin by writing in your success journal about the present life roles in which you feel you already express your positive personality traits or authentic self.

Develop an Assertive Communication Style

Psychological researchers have found that assertive communication skills are required for one's health, well-being, and success. What is an assertive communication style? How does it differ from nonassertive and aggressive communication styles? How will developing and using an assertive communication style contribute to your personal empowerment, physical and mental health, and success in college and life?

Assertive Communication Style—Involves standing up for your personal rights; expressing your thoughts, feelings, and beliefs in direct, honest, and appropriate ways that do not violate another person's rights; and showing respect for the other. The assertive message expresses "who you are" and "how you feel" and it is said without dominating, humiliating, or degrading the other person. The goal of assertion in communication is "mutuality." Therefore, using it will improve your ability to experience equitable relationships with others. Mutuality is achieved by getting and giving respect, asking for fair play, negotiating a compromise when the needs and rights of two people in conflict clash. In assertive communications, neither person sacrifices basic integrity since both get some of their most important needs met (Jakubowski & Lange, 1978).

Nonassertive Communication Style—Involves violating your personal rights by failing to express honest thoughts, feelings, and beliefs in direct, honest, and appropriate ways; permitting others to violate your rights; and expressing yourself in an apologetic, timid, self-effacing manner which allows others to easily disregard you. It involves showing a lack of respect for your needs, violating another person's rights by showing deference instead of respect, showing disrespect for the other person's ability to communicate honestly, and taking responsibility for the other person's actions and problems. Nonassertive messages tell the other: "I don't count." "You can take advantage of me." "My feelings don't matter, only yours do." "My thoughts aren't important, yours are the only ones worth listening to." "I am nothing, you are superior." The goals of nonassertive communications include appeasing others and avoiding conflict at any cost (Jakubowski & Lange, 1978).

Aggressive Communication Style—Involves directly standing up for your own rights and expressing thoughts, feelings, and beliefs in a way that is dishonest, inappropriate, and violates the rights of the other person. In aggressive communications, winning is assured through use of psychologically abusive techniques that cause the other to become weaker and less able to communicate assertively, including humiliation, degradation, belittling the other, and overpowering the other. Aggressive messages tell the other: "This is what I think—You're stupid for believing differently." "This is what I want—What you want is not important." "This is what I feel—Your feelings do not count." The goals of aggression include domination of the other, winning at all cost, and forcing the other person to lose (Jakubowski & Lange, 1978).

A review of the psychological literature reveals that using an assertive communication style is most conducive to your personal empowerment because it allows you to be your authentic self, express your true needs and feelings while respecting the rights of yourself and others, and achieve mutuality with others. Even though being nonassertive may seem to be a way to keep peace in the short run, research reveals that it will take its toll on one's physical and mental health in the long run in the form of somatic symptoms and lowered self-esteem. An aggressive person may seem to "win the battle" in the short run by bullying others, but will probably "lose the war" in the long run as he or she proceeds to destroy his or her relationships with others (Beck, 1988; Schwartz, 1994).

Does using an assertive communication style improve one's interactions with people who are evaluating her or his performance in college and at work? In a study of the relationship between subordinates' assertive communication style and interactional behavior of supervisors conducting evaluations, the researchers systematically varied the communication style of a confederate (a student acting as a subordinate), who exhibited either high or low levels of assertiveness during their evaluation by a supervisor. Supervisors were asked to rate the confederate's performance on a skills test and then to provide evaluative feedback. When following the high assertiveness communication script, "...the confederate directly stated opinions of his or her performance, cited specific examples to support those opinions, asked ...questions of clarification, and engaged in eye contact and forward body posture" (Korsgaard, Roberson, and Rymph, 1998, p. 737). When following the low assertiveness communication script, "...the confederate made vague or noncommittal statements, asked indirect questions ..., and engaged in low eye contact and slumped body posture" (p. 737).

Supervisors' responses during their evaluation were audio taped and then analyzed by trained raters who were unaware of the condition or *hypotheses* (predicted outcome). The interactional behaviors measured were:

- *Consideration*—The extent to which the supervisor acknowledged and showed consideration of the confederate's views, and

- *Justification*—The extent to which the supervisor provided an adequate explanation for his or her decision.

As expected based on the results of previous research, the supervisor exhibited significantly more interactionally fair behavior when the confederate acted in a highly assertive manner. The finding implies that if you want people who are evaluating you to pay attention to what you are saying and to treat you fairly, you are best able to achieve those goals if you use an assertive communication style. Therefore, it will be well worth your while to learn how to behave in a more assertive manner if you do not already do so.

If you feel that you need to become more assertive, follow these simple exercises. Pretend you are watching a movie of yourself acting nonassertively, as defined above, in a specific situation such as talking to a professor about your grades or on a job interview. Then imagine yourself behaving in an aggressive way in that specific situation. Now imagine yourself acting assertively in that same situation. If desired, role play a scene with a classmate, trusted friend, or counselor. You can role play acting assertively in a variety of situations such as going to a party where you don't know anyone, questioning a professor about a grade, going on a job interview where the interviewer makes inappropriate comments about your appearance, or asking your boss for a raise. Affirm that you are ready and able to act in this same assertive manner in real life situations. When ready, act assertively in real life situations.

Imagine and Write about Many Positive Possible Selves

The self is a changing entity and we are able to imagine many positive *possible selves*. What are the careers, hobbies, and roles in life you have thought about pursuing? Have you considered many different occupations? Do you project marriage, family, and other relationship roles for yourself? Have you ever thought about adopting a child or becoming a foster parent? Do you participate in a religious community? What are the possible selves you can project onto the imaginary movie screen in your mind that are most consistent with your own personality traits, interests, abilities, and goals?

Research indicates that people who have a larger number of positive possible selves are emotionally healthier. Following a traumatic event, people who can envision many possible selves are better able to cope with the situation (Morgan & Janoff-Bulman, 1994). People who have greater self-complexity are less likely to become depressed and have stress related illnesses (Linville, 1987). Although both optimistic and pessimistic college students—when asked to describe their future selves—were able to imagine positive futures, the optimistic ones had a greater expectation of actually attaining a positive self than did those who were pessimistic (Carver, Reynolds, & Scheier, 1994).

Recent research finds that students instructed to write about their best possible selves for 20 minutes each day for four consecutive days had significantly improved moods (King, 2001). Students who wrote about their best possible selves had significantly fewer visits to the campus health center for illness than did a control group who wrote about a neutral topic. This research implies that you can increase your ability to cope with traumatic or stressful life events and safeguard your physical and mental health by imagining a large number of possibilities, and expanding your imagined repertoire of the social roles, activities, and interests which you might cultivate—your possible selves. Perhaps you might like to write each day about your best possible future self to improve your mood and health.

Develop Self-Efficacy to Accomplish Your Tasks

Perceived *self-efficacy* is concerned with one's judgments of his or her capability of performing a specific task (Bandura, 1997). Collins (1983, as cited in Bandura, 1997) conducted research in which children selected at low, medium and high levels of math ability were given difficult math problems to solve. At each level of math ability, children with high self-efficacy were quicker to discard faulty strategies, solved more problems, and chose to rework more of those problems they failed and did so more accurately than children of equal ability who doubted their efficacy.

Bandura believes that self-efficacy may vary from one task to another. For example, you may have high self-efficacy for playing basketball, but low self-efficacy for writing term papers. Research in a variety of areas finds that the more self-efficacy you have for accomplishing a particular task, the more likely you are to attempt the activity, to try hard at it, to persist if at first you don't succeed at it, and to ultimately succeed at the task (Shaefers, Epperson, & Nauta, 1997). Even your health is impacted by your self-efficacy for stopping smoking, abstaining from alcohol, staying physically fit, and tolerating pain such as of migraine headaches and childbirth (Maddux, 1991).

Do you believe that you have the ability to achieve your desired life goals? People who believe that they do have the ability to achieve specific goals and turn their future life dreams into their reality have a positive sense of self-efficacy in those areas (Bandura, 1997). Lesser self-efficacy concerning one's ability to achieve their desired goals negatively impacts performance in specific areas of achievement. For example, some girls and women have lesser self-efficacy in their ability to perform successfully in high-level, male dominated careers such as engineering and physics due to cultural stereotypes that do not depict females in these positions. Statistics show that as a result only 9.2% of the doctorates awarded in engineering and 19.7% in physical sciences were awarded to women (U.S. Census Bureau, 1993).

Do researchers still find gender differences in factors predicting persistence of women and men in nontraditional occupations? In a recent study, researchers examined factors related to persistence of 278 undergraduate students (135 women and 143 men) in engineering courses (Schaefers, Epperson, & Nauta, 1997). Of the women, 93 were persisters and 42 were non-persisters. Of the men, 105 were persisters and 38 were non-persisters. In that study, ability was measured using the students' first-semester college GPAs, cumulative GPAs, and scores on the Mathematics portion of the American College Test (ACT-Math). Self-efficacy was measured using scales assessing self-efficacy in mathematics and in one's ability to complete courses required for scientific and engineering occupations.

Support and barriers to persistence were measured using scales that assessed the perceived classroom climate, teacher support and competition as well as social support received from people in engineering, mathematics, and science. Interest congruence was assessed by examining the fit between respondent's pre-college scores on the unisex edition of the ACT Interest Inventory (UNIACT) American College Testing Program, 1981), and their original choice of the engineering major in college. The six scales included in the UNIACT are: Technical, Science, Arts, Social Service, Business Contact, and Operations. These scales correspond respectively to Holland's (1985) Realistic, Investigative, Artistic, Social, Enterprising, and Conventional occupational themes, discussed in a later chapter on selecting a college major and career.

In contrast to previous researchers, Schaefers et al. (1997) did not find gender differences in either persistence or factors predicting persistence. Instead, they found that persistence rates of women and men were not significantly different and gender did not moderate any of the relationships between predictor variables and persistence. Ability of students was the best predictor of persistence, and first-semester GPA was the best of the ability measures. Measures of math and science self-efficacy, perceived social support and barriers to pursuing a career in engineering, and interest congruence with choice of an engineering major each significantly added to the prediction of persistence beyond the contributions of the ability measures.

What are the implications of this research for you? The finding that the first-semester GPA was the best predictor of persistence indicates that early interventions designed to remedy college student's deficits in skills might help increase persistence in engineering and science programs. The finding that ability, self-efficacy, perceptions of support and encouragement, and interest congruence were important factors predicting persistence for both women and men implies that these are important factors for you to consider when thinking about your own career choice.

Low self-efficacy can lead to failure when a person's expectations lead him or her to behave in a manner that makes the prediction come true, as shown in the cycle of success figure below. If you believe you are capable of accomplishing a task or goal, such as getting good grades in college, the more likely you are to put in the effort to do it and to achieve the goal. Since one success leads to another, you then begin to see yourself as a successful student. On the other hand, if you have a low sense of self-efficacy for doing college work, you will believe you are unable to do well in college and will hardly even try. This failure to study enough to pass tests will lead to failure on tests and to the fulfillment of your own negative prophecy.

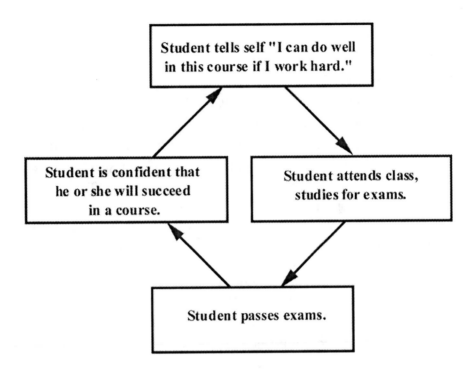

Figure 2.
Cycle of Success: Positive Self-Efficacy

Do you believe you are capable of getting good grades in your college courses? What skills do you need to learn in order to be able to become capable of getting good grades in the college courses in which you have low self-efficacy now? Get help learning these skills from the tutoring center or your professor.

Develop Your Emotional Intelligence

Emotional Intelligence is defined as "the ability to perceive, express, understand, and manage emotions" (Ciarrochi, Chan, Caputi, & Roberts, 2001, p. 26). Psychologists studying emotional intelligence have examined people experiencing a variety of life events to determine the life outcome. *Life events* include positive ones such as marriage, negative ones such as the death of a loved one, minor daily hassles such as driving in traffic, and uplifting events such as going to a movie with a friend. *Life Outcomes* refers to how the individual reacts and adapts to these events. One person who loses his or her job may become depressed and suicidal. Another may be disappointed but begin a job search with the attitude that he or she can get another job. "Today we believe that if you are emotionally intelligent then you can cope better with life's challenges and control your emotions more effectively, both of which contribute to good mental health" (Taylor, 2001, p. 67).

Mayer and Salovey and their colleagues have defined emotional intelligence as a set of interrelated abilities organized along four dimensions:

- Identifying and expressing emotions
- Using emotions
- Understanding emotions
- Managing or regulating emotions (Salovey, 2001, p. 168).

People high in emotional intelligence are also better able to recognize the emotions of others and to use this information to guide their thinking and actions (Mayer & Salovey, 1993).

What is the relationship of emotional intelligence to education? First of all, emotional intelligence is a set of skills that can be improved through education. The elementary, middle and high schools are beginning to introduce preventive intervention programs. These programs are aimed at such areas as prevention of violence through such training as conflict resolution, by teaching students how to recognize their feelings and empathize with the feelings of others and solve problems without resorting to violence. Helping children to participate in service to their communities is another way that emotional intelligence skills are now being developed in students (Elias, Hunter & Kress, 2001).

Research on emotional intelligence finds it to be positively related to goal orientation and life satisfaction, and to negatively influence depression symptomatology (Martinez-Pons, 1997). This research was conducted with college students as well as with a cross section of people aged 18 to 60 years. Thus, people who are able to discriminate among their feelings, and have the ability to regulate their emotions and moods are more goal oriented, have a greater sense of satisfaction and fulfillment in life, and are less depressed.

Some other psychologists have a broader definition of emotional intelligence. Albert Mehrabian (2000) defines emotional intelligence as the individual's level of success in various areas of life. "In particular, emotional intelligence has been used as an overarching construct to describe individual differences associated with life success that are not specifically measured with traditional intelligence test measures. (Mehrabian, 2000 p. 134).

The various areas of life Mehrabian includes are:

- *Emotional Success*—General happiness and satisfaction with life.
- *Relationship Success*—Satisfactory, harmonious and productive interpersonal relationships.
- *Physical Success*—Health and fitness with minimal recourse to drugs and medical intervention.
- *Work Success*—Work satisfaction and dedication, growth in the workplace (pp. 133–134).
- *Career and Financial Success*—Career optimism and dedication, wise and successful saving, spending and investing habits.

To determine what are the individual differences that account for differences in success in the five categories and *Overall Success* (a combination success score for the five categories),

Mehrabian (2000) assessed individual differences on 32 dimensions using a sample of 302 people (107 men, 195 women). He also had peer ratings of all participants' level of success in the five areas plus overall success. After the administration of many scales and statistical analyses of all of the data, Mehrabian concluded the following characteristics were most strongly related to success in order of importance as follows:

1. Psychological adjustment and a relaxed temperament
2. Employee productivity and reliability
3. Disciplined goal orientation and achieving tendency
4. Does not use emotional thinking
5. Integrity and emotional empathy
6. Overall success (a combination of the first five)
7. Overall physical attractiveness and intelligence

Let's take a closer look at what each one of these characteristics related to success means.

Psychological Adjustment is the most highly correlated psychological characteristic with each of the types of success. Pleasantness and taking pleasure in life are a general index of psychological adjustment. Other characteristics in this factor related to success are low arousability, which means that one is not easily upset by things, and dominant characteristics (e.g., being self-assured, assertive, and competitive versus being submissive, humble, and tense). This cluster of traits, pleasantness, low arousability, and dominant characteristics is called *Relaxed Temperament*.

The second most highly correlated psychological characteristic with each of the types of success was *Employee Productivity and Reliability*. This characteristic was measured by The Covert Index of Employee Productivity and Reliability, which provides an indication of "...the overall honesty, dependability, reliability, and interpersonal effectiveness of an employee" (Mehrabian, 2000, p. 162).

The third most highly correlated psychological characteristic with each of the types of success was *Disciplined Goal Orientation* and *Achieving Tendency*. This characteristic involves being willing to *delay gratification* or sacrifice immediate pleasures to achieve more distant, but more rewarding goals. *Delay of Gratification and Patience* were the two most important aspects of this orientation, and two aspects that were negatively related to goal orientation were *Impulsivity* and *Procrastination*. *Achieving tendency* refers to the desire to pursue achievable goals and to overcome failure.

Successful people do not use emotional thinking. *Emotional Thinking* refers to an excessive influence of one's emotions on one's thought processes. An example of an item from the scale used to measure emotional thinking is "I don't lose my objectivity in emotional situations" (Mehrabian, 2000, p. 161).

Integrity means honesty, trustworthiness, dependability, reliability, and generally prosocial versus antisocial behaviors. After Relaxed Temperament, Integrity is the strongest correlate of Emotional Success (general happiness and satisfaction with life). Integrity, Relaxed Temperament and Disciplined Goal Orientation were tied as the three top correlates of *Work Success*.

Overall Success was most highly correlated with *Relaxed Temperament*, followed by *Achieving Tendency*.

Physical Attractiveness was a particularly important correlate of relationship success. Physical Attractiveness was also related to Relaxed Temperament, and is generally a modest asset in achieving success in various areas of life. *Intelligence* was also related to all areas of life success.

Participants who had higher scores on the Emotional Intelligence Scale were found to pay greater attention to feelings, have greater clarity of feelings, more mood repair, greater optimism and less pessimism, less depression, and less impulsivity. Among a sample of freshman, students with higher scores on the Emotional Intelligence Scale were found to have higher grades at the completion of the freshman year (Schutte, Malouff, Hall, Haggerty, Cooper, Golden & Dornheim, 1998).

You have the power within you to succeed in college and lead a happy and successful life. This section gives you the building blocks for that life. Take a relaxed attitude toward life. Be pleasant toward others rather than judgmental and disagreeable and let go of turmoil. Make decisions and deal with the inevitable problems of life in as rational a way as possible. Although it is important to enjoy the pleasures of life, it is necessary to learn when to delay gratification, have self-discipline, and be conscientious in order to achieve your goals, like Karla who is featured in the Success Profile below. Physical attractiveness and intelligence may be characteristics you don't think you have much control over, but exercise, enough sleep, good nutrition, and not smoking, not using drugs, and good hygiene practices all lead to greater physical attractiveness and functional intelligence.

Success Profile—Karla

Karla is from Oulu in the north of Finland. She first came to the United States to stay with a cousin of her mother's in West Lafayette, Indiana to attend the 11th grade in an American public school. She returned to Oulu to complete her senior year of high school. Unlike American high schools, students specialize in a subject in high school, because upon graduation they can go straight into a Master's program. Karla, whose mother is a social worker and father is a retired businessman, knew from an early age that she wanted to be a psychologist. In high school in Finland, she took five courses in psychology and one in psychology in the American high school she attended for one year. In Finland, in order to graduate from high school, students must take the Matricular exam consisting of eight essays. The student may select, however, the areas in which they wish to take the essays. Karla selected all eight of her exams to be from psychology. She scored in the top 1% on this exam and was awarded a small scholarship.

When attending the 11th grade in Indiana, she met her boyfriend, who was originally from Columbia, South America. He was one year ahead of her in school, and the year she completed high school in Sweden, he attended Brown University in Providence, RI. So, when Karla graduated from high school, she applied to colleges in the Providence, RI area. She lived in the residence hall at college during her first two years of college and was a resident assistant during her second year. For her junior year, she moved into an apartment with her boyfriend. During her senior year she lived alone because her boyfriend graduated a year ahead of her and went to graduate school in California.

Karla has a 3.92 GPA. She said that one reason that she has been successful in college is that she was able to obtain a job in the college library in a department where she is able to complete her responsibilities quickly and spend most of her time there studying. Her study strategies include reading or at least skimming the chapter of the text assignment for that class before going to class. She said that by reading the assignments before class, you do not fear the professor asking a question and look smart when they do. She reads the summary and outline of a chapter first. Then she takes notes as she reads each chapter. She also makes up flash cards for material that has to be memorized. Her boyfriend impressed on her the need to systematically study the material. Before an exam, she studies the lecture notes and her notes from the readings at the same time, comparing how the material was covered in class and in the reading.

During her freshman year, Karla went to see one of the psychology professors about the college's Honors program. After her conversation with him, he suggested they collaborate on some research. One of her professors introduced her to a retired professor of Finnish ancestry who helped her meet Finnish people in the Boston area. It was through these contacts that she obtained a job working on a smoking cessation project at Harvard University between her freshman and sophomore years. During fall of her sophomore year, her professor recognized her dedication to psychology and asked her to become involved in research with her as the other project at Harvard University was completed. She began her Honor's research project during her junior year working with another professor.

Karla joined the psychology club during her freshman year, and in her sophomore year was admitted to Psi Chi, the psychology national honor society. Karla was President of Psi Chi during her senior year. She recommends that students join their college's club in their major and, if eligible, become a member of the honor society as well. In the fall of her senior year, Karla presented a poster depicting the results of her research at the Psi Chi poster session at the New England Psychological Association (NEPA) annual meeting. It was at that meeting that Karla was recognized with the Honors Undergraduate Scholars award by NEPA. At senior Cap and Gown day, Karla was awarded the prize for the outstanding student in psychology and the prize for the best Honor's project from any department in the college for that year. Karla graduated Summa Cum Laude.

Select a Major that Is Compatible with Your Personality, Interests, and Abilities

Beginning college students are typically required to take a variety of general education courses that help students gain knowledge in the liberal arts before specialization. If you are just starting college, explore areas in which you are interested by taking required courses and electives in those areas. Many of the required first- and second-year general education courses are designed to help you develop the basic academic skills that you will need to perform any type of work (e.g., reading, conducting research, writing, mathematics, science, communication, and computer literacy). Other courses such as those in the social sciences and the humanities are also designed to increase your general knowledge and to expand your view of the world and people living in it. These courses will help you to live a more productive, enriched life. As you achieve success in your classes, your self-efficacy in several areas will increase. How do we know that your self-efficacy will increase with exposure to particular educational experiences?

Photo courtesy of Bristol Community College.

Researchers have assessed the effects of interventions designed to enhance self-efficacy on the math/science self-efficacy and career interests, goals, and actions of career undecided college students (Luzzo, Hasper, Albert, Bibby, & Martinelli, 1999). First year college undergraduates (55 women and 39 men) who possessed at least a moderate level of math ability and career undecidedness were randomly assigned to one of four conditions. These conditions included:

- Performance accomplishment only—participants successfully completed number series tasks that ware described as a test of their math ability.

- Vicarious learning only—participants watched a video in which two graduates of the university described how they had been undecided about their college major at first but then went on to have successful careers in math-science fields.

- Combined performance accomplishment with vicarious learning.

- A control group that didn't receive any intervention.

Math ability was measured using the American College Test for Math (ACT-Math). Math self-efficacy was measured using self-report scales that assessed participants' self-efficacy for successfully completing math/science college courses and pursuing a career in technical and scientific fields or occupations requiring education in math and science.

The pre- and post-treatment assessments showed significant effects of the performance accomplishment and combined treatments on self-efficacy, selection of future courses, and indication of choice of a major (Luzzo et al., 1999). People who successfully completed the series of math tasks were more likely to elect to take math courses in the future and to select a college major in fields requiring math or science. The results of this research suggest that your self-efficacy in specific areas will also increase as you successfully complete related college courses. Once your self-efficacy in a particular area increases, you may find yourself opting for more courses in similar subjects or even selecting a career and college major in a related area.

Investigate your options and choose a college major that will help you prepare for the career that you think is consistent with your personality, interests, talents, and abilities. To help you accomplish this task, you can access a useful college major to career converter tool on the Internet at http://campus.netscape.monster.com/tools/careerconverter/. The converter, which is provided by Monster.com, Inc., provides a listing of career opportunities reflective of various academic majors. Once you really identify and select a college major, identify a tentative plan outlining the courses you need to take in order to complete your selected college program by your anticipated graduation date. Locate other students who share your career interests and ask them to form a study group with you. Join the club and/or honor society associated with your major at your college or university.

Success Recommendations

This section contains a summary of the main points in this chapter to help you reflect on and recall what you have learned.

- **Develop High Self-esteem in Personally Valued Areas.** Determine the areas of your life in which you have high and low self-esteem. Do you desire to focus on increasing your self-esteem in any of the areas in which you have low self-esteem at this time? Note one specific area of your life in which you would like to increase your self-esteem and the steps you think you need to take to implement that change.

- **Close the Gap Between Your Real and Ideal Selves.** Start by listing the ten most highly valued characteristics you would like your ideal self to possess. Then rate yourself on a 7-point continuum between your ideal self and your real self. You can create a scale like this for every characteristic you want to develop and rate yourself on a monthly basis to measure your progress toward becoming your ideal self. If you are seeing a therapist or counselor, this exercise can also help you to determine those areas that might be useful to focus on during your therapy sessions.

- **Develop a Complex Self-concept.** Your self-concept is influenced by both the important roles you play (i.e., son or daughter, student, mother or father, chemist, boyfriend/girlfriend, etc.) and group identities (team member, etc.). You can enhance your self-esteem by developing your interests and abilities and having multiple roles by participating in extra-curricular activities such as athletics, the debate team, and the theater group, or work roles such as research assistant to a professor in your major.

- **Develop the "Big Five" Positive Personality Characteristics.** How would you rate yourself on each of the positive "Big Five" personality traits—Extraversion, Agreeableness, Conscientiousness, Emotional Stability, and Openness to Experience? Developing self-insight about your personality will enable you to make changes in areas that would lead to more college and personal success such as being more open to experience or agreeable, for example, if those are areas in which you need to improve your personality.

- **Identify Present Life Roles that Allow You To Be Your Authentic Self.** Think and write about your present life roles that allow you to feel authentic and express your positive personality traits. Doing so will help you envision how you can incorporate these or similar roles in your future life.

- **Develop an Assertive Communication Style.** You have a much better chance of achieving your goals while at the same time improving your interpersonal relationships if you use an assertive rather than a non-assertive or aggressive communication style.

- **Think of All of Your Possible Selves and Roles.** Identify and write about all the possible selves or future roles you could have that would allow you to feel authentic and express your positive personality traits. What career paths might you choose? What kind of hobbies could you possibly develop? What personal life roles are possibilities for you?

- **Increase Your Self-Efficacy for College Course Work.** Identify the college courses for which you have high or low self-efficacy. Then, determine the skills you need to learn to increase your self-efficacy in courses for which it is low as well as the resources available to help you.

- **Develop Emotional Intelligence Skills.** Develop the emotional intelligence skills associated with a relaxed temperament, disciplined goal orientation, achieving tendency, and integrity in order to be successful in college and happy in life. Avoid emotional thinking, impulsive behavior, and procrastination, which will jeopardize your success. Maintain a physically attractive appearance to achieve success in relationships. Develop your natural intelligence and abilities to achieve success in all areas of life.

- **Select a College Major.** Investigate your options and choose a college major that will help you prepare for the career that you think is consistent with your personality, interests, talents, and abilities.

Chapter Four
Develop Successful Learning Styles

Psychologists and educators have also looked at individual differences in approaches to mental processing such as cognitive styles (preferred perceptual modes for receiving and processing information), thinking styles (preferred ways of using the mental abilities one has), and personality (the enduring traits or characteristics of the person) (Sternberg & Grigorenko, 1997). Learning is an area where these differences in styles can have potential importance and research attention has been given to learning styles, which arise from both cognitive and personality approaches. A number of different scales have been developed to measure these different cognitive, learning, and personality styles. It is only very recently that research is being conducted to assess the relationship between learning and cognitive styles, learning preferences, personality, and academic achievement. We discuss that research and the implications for you in this chapter. We help you gain insight into your preferred cognitive receptive, learning, information processing, and evaluation styles. This self-knowledge will enable you to build on your areas of intellectual strengths and learn strategies for successfully compensating for your areas of weakness in learning situations.

Identify Your Multiple Intelligences

If you are like most students, you will be more enthusiastic and more motivated to achieve if you are doing college work that allows you to explore your interests and to develop and use your own unique talents. And, you will have a better chance of achieving proficiency and success when using these gifts doing professional work that you love. Vocational counselor Marsha Sinetar (1989) advises: *Do what you love, the money will follow.*

How do you identify your unique intellectual gifts and the type of work you love to do? In *Seven Frames of Mind* (1983), Harvard psychologist Howard Gardner defined seven intelligences: verbal-linguistic; logical-mathematical; visual-spatial; bodily-kinesthetic; musical-rhythmic; intrapersonal; and interpersonal. He points out that everyone has a unique combination of intelligences, which influences the types of academic courses and professional fields in which one is interested as well as her or his approach to new learning situations. In *Intelligence Reframed*, Gardner (1999) added another intelligence, naturalist. Those eight intelligences or frames of mind and the skills and abilities associated with them are provided in the Table below along with examples of related courses and college programs. This information will to help you gain insight about possible college majors and career paths that would enable you to utilize your strengths as well as general education courses that will help you gain more strength in other, less-preferred areas.

Table 1.
Multiple Intelligences, Abilities and Interests, and Related College Courses and Programs

Intelligences	Abilities & Interests	College Courses & Programs
Verbal-Linguistic	Speaking, reading, writing, learning languages	Communications, Education, English, History, Humanities, Languages, Literature, Philosophy, Religion, Psychology, Sociology, Speech, Writing
Logical-Mathematical	Analyzing, reasoning, solving logical and mathematical problems, computing	Accounting, Chemistry, Computer Science, Engineering, Law, Logic, Mathematics, Medicine, Physics
Visual-Spatial	Visualizing and mentally rotating a geometric object in space, creating art, following spatially oriented directions	Architecture, Art, Aviation, Computer Science, Engineering, Fashion design, Graphic design, Interior design, Landscaping, Multimedia design
Bodily-Kinesthetic	Activities that require gross motor skills and body balance	Dance, Physical Education, Sports, Physical Therapy, Theater
Musical-Rhythmic	Playing a musical instrument, understanding music theory, composing music	Music education, Theory of music, Music composition, Musical performance, Sound engineering
Intrapersonal	Ability to gain self-insight and become personally competent, be self-directed, be a leader	Artist, Counseling, Creative writing, Education, Human Relations, Law, Management, Psychology, Religion
Interpersonal	Ability to relate well with others and to become socially competent	Counseling, Criminal Justice, Education, Human Relations, Law, Medicine, Nursing, Political Science, Psychology, Social Work
Naturalist	Enjoys being in nature, recognizes details and fine distinctions among various plants, animals, rocks, clouds, and natural formations	Agriculture, Astronomy, Biology, Botany, Forestry, Geology, Horticulture, Marine Biology, Meteorology, Oceanography, Science, Zoology

Gardner notes that because schools have focused so much attention on developing verbal-linguistic, logical-mathematical, and visual-spatial skills, students who were not particularly gifted in these areas were made to feel that they were not very smart. They were also made to feel that the areas in which they were gifted were not valued in our culture, which caused many of them to lose motivation for achieving in academic work or in life (Gardner, 1983; 1999). Consequently, many people in our society did not have an opportunity to develop their talents to the fullest because what they loved to do and their talents and abilities were not valued in their schools.

Some community college students, who perform very well in college, recall that they felt "stupid" in grade school because of messages from teachers or guidance counselors. For example, Anna, a 32-year-old student in a child development class recalled being assigned to a special education class and being labeled "stupid" because she lacked English language skills when she entered the first grade. She said that it has taken her many years to realize that she "wasn't stupid," but may have appeared so since she couldn't speak as fluently as most of the other children because she came from a home in which English was not the primary language. Now, her goal is to be a bilingual elementary school teacher. Some community college students with undiagnosed learning disabilities recall teachers and guidance counselors telling them that they were "not smart enough to go to college."

Other community college students recall the loss of self-confidence when they were told that they didn't have high IQ test scores or good enough SAT scores to be admitted into a university of their choice. It typically takes a semester or two of successful performance in college for these students to gain back their lost self-confidence and begin to feel positive about their abilities for passing tests and successfully completing college work.

Most of us have an idea of our ability and aptitude, or potential, for academic subjects such as math and verbal ability because these were the areas in which we were tested by intelligence, aptitude and achievement tests in school. Gardner argues that the education system should stop making people feel like failures and, instead, teach them to appreciate and develop their natural talents while striving to become as competent as possible in all of these areas. We wholeheartedly agree with him that all of the intellectual abilities that Gardner has identified are important for achieving success in college and life. Think and write in your success journal about your unique blend of intelligences and how you might use that information to choose courses and a college major.

Identify the Sensory Perceptual Style You Prefer to Use for Learning. Use the Best Modality for the Material You Are Studying

Psychological researchers have found that people vary in their preferred cognitive reception style (the perceptual modality they prefer to use to learn new information) and approach learning situations differently. For example, some students may prefer to learn by listening and prefer classes with lectures, whereas others may have to struggle to follow that abstract style of presentation. Some students may be able to quickly digest the material in the text from reading it whereas others may benefit more from class discussions, videos, or hands-on learning opportunities. Some researchers have found that people perform better when they are able to process information using their preferred information reception style (e.g., Boulmetis & Sabula, 1996; McClanaghan, 2000). Other studies, however, do not support the idea that teaching in a student's preferred modality increases learning. A meta-analysis, a statistical integration of the research conducted on studies with elementary and secondary students, found "no appreciable gain" by teaching according to the student's modality preference (Kavale & Forness, 1987). A recent article in *American Educator* concluded that

> ...children do differ in their abilities with different modalities, but teaching the child in his best modality doesn't affect his educational achievement. What does matter is whether the child is taught in the content's best modality. All students learn more when content drives the choice of modality (Willingham, 2005, p. 31).

Although it is important to identify your preferred receptive style, it is necessary that you use the best modality for the material you are studying. For example, if your preferred modality is listening and you are taking an English literature class, you will have a lot of reading and must read and grasp the ideas of the written material. Therefore, it is important for you to build skills associated with your less preferred reception styles so you will be able to learn new information in all types of college courses and work situations.

One way to identify your preferred cognitive information reception style is to think about your past and present learning experiences. Do you prefer to learn by reading or viewing overheads or seeing videos? Or do you prefer to sit and listen to a lecture? Can you remember what you hear in a lecture? Maybe you like hands-on learning such as working with materials in science labs or performing activities in physical education or theater courses. Several cognitive reception styles or perceptual modality preferences have been identified:

- *Aural learners*—Prefer to learn by listening to a lecture, stories, or audio tape.
- *Visual learners*—Prefer to learn by reading textual material or an outline of it as well as seeing graphs and pictorial illustrations, Power Point presentations, and videos.
- *Tactile/Kinesthetic learners*—Prefer to learn by touching and doing "hands on" activities.
- *Global learners*—Prefer to learn by participating in a combination of aural, visual, and hands-on experiences.
- *Mixed Modality learners*—Have no preference for a perceptual modality—more common among adults than among children, indicating a developmental process. (Boulmetis & Sabula, 1996).

Many people have a second perceptual modality by which they prefer to learn as well. Having a secondary modality preference does not detract from but rather enhances information processing. A distinction can be made between perceptual modality preference and perceptual modality strength. A modality preference is the preferred perceptual route. A modality strength is superior functioning in one or more perceptual channels. "Approximately 30 percent of the population have a visual modality strength, 25 percent have auditory, and 15 percent have kinesthetic. The remaining 30 percent are thought to have mixed modality strengths" (Barbe & Milone, 1981 as cited in Boulmetis & Sabula, 1996, p. 15).

You may not have a perceptual modality preference for learning and can learn well in any situation, whether the material presented is visual, auditory, tactile/kinesthetic, or a combination of the modalities. Think about how you like to learn and determine whether you have a preferred perceptual modality or information reception style or not. If you do, you can tailor your studying to best fit that style, if it is appropriate to the nature of the subject matter being learned.

For example, if you are a visual learner, you might draw illustrations or tables to summarize your lecture notes. If you are an auditory learner, you might want to ask permission to tape record your classes and listen to the tapes rather than studying from written notes in preparation for an exam. If you are a tactile/kinesthetic learner, be sure to do all of the "hands on" activities and exercises in your text. If you are fortunate to learn equally well in all perceptual modalities, you might want to use a combination of methods in studying for your courses.

Photo courtesy of Bristol Community College.

Analyze Your Professors' Preferred Teaching Styles

Does it matter if the style the professor uses to present information doesn't match your preferred information reception style for learning or your perceptual modality preference? In recent research conducted with students in a Licensed Practical Nursing (LPN) Program, 28 of the 63 students tested had one or more perceptual modality preferences, whereas 35 students did not have a preference. Ten of the 28 participants with a perceptual modality preference received training in nutrition that matched their modality preference and 18 participants received training that did not match their modality preference. Students were given a pre-test and after three hours of instruction in nutrition were given a post-test. The results showed significantly higher achievement of students when instruction matched their perceptual modality preferences than when the instruction did not match their perceptual preferences (Boulmetis & Sabula, 1996). The results of this research show that students who have a perceptual modality preference can learn new information easier when there is a match between the professor's teaching style and their own modality preference.

Are you in a class in which you feel that the professor is presenting material in a foreign language or is so dull and boring that you can't seem to pay attention? If yes, think about whether your professor's preferred teaching style is the same as or different from your preferred information reception style. Some professors use overheads or Power Point presentations on which they visually present structured notes and diagrams, whereas others talk without any visual presentations. Look at the summary of teaching strategies and associated cognitive reception styles, in the Table below, and identify your professors' styles.

Table 2.
Teaching Methods and Associated Cognitive Reception Styles

Professor's Teaching Methods	Professor's Reception Style
Lectures, tells stories, plays tape recordings	Aural
Shows graphs and pictorial illustrations, outlines of text, Power Point presentations, and videos	Visual
Shows demonstrations, arranges in-class "hands on" activities.	Tactile/Kinesthetic
Provides a combination of aural, visual, and tactile/ kinesthetic experiences.	Global

If there seems to be a mismatch between your style and that of your professor, try to compensate by transferring as much of the learning as possible into your preferred learning style. Look at the list of strategies associated with each information processing style in the section above that you could use to transfer the material into your preferred style. You can also practice your non-preferred style in order to improve your performance in the class and become a global learner. Some professors tell their students that the tests will cover only material from their lectures. First of all, the student should not miss any classes. Then students must pay close attention to what is being said. If they are auditory learners they can listen attentively. If they are visual learners, however, they must write careful notes, perhaps rewrite the notes, and read and reread the notes regularly.

Most current textbooks present information in a way that appeals to all types of learners. They summarize the key concepts in each section in both textual and graphic form, provide hands-on activities for students to work on alone or in class, include various styles of practice test questions, and now have websites as well that provide further exercises and activities.

This can be somewhat overwhelming to a student, and the student should select which of these learning aids to attend to based on their time constraints and preferred learning style.

Draw Diagrams to Visually Summarize Important Information

According to Barbe and Milone (1981, as cited in Boulmetis & Sabula, 1996), about one-third of the population are visual learners. Visual learners prefer to learn by reading textual material or an outline of it as well as seeing graphs, pictorial illustrations, Power Point presentations, and videos, as noted above. Are you primarily a visual learner? Whether or not you are primarily a visual learner, you can enhance your learning of complex material by studying illustrations such as tables, graphs, flow diagrams, and concept maps in your text that summarize the key points concerning important processes, principles, theories, findings, and topics or drawing these types of illustrations into your notes.

Graphs are used to summarize quantitative information. An example of a type of graph is the figure in Chapter One showing data from the U.S. Census Bureau (2004) depicting the positive relationship between income and degree earned. You can use graphs to help you understand results of problems in your math courses.

A flow diagram, such as the one depicting the Information Processing Model shown in Chapter Five, is used to illustrate the sequence of operations or steps in a process.

A concept map, such as the one provided below, is used to illustrate the relationship between a key concept or central topic and the components of it. (The effective strategies for learning new information shown in the concept map are discussed in detail in Chapter Five.)

In order to construct a graph, you need to determine the relationship the data expresses. In order to construct a flow diagram, you need to identify the steps in the process you are trying to learn and then decide the sequence in which they occur. In order to construct a concept map, you need to first identify the components of a key concept you are trying to learn and then decide how they are related to the concept and to one another. Thus, drawing these illustrations involves a deep level of information processing that enables you to organize and to understand the material.

Therefore, these visual learning tools will enhance your ability to encode, store, and retrieve important complex information when needed. When you review graphs, flow diagrams, and concept maps when studying for an exam, you will save a great deal of time. If you are a primary visual learner, you may even be able to see your graphs, flow diagrams, and concept maps in your mind's eye during the exam. Additionally, you can also use concept maps to organize your ideas for an essay or paper.

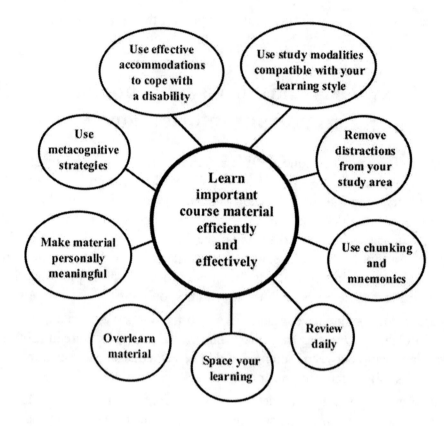

Figure 3.
Concept Map Summarizing Effective Strategies for
Learning New Information

Seek Out "Experiential" Learning Opportunities

Most students' can learn a great deal of information about the key concepts and theories in their field of interest through traditional classroom educational experiences. However, some students have been found to learn better when more active, "hands on" experiential methods are used (Bartlett, 1996). It is also well known that some types of learning can be best acquired through experiential learning and life experiences. Consequently, many educational and career training programs require some type of clinical work, internship, or service-learning (a method of experiential learning that links the college classroom with organizations in the community). In the past, clinical work and internships have been used to train professionals such as doctors, nurses, clinical psychologists, social workers, and teachers. At present, service-learning is expanding to other fields as well.

What is the difference between these methods of learning? How does "hands on" service-learning experience benefit students? Traditional classroom lecture and discussion learning primarily involves imparting factual information and facilitates the formation of abstract concepts and generalizations. On the other hand, service-learning begins with a concrete experience, moves through observation and reflection to the formation of abstract concepts and generalizations, then to testing implications of concepts in new situations, and finally it begins again by reinforcing what has been learned through a new concrete experience (Kolb, 1984).

How might a service-learning experience be structured? Strober and McGoldrick (1998) described service-learning experiences of students enrolled in an upper level course titled Women and Gender Issues in Economics, which focused on micro- and macroeconomics principles. Students were given three project options for earning 15% of their grade: participating in the service project, doing a traditional research paper, or writing a biography of a female economist. Seventeen of the 19 students chose the service project and each one of them subsequently worked for 15 hours in a variety of community organizations, such as women's shelters and resource centers, which have an economic impact on women. Students also kept journals of their reflections about their work and learning experiences and the perceived benefits, completed research papers, prepared poster presentations describing their service-learning experiences, and completed exit questionnaires. Analysis of student journal entries, papers, posters, and exit questionnaires revealed that students perceived that they benefited from the service-learning experiences. Faculty and community organization responses to this economics course student learning experience were also positive. When describing the benefits of a structured service-learning experience, Strober and McGoldrick (1984) quote Phillips' well-known statement that:

> We remember 10 percent of what we hear, 15 percent of what
> we see, 25 percent of what hear and see, 60 percent of what
> we do, 80 percent of what we do with active reflection, and 90
> percent of what we teach. (p. 375)

The results of this research suggest that you will benefit by actively seeking out opportunities for "hands on" service-learning, work, or tutoring experiences that are related to your field of interest. Not only will these types of experiences help you acquire expertise and work skills in your field of interest, but they will also afford you the opportunity to see if you like doing a particular type of work. Another benefit is that you will be in a better position to attract suitable mentors and role models in the community to guide and advise you.

Identify the Learning Mode You Have a Tendency to Emphasize

One of the most frequently used measures of learning styles is the Learning Style Inventory (LSI) based on Kolb's Theory of Experiential Learning (Kolb, 1984; Kolb, Osland, & Rubin, 1995). The LSI measures the individual's relative emphasis on the four modes of learning measured by the scale:

Concrete Experience (CE)—The focus is on being involved in experiences and emphasizes feeling and enjoyment of relating to others. The orientation is an intuitive "artistic" approach to solving problems. People with a high CE score on the LSI probably would enjoy a class that emphasizes practical application of things that they feel are personally meaningful such as an applied psychology course.

Reflective Observation (RO)—The orientation is towards understanding the meaning of ideas and situations. The focus is on careful observation and reflection as opposed to action and practical application. People with a high RO score on the LSI probably would enjoy a class that emphasizes demonstration such as a science lab.

Abstract Conceptualization (AC)—The focus is a logical, scientific orientation. People with this approach value planning, manipulating abstract symbols, and analyzing quantitative data. People with a high AC score on the LSI probably would enjoy math classes.

Active Experimentation (AE)—People with this orientation emphasize practical applications and are good at getting things accomplished. They focus on influencing people and changing situations. People with a high AE score on the LSI probably would enjoy a "hands on" computer or science lab.

According to Kolb et al. (1995), each person's learning style is a combination of the four categories, and effective learners rely on the four different learning modes, which are based on two dimensions: converging versus diverging and assimilating versus accommodating.

- *Divergent Learning Style*—Emphasizes Concrete Experience (CE) and Reflective Observation (RO). People with this orientation are imaginative and interested in people.

- *Convergent Learning Style*—Is the opposite of the divergent style. Convergers are high in Abstract Conceptualization (AC) and Active Experimentation (AE). The strength of this approach is reasoning. People with this orientation prefer dealing with technical tasks rather than with people.

- *Assimilative Learning Style*—Characterized by Abstract Conceptualization (AC) and Reflective Observation (RO). The strength of this approach is reasoning and the ability to create theoretical models and in assimilating disparate observations into an integrated explanation.

- *Accommodative Learning Style*—Characterized by Concrete Experience (CE) and Active Experimentation (AE), which is the opposite of the assimilative style. People with this style are action orientated and solve problems in an intuitive trial and error manner.

The scores on the LSI indicate which modes of learning an individual emphasizes. "The key to effective learning is being competent in each mode when it is appropriate" (Kolb et al., 1995, pp. 51–52).

Are there sex differences in the tendency to emphasize these learning modes? Gender differences in learning modes were found with Kolb's LSI among a sample of university students. Women's scores were more evenly distributed than men's across the four categories, with Diverger (interested in people) and Converger (prefers technical tasks) being the greatest number. Men on the other hand, were least likely to be in the Diverger category and most likely to be Assimilators (prefers reasoning and creating theoretical models) (Philbin, Meier, Huffman, & Boverie, 1995).

In a recent study with undergraduate business and management students in England, the Learning Styles Inventory (LSI) was administered and students were then asked about their learning style preferences. Men who prefer to deal with the world through Active Experimentation (AE) and Reflective Observation (RO) as measured by the LSI prefer learning methods that involve social interaction. Women who have a higher preference for autonomy have higher verbal preference and lower imagery preference (Sadler-Smith, 2001).

What learning modes do you tend to emphasize? How do you typically approach learning situations? Read the descriptions for each of the four different learning modes above and identify the ones that best describe you. Then, look at the examples of preferred learning situations associated with your preferred learning style in the Table below.

Table 3.
Kolb's Learning Styles and Preferred Learning Situations

Learning Style	Learning Situations
Divergent	Counseling, Human Relations, Sociology
Convergent	Computer science, Math, Science
Assimilative	Math, Psychology, Science
Accommodative	Art, Counseling, Graphics design, Humanities

Once you determine the learning mode you tend to emphasize, begin to think about how you might be able to become a more effective learner by being competent in using each of the modes, as appropriate. For example, if you find that you rely on concrete experience, taking classes in which the scientific method is taught may help you develop the capacity for abstract conceptualization.

For First-Year Academic Success, Develop Your Executive and Internal Thinking Styles

Robert J. Sternberg (1994; 1997) has proposed another approach to learning and thinking styles based on the Theory of Mental Self-Government (MSG), which is modeled after governments. "Just as governments carry out legislative, executive, and judicial functions, so does the mind" (Sternberg & Grigorenko, 1997, p. 707):

- *Legislative Style*—Characterizes people who enjoy creating their own rules and doing things their own way.

- *Executive Style*—Characterizes people who prefer structured tasks and who rely on existing methods.

- *Judicial Style*—Characterizes people who like to analyze and evaluate the existing rules and procedures.

The scope of mental self-government is dichotomized as either

- *Internal*—Exemplified by people who like to work alone, or
- *External*—Exemplified by people who prefer accomplishing tasks by working through interaction with others.

Research conducted with undergraduate students in Spain compared the Learning Styles Questionnaire (LSQ) (a variation of Kolb's LSI) with the MSG Thinking Styles Inventory (developed by Sternberg and Wagner, 1991, as cited in Sternberg & Grigorenko, 1997) in relation to their influence on academic achievement (Cano-Garcia & Hughes, 2000). Four of the subscales of the two inventories were the best predictors of academic achievement after all statistical analyses were completed: Executive and Internal from the MSG Thinking Styles Inventory were positively related to academic achievement. Legislative from the MSG and Concrete Experience from the LSQ were negative predictors of academic achievement.

What are these subscales and how might you incorporate what they are measuring into your learning and thinking styles? The MSG Thinking Styles Inventory is based on Sternberg's Theory of Mental Self-Government discussed above (Sternberg & Grigorenko, 1997). What this means is that students who prefer that someone else defines and structures what they have to do and who like to work alone get the highest grades. On the other hand, students are least likely to perform well academically who enjoy creating their own rules and doing things their way as well as those who focus on feelings and relating to others, at least among the first-year psychology students studied (Kolb, 1984; 1995).

The implication of this research is consistent with the message of Chapter One. In order to succeed in college you need to follow the rules and regulations of the college or university you attend. When a professor gives you a syllabus telling you what the assignments are, you have to turn in the assignments required on the dates on which they are due. If the assignment asks for a paper based on library research from journals in a particular field, you write a paper based on journal articles and not based on interviews with people or your opinions. If you attend a large university, your classes may be very large, with few opportunities to express your creativity and influence the form or structure of the course. You should play by the rules. As you move to higher-level courses, you may have the opportunity to participate in seminars where you may be able to have a role in the direction of the discussions and ideas examined in the class. Grades in college do not necessarily correlate with creative successes in a career after you graduate.

Learning of Complex Material Requires Mastery Goals and Deep Processing. Performance Approach Goals and Surface Learning (but Not Performance Avoidance Goals) Can also Lead to Exam Success for Less Complex Material

Schmeck (1988) suggested that people's learning styles differ in whether they use "deep" or "surface" processing, which also has implications for college achievement. Deep processing has also been labeled elaboration or critical thinking. It involves challenging information and integrating it with previously learned knowledge and experience. On the other hand, surface processing involves repetitive rehearsal and rote memorization of information (Elliot, McGregor & Gable, 1999). Research with first and second year students in the Netherlands found that surface learning is associated with a tendency toward external regulation, such as teacher's instructions, whereas deep learning is associated with a tendency to self-regulate (Vermetten, Lodewijks, & Vermunt, 2001).

Whether you prefer one or the other of these styles is related to goal orientation. Achievement motivation involves goals involving competence: (a) learning goals which are focused on increasing competence, understanding or mastery of something new, and (b) performance goals, in which individuals seek to gain favorable judgments of their competence, or avoid negative judgments of their competence (Dweck, 1986). Recently, performance goals have been divided into two goals: a performance-approach goal focused on the attainment of high achievement relative to others and a performance–avoidance goal focused on the avoidance of failure relative to others (Elliot, McGregor, & Gable, 1999).

Research conducted with 164 students, in an introductory psychology course, assessed student achievement goals and performance on an exam in a college classroom (Elliot, McGregor, & Gable, 1999). The three goals assessed were:

- *Learning or mastery goals*—Characterized by a desire to learn
- *Performance-approach goals*—Characterized by a desire to be judged favorably relative to others
- *Performance-avoidance goals*—Characterized by a fear of performing poorly relative to others

Students who had learning or mastery goals or performance-approach goals did well on the exam, whereas students with performance-avoidance goals tended not to do well on the exam. Students who held learning or mastery goals were most likely to use the study strategy of deep processing, and persistence, and effort. Students with performance-approach goals used surface learning, but also persistence and effort. Students with performance-avoidance goals used surface learning but had a disorganized approach to studying. The study strategies that were related to successful exam performance in an introductory psychology course were either surface or deep processing, when combined with persistence and effort, whereas disorganization led to poor performance (Elliot, McGregor, & Gable, 1999). However, Grant and Dweck (2003) have recently found evidence suggesting that only deep processing leads to exam success in a course in which complex material needs to be mastered such as a challenging chemistry class for premed, engineering, and science majors offered at Columbia University. Thus, there is research evidence that the type of processing that leads to successful performance on exams may depend on the complexity of material to be mastered, as one might expect. Deep processing may lead to exam success when elaboration or critical thinking is required whereas surface processing may lead to exam success when repetitive rehearsal and rote memorization of information is required.

What implications does this research have for studying for exams? You want to be motivated by mastery goals (a desire to learn), or performance-approach goals (doing well relative to others) in your basic introductory courses. The goal you don't want to have is the performance-avoidance goal, which is a fear of failure, of not doing as well as others. Students with this goal do not do well on exams because they are disorganized in their approach to learning. In courses in which there is a high level of complexity such as challenging chemistry or other science courses, a mastery approach, which leads to deep processing, is predictive of high exam performance. Either surface learning or deep learning strategies can lead to doing well on an exam, when combined with persistence and effort, in courses with less complex material. Surface learning combined with a disorganized approach to studying leads to exam failure in all courses. The moral of the story is that you should plan your study strategy according to the complexity of the material you are studying and carry it out with persistence and effort.

Work at Developing a Rational-Analytical Style of Processing and Evaluating Information

Recently, two fundamentally different types of information processing styles have been proposed by psychologists representing a broad spectrum of theoretical orientations—one is known as *intuitive-experiential*, and the other as *analytical-rational* (Epstein, Pacini, Denes-Raj, & Heier, 1996). The intuitive style of information processing is preconscious, emotional and automatic and operates primarily at the nonverbal, holistic level. The rational style of information processing is intentional and primarily verbal and is guided by abstract, general rules, analysis, and logic. Based on research on 184 undergraduate students, Epstein and his colleagues determined that the scores from a *Need for Cognition Scale* (NFC), measuring the analytical-rational dimension, and a *Faith in Intuition Scale* (FIS), measuring the intuitive-experiential dimension, are in fact two separate modes of processing information.

Epstein et al. (1996) then administered a shortened version of these Need for Cognition (NFC) and Faith in Intuition (FIS) scales to 973 students as well as measures of personality and adjustment and grade point average (GPA). Despite the stereotypes of women as being more intuitive and less rational than men, no significant gender differences were found in rational vs. intuitive information processing styles. Students scoring high in the analytical-rational scale were more dominant, had higher self-esteem, and greater satisfaction with their health than students scoring low on the scale. The high analytical-rational scale scorers also had higher SAT scores and GPAs in college than did low scorers. The high scorers were also less likely to hold racist attitudes, to suffer from depression and anxiety, to feel stressed out by college life, to drink alcohol and when they did drink, to drink less alcohol than did students scoring low in analytic-rational styles. Need for Cognition Scale (NFC) scores were also positively correlated with degree of traumatization and abuse, especially emotional abuse before the age of 16. This correlation suggests that distressing experiences may stimulate people to think seriously about their lives. In the absence of such experiences, people may be less prone to develop such an interest (Epstein et al., 1996, p. 399).

Students scoring high on the intuitive-experiential scale were also more dominant and had higher self-esteem, and were less depressed than students scoring low on this scale, however, the relationship was weaker than for the analytical-rational styles and these characteristics. The intuitive style was not related to either SAT scores or GPAs. Although women with high scores on the analytic-rational dimension do have a positive psychological adjustment, they have a tendency to avoid close, emotional relationships. Men and women scoring high on the intuitive-experiential dimension have a secure style in romantic relationships.

Information processing style is not simply determined by personality preference. Whether one type of information processing is preferred over another is also determined by the nature of the material being processed, one's mental set at the time, and whether the information threatens or enhances existing beliefs and goals. Epstein and his colleagues (1996) asked students to respond to people in various situations and to make evaluations of the outcome. They were able to shift back and forth between the rational and intuitive modes of processing according to different perspectives they were asked to take. The finding that students are able to change their style and process information either rationally or intuitively indicates that although the two styles are independent, individuals can adopt both perspectives depending on the situation. The exception to this flexibility is women very high in intuitive style, tending to use this style with differing instructions.

Motivational factors also play a role in whether an individual uses an analytical or intuitive style in evaluating information. In a series of four experiments, biases in reasoning about students' future occupations were predicted not only by a student's preference for an intuitive style, but also by whether the problem was threatening to one's career goal (Klaczynski, Gordon, & Fauth, 1997). Depth of processing (a rational approach) was greatly increased when the material presented was threatening to one's career choice; reasoning on the goal-enhancing and neutral problems was less sophisticated. This shows that when we are motivated by a goal, we are capable of more rational-analytical reasoning processes, regardless of intellectual ability, which was found by Klaczynski and his colleagues not to predict information processing style as well as the underlying motivation for reasoning did.

What are the implications of this research for you? Students who have an intuitive information processing style learn better from personal experience and concrete examples. Those with a rational style learn best from a presentation of facts and logical arguments. It is not surprising that students with the rational style receive higher grades in college since most college courses are based on factual information and logical arguments. One can still maintain an intuitive style in relationships. To improve college performance, however, work to develop a rational style with regard to college courses, since that is the type of learning and thinking processes required in most college classrooms. As the research has demonstrated, most college students, regardless of intelligence, are capable of using a rational style of information processing when they are motivated to do so.

If You Have a Learning or Physical Disability, Use Effective Accommodations for Coping with It

Do you typically have trouble paying attention to your professors' class lectures or taking good notes? Do you typically spend a great deal of time studying only to find that you have trouble understanding what you have just read? Have you always had problems doing school work? Do you know or suspect that you may have a learning skills deficit or learning disability that is making it harder for you to achieve in college than it is for other students? If yes, contact the learning specialists in the center for developmental education at your college for assessment and assistance in identifying any tutoring services or special accommodations that you might need to optimize your chances of success in college. All state and private community colleges, colleges, and universities that receive funding from the United States government have these types of services. They are legally obligated to provide them for students with disabilities, as outlined under Section 504 of the Rehabilitation Act of 1973 and Individuals with Disabilities Education Act (1990).

Even though it is their legal right to ask for assessment and accommodations, some students who suspect that they might have a learning disability hesitate to ask for accommodations thinking that they should try to succeed without them. However, students who need and use appropriate accommodations for learning disabilities vastly increase their chances of success. The diagnoses and information about any services provided are kept confidential. Professors are not informed about any disability unless the student gives written permission or tells the professor.

How are learning disabilities assessed? Diagnosis usually begins with a detailed history of the student as a learner. Has the student always had problems in school or at work? Then, a test for diagnosing the suspected learning disability would be administered to the student by a trained learning specialist. For example, the adult version of the Computer-Based Academic Assessment System (CAAS) might be used to diagnose specific reading disabilities among college students. The CAAS uses four computer-presented tasks that measure speed and accuracy of reading performance to assess underlying component processes involved in reading. These include perceptual processing response time, a letter identification task, a word and pseudoword (with one letter of each word changed) naming task, a semantic or sentence processing knowledge task, and a phonological (rhyming and spelling) awareness processing task. Researchers have found that the adult version of the CAAS can not only discriminate between college students who have a reading learning disability and those who do not, but it also can pinpoint the specific underlying reading processes that the student has difficulty performing (Cisero, Royer, Marchant, & Jackson, 1997). Once a specific problem is identified, the learning specialist may recommend accommodations to help the student successfully complete her or his course work.

What types of accommodations are provided for students with learning disabilities? The accommodations needed are determined once both the specific type of learning disability and the seriousness of it are identified. Some students with Attention Deficit Disorder (ADD) who have difficulty paying attention to lectures are allowed to ask their professors if they can tape record their classes and to ask for extra time when taking exams. Students with serious difficulty reading and comprehending exam questions due to conditions such as dyslexia (a learning disorder marked by impairment in one's ability to recognize and understand written words) might be allowed to take exams in another supervised testing location with extra time to complete it. Some students with severe learning or physical disabilities might have a scribe take class notes for them as well as a tutor to read exam questions aloud and record their answers for them. Many colleges and community colleges have computerized technology that provides assistance with reading and test-taking tasks for hearing and sight impaired students.

Once students find out they have a specific learning disability and identify effective strategies for coping with it, they usually feel relieved and perform very well in college. Yet, some students—especially mature ones who attended school before diagnosis of learning disabilities was common—struggle needlessly because they do not realize they have a learning disability and need help.

For example, Marcy was very surprised to recognize herself in the profiles of people with attention deficit disorder (ADD) in a movie shown in her psychology of personal adjustment class. ADD is a learning disorder characterized by an inappropriately low level of ability to pay selective attention to information entering one's sensory register from the senses or in short-term memory. Even though she seemed to be a fairly good student, Marcy said that she always had to struggle and spend enormous amounts of time studying in order to achieve average grades in school. She said that she had been enrolled in college ten years earlier but had dropped out because she thought she was "too stupid to earn a college degree." She felt that she was not as smart as her friends who seemed to sail through college spending a lot less time studying than she did but earning much higher grades.

Unlike her friends who were college graduates, Marcy had spent the decade since she dropped out of college in low paying, dead-end jobs. She returned to college determined to earn a degree and pursue a higher paying, more meaningful career. She was struggling to achieve her goals when she recognized herself when exposed to information about people who had trouble paying attention or finishing tasks.

After Marcy saw the movie on Attention Deficit Disorder (ADD), she visited the learning specialist at her community college and was subsequently tested. She was diagnosed as having a mild case of ADD and began the process of learning effective study and test-taking strategies for coping with it. As with so many students who are diagnosed with learning disabilities, Marcy was very relieved to find out that she is "not stupid." Instead, she has discovered that she is a very intelligent and creative woman who just happens to have ADD. Marcy is currently considering becoming a special education teacher so that she can help children who also have difficulties learning in school.

If you suspect that you might have a learning deficit or disability, contact a learning specialist at your college's tutoring center. Ask for help in identifying the source of your problem as well as effective strategies you can use to improve your performance in academic tasks. Sometimes all that is needed is some tutoring in reading or training in study skills. If desired, you may speak directly to your professor who may suggest other accommodations, as did Stacey who is featured in the Success Profile below.

Success Profile—Stacey

Stacey is a student who had psychological testing that identified her as having dyslexia. Stacey is a 28-year-old woman with large blue eyes and blond hair who has had to accommodate to learning disabilities throughout her educational career. She was originally diagnosed in the 3rd grade when she moved to a new school and the teachers there sent her for testing. Stacey has disabilities in reading, math, and writing. She has a very good vocabulary, but has difficulty with organization in writing. In elementary school, Stacey was in special education classes and when in a regular classroom she went out to resource rooms. In high school, she was in the general classes, not the college prep classes. For the last two years of high school, Stacey went to the regional vocational high school, alternating two weeks in the vocational school and two weeks in the general high school classes. She received a lot of support from her teachers in high school. She was taking courses in child development in the vocational school so that she could get a job working in a daycare center when she graduated.

The summer right after graduation, however, Stacey went to a private junior college in a neighboring state. She lived there and that was a very difficult time for her as she was away from home for the first time living in a dorm and her parents were going through a divorce. Stacey talked to an advisor and worked with tutors, so she was able to complete three courses that summer with As and Bs. After that summer, she moved home and went to the community college on a part-time basis and worked full-time. Stacey said that she felt that she needed to be able to do multiple things, rather than going to school full-time and only studying. She needs balance—time away from course work. Consequently, Stacey was also working in a school for behaviorally disordered children and adolescents who had been physically and sexually abused. She went through many training sessions in areas such as the use of behavior modification. Stacey continued going to school, taking one or two courses a semester. She graduated with an Associate's degree in General Studies.

Stacey transferred to a four-year college with the goal of earning a Bachelor's Degree and becoming a special education teacher. Before she could get accepted into the education program and take the methods classes, however, she had to pass a national standardized test. Stacey failed the exam twice because she doesn't do well on standardized tests. Now, she has decided to become a psychology major. Stacey has had tutors that she hires and pays for herself to help her every semester.

Currently, Stacey works full-time at a local hospital in a psychological research program. At work, her supervisors say she is thorough because she focuses on her work and documents everything. She takes all of her courses at night. Stacey has been in college for ten years and has more than enough credits for graduation, but she still needs five courses required in the psychology major because she took a number of education courses.

Stacey has to work very hard in her college courses. Her fiancé, who works full-time for a cable company and did not attend college, is willing to spend time with Stacey helping her study by testing her with flash cards she makes up from her textbook. She also explains to him what was discussed in class as a way of helping her to process and remember the information. Her fiancé is finding the coursework interesting, and he may take classes as well. Last weekend they rewarded themselves by going to a Boston Red Sox game on Sunday after spending all day Saturday studying.

Despite her hard work, Stacey did not do well on the first test in her psychology class. She initiated a discussion with her professor about the nature of her learning disability. One of the problems is that she cannot take notes and listen at the same time. Her professor told Stacey to just sit and listen and not take notes and then said she would give her the overhead transparencies shown during the class if Stacey agreed that she would return them the next day. This system worked so well that Stacey got an "A" on the next exam. Because of working and her learning disability, Stacey is only able to take one course a semester. But, her hard work has paid off. Stacey is now a senior with a 3.6 GPA (on a 4-point scale).

Stacey is planning to go into a Master's program after graduation. She plans to continue working and going to school part-time, in either the counseling program at the college she attends or into a marriage and family counseling program at the state university.

Success Recommendations

This section contains a summary of the main points in this chapter to help you reflect on and recall what you have learned.

- **Identify Your Multiple Intelligences.** In recent years psychologists have been expanding their definition of intelligence. Howard Gardner, a Harvard psychologist, has identified eight different forms of intelligence: Verbal-Linguistic, Logical-Mathematical, Visual-Spatial, Bodily-Kinesthetic, Musical-Rhythmic, Intrapersonal, Interpersonal, and Naturalist. Think and write about your unique blend of intelligences and how you might use that information to choose courses and a college major.

- **Identify the Sensory Perceptual Style You Prefer to Use for Learning.** Observe yourself in learning situations in order to gain self-insight about the types of information you learn most easily and the learning strategies you tend to use. Knowing this information can help you identify strategies you can use to improve your reading, studying, note-taking, and test-taking techniques.

- **Analyze Your Professors' Teaching Styles.** Think about the teaching methods used by your favorite professors in order to gain self-insight about the teaching style you prefer. Knowing this information can help you identify strategies you can use to take advantage of your strengths while striving to become a more global learner.

- **Draw Diagrams to Visually Summarize Important Information.** Draw graphs, flow diagrams, and concept maps, if appropriate for the type of material you are learning, to enhance your ability to encode, store, and retrieve important information for exams. These visual information organization tools will also save you a great deal of time when studying for an exam.

- **Seek Out "Experiential" Learning Opportunities.** Actively seek out opportunities for "hands on" service-learning, work, or tutoring experiences that are related to your field of interest. Not only will these types of experiences help you acquire expertise and work skills in your field of interest, but they will also afford you the opportunity to see if you like doing a particular type of work. Another benefit is that you will be in a better position to attract suitable mentors and role models to guide and advise you.

- **Identify the Learning Mode You Have a Tendency to Emphasize.** Gain self-insight about your learning style and the strengths and abilities associated with it. This knowledge will enable you to identify ways you can build on your cognitive strengths, compensate for your weaknesses, and improve your ability to learn in various types of classes and work situations.

- **For First-Year Academic Success, Develop Your Executive and Internal Thinking Styles.** In order to succeed in college, you need to play by the rules. Be sure to follow the rules and regulations of your college or university. You must also adhere to your professors' directions when completing assignments.

- **Realize that Either Surface or Deep Learning Styles, and Either Mastery or Performance Approach, Plus Persistence and Effort Lead to Exam Success.** Strive to be motivated by either mastery goals (a desire to learn) or performance-approach goals (doing well relative to others). To perform well on exams, you can use either

85

surface learning or deep learning strategies, as appropriate for the complexity of the material you are studying. The moral of the story is that you should plan your study strategy and carry it out with persistence and effort.

- **Develop a Rational-Analytical Style of Processing and Evaluating Information.** Gain self-insight about your temperament, how you approach your environment, and how you prefer to solve problems. To be a successful student, however, work at developing a Rational-Analytical style of processing and evaluating information.

- **If You Have a Learning or Physical Disability, Use Effective Accommodations for Coping with It.** If you suspect that you may have a learning or physical disability, seek help. Contact a learning specialist in the center for developmental education at your college. Ask him or her for an assessment of your learning abilities as well as assistance in identifying any tutoring services or special accommodations that you might need to optimize your chances of success in college.

Chapter Five
Process Information Efficiently and Learn Effectively

This is the information age. From the multiple channels of television stations we can receive on our cable systems, to the seemingly limitless information available on the Internet, to the volumes of books and plethora of newspapers and magazines, to the fast paced lives we live in cities and suburbs, we are inundated with information on a daily basis. How can we evaluate this information and decide what is important and what is trivial? How can we process this information selectively and efficiently, maintain our sanity, and remember and utilize the information that is important to functioning in our daily lives and achieving success in college courses?

In this chapter we provide students with effective strategies for dealing with information overload based on over 100 years of research on learning, memory and, more recently, information processing. This information will empower you to develop metacognitive skills, which are mental skills that enable you to have knowledge or awareness of your thinking and to monitor and control those mental processes. Developing and using metacognitive skills will help you improve your ability to study more efficiently and to perform more effectively in test taking situations.

Understand How the Information Processing Model of Memory Explains How You Process and Learn Information

How do we receive and process information entering our sensory systems from stimuli in our environment, process and store it in memory, and retrieve it for use when needed? Memories are stored in neural networks distributed throughout various areas of the brain and the complex processing involved in storing and retrieving information is still not completely understood (Baddeley, 2002; Smith, 2000). Despite the complexity of the processes, many psychologists still use an updated version of a three-stage model of interacting memory systems, originally proposed by Atkinson and Shiffrin (1968), to explain how the human information processing system works. We provided a discussion of an updated to version of this model because we know that this information will help you to understand how to study different types of information you need to learn for your college courses.

The three stages of memory depicted in the figure below are the sensory memory stores, short-term memory stores in working memory, and long-term (permanent) memory stores. These memory stores differ in the amount of perceptual inputs they can store, the duration of time over which the inputs can be retained, and the types of control processing that can occur in them (Atkinson & Shiffrin, 1968; Baddeley, 2002).

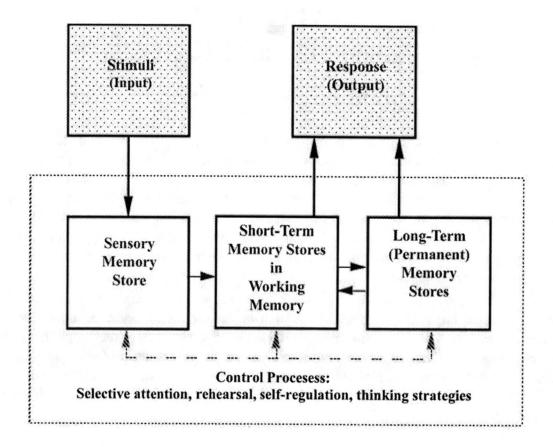

Figure 4.
Information Processing Model of Memory

Sensory Memory—The first stage in information processing is activated as stimuli in the environment impinge upon one's senses causing perceptual data to be input into one's sensory memory store. Sensory memory storage occurs automatically as the areas of one's brain involved in processing modality specific perceptual inputs (e.g., visual, auditory) are stimulated. Thus, a low-level, unconscious, effortless type of processing of sensory information takes place in the sensory memory stores. The sensory memory store holds a large amount of sensory data for a fraction of a second so that one can have a chance to recognize stimuli in the environment and decide if it should be given some attention (Sperling, 1960). Data in one's sensory memory store that is not attended to is constantly being replaced by new data impinging upon one's senses so that we can remain aware of new stimuli in our shifting environment.

Short-Term Memory Stores in Working Memory—The second stage in information processing is activated as perceptual data related to sensory stimuli that receive selective attention are transferred from one's sensory memory stores to one's modality specific short-term memory (STM) stores, which are distributed in various areas in the brain (Baddeley, 2002; Ungerleider, 1995). Short-term memory (STM) stores, in contrast to sensory memory stores, have a limited capacity and can only hold between five and nine chunks of information for a short period of time, perhaps up to 30 seconds (Baddeley, 1992; Miller, 1956). One can rehearse (repetitively verbalize or think about and subvocalize) and refresh the information and, thereby, retain it longer in short-term memory (Baddeley, 2002; D'Esposito et al., 1995).

In Atkinson's and Shiffrin's (1968) original model, short term memory was described as a simple rehearsal buffer and the research evidence cited above was congruent that view. More recent research on people with short-term memory deficits and studies using new brain imaging technologies, however, have demonstrated that a profusion of complex information processing occurs in different areas of the brain during this stage (Baddeley, 2002; Logie, Cocchini Della Sala, & Baddeley, 2004). Baddeley (2002), therefore, proposed a model of working memory that incorporates the characteristics formerly attributed to short-term memory, accounts for the findings of recent research, and explains how complex information processing tasks appear to be accomplished in the brain. The four elements in Baddeley's working memory model are the

- *Executive control system*—Controls the deployment of attention, dividing attention, and switching the focus of attention. It is also involved in maintenance rehearsal that can be used to retain information in short-term memory.

- *Phonological rehearsal loop*—Contains a phonological store for temporary or short-term verbal memory storage and an articulatory rehearsal system that facilitates language acquisition by enabling subvocal articulation rehearsal of coded verbal and auditory perceptual inputs from the sensory memory stores. It also has links to long-term memory for retrieving information about language.

- *Visuospatial sketchpad*—Multicomponent element enables temporary storage and mental manipulation of visual and spatial information, maintenance of one's spatial orientation, and solving of visuospatial problems. The sketchpad forms an interface between visual and spatial information accessed either through the senses or from long-term memory.

- *Episodic buffer*—A temporary, limited capacity storage system for integrated episodes or scenes using different codes (verbal, auditory, visual, spatial) from the phonological rehearsal loop and the visuospatial sketchpad components of working memory. This element allows one to consider multiple sources of information simultaneously and, thereby, create a model of the environment that one can manipulate to solve problems and plan future behavior.

As the discussion above indicates, you will be relying on the working short-term memory elements to learn your course material and to complete answers on your exams. The executive control system will enable you to focus your attention on perceptual data related to particular points of interest that you hear in your lectures and rehearse it to retain it in short-term memory. The phonological rehearsal loop and the visuospatial sketchpad will enable you to temporarily store and compare and contrast perceptual inputs from the sensory stores that you are rehearsing (verbal, auditory and visual, spatial, respectively) with similar or related information you retrieve from your long-term memory in order to help you interpret the meaning and relevance of the incoming data and transfer it to your long-term memory stores. The episodic buffer will enable you to temporarily store and integrate different types of perceptual data segments related to the lecture (verbal, auditory, visual, spatial) coming from your sensory stores with data already stored in your long-term memory that you consciously retrieve and to integrate and combine these segments into a meaningful answer for you to use on your exam. The parts of the information from the lecture that you do not fully process and store in long-term memory are not maintained in your short-term stores and so you forget them.

Long-Term (Permanent) Memory Stores—As with short-term memory stores, there are modality specific long-term memory (LTM) stores distributed in various areas of the brain (Ungerleider, 1995). In contrast to short-term memory stores, the long-term memory stores can hold an unlimited amount of information for a long time, ranging from hours to a lifetime, even though one is not consciously aware of what's stored in it. All forms of long-term memory rely on permanent changes in strength of neural connections between sending and receiving neurons, which make it easier to get the same effect in the future (Bliss & Collingridge, 1993). This is why it's easier to recall the information you frequently use. Depending on which connections among neurons are altered, different types of long-term memories will be stored (Eichenbaum, 1997; Schacter, 1994).

Two long-term memory systems have been identified: declarative (explicit) and procedural (implicit) (Schacter, 1992; Squire, Knowlton, & Musen, 1993).

- *The declarative (explicit) memory system* handles explicit factual information concerning what one knows, such as the words and sounds of one's favorite song and a visual image of how the band looks. These memories can be retrieved at will from long-term memory stores and represented in one's short-term memory stores in working memory. Two types of declarative memories have been identified: semantic and episodic.

  — *Semantic memories*—Encyclopedic memories about general facts that are not associated with a specific time, place, and circumstance such as the meanings of words, concepts, and facts or general knowledge about one's world (Schacter, 1992; Tulving, 1993). This is the type of memory you'll need to call on to remember the facts you will need to learn for your classes and exams. Learning and retrieving semantic information requires effortful processing. For example, you need to understand the meaning of material that you are trying to learn so that you will know what other information it is related to and, therefore, should be stored with in LTM as well as how to retrieve it when needed. We discuss strategies that you can use to make semantic information processing easier for you in the sections below.

  — *Episodic memories*—Autobiographical memories are personal facts and events (episodes) about what you have seen, heard, or done that are associated with a particular context—a time, place, and circumstance in which specific events took place (Schacter, 1992; Tulving, 1993). Storing and retrieving episodic memories, in contrast to semantic memories, do not require as much conscious, effortful processing. This is especially true for memories of events that are personally meaningful to you or associated with strong emotions such as the events surrounding the untimely death of Princess Diana in 1997, your first date, or your high school graduation.

- *The procedural (implicit) memory system* handles implicit memories of knowing how to do some actions, skills, operations, or perform some conditioned behaviors (Schacter, 1992; Squire, Knowlton, & Mussen, 1993). Procedural memories such as riding a bike, using the computer, driving a car, or smoking in response to stress are considered to be implicit because, once learned, they do not require intentional remembering to carry out. Nevertheless, they influence one's behavior and thinking in predictable ways.

As the discussion of long-term memory indicates, learning semantic information—the type required for your college courses—requires effortful encoding strategies. Sometimes college freshmen who were not challenged in high school do not do well on their first exams in college because they continue to rely on effortless encoding strategies such as simply reading the book once, memorizing definitions of words rather than thinking about the meaning of them, or passively listening to the course lectures. In the sections below, we discuss specific study strategies that you can use to learn new information for your college course efficiently as well as to understand how to select study strategies that are appropriate for mastering the various types of information required for answering your exam questions.

Plan Your Search When Seeking Specific Information

The computer technology revolution has ushered in an explosion of information. Concomitantly, it has provided the opportunity to quickly and easily locate and read specific material embedded in the avalanche of information on the Internet, in libraries, and in the media. One aspect of contemporary functional literacy is *information literacy*, which includes knowing what information is relevant for the task at hand and reading to locate the relevant information. Consequently, employers want to hire college graduates with a high level of functional literacy, which includes the ability to read and interpret documents (Pryor & Schaffer, as cited in Mittelhauser, 1998). Research indicates that this is a distinct cognitive task from reading to understand and recall material (Dreher & Brown, 1993).

A typical assignment for college students is to select a topic and write a term paper about it based on a search of the literature. Or, the paper may be more restricted and you may have three or four papers to write during the course of the semester on one or more topics. Sometimes you just need to search for information within your textbook that you need to include to answer a take home final or to review for an exam. An unsystematic approach to searching for information is characteristic of unsuccessful searchers (Dreher & Guthrie, 1990). What is a successful search strategy?

To answer this question, Dreher and Brown (1993) conducted an experiment with college students who were asked to locate information in an introductory psychology text of more than 800 pages that included a table of contents, 19 chapters, four appendices, a glossary, and an index. Half of the tasks contained terms that could be searched in an index and half of the tasks required that a search term be generated by the participants. Half of the participants were also randomly assigned to a prompt condition in which they were read and then given cards with the following questions: "How will you proceed? What parts of this textbook will you use? Why? What specific topics or key words will you look for? Why?" (p. 666). Results

91

of the experiment showed that engaging in planning before the search task (as prompted by the questions) significantly raised the success level of their search performance. Performance was also better when terms were in the index of the text. How much prior knowledge you have on the topic you are searching also must be taken into consideration when planning your search strategy. Learn the research skills you need to process information efficiently to be successful in college and to get a high paying professional job after you graduate.

Be a Self-Regulated Learner

A self-regulated learner is one who performs the academic tasks that are required in college such as attending class, studying for and performing well on tests and writing papers and doing other activities assigned for a course and completing them by the due date. They regulate their activities in order to achieve their short-term and long term goals.

In order to determine those non-intellectual factors that are keys to academic success, the authors along with their colleagues Peter Merenda and Gary Burkholder (2002) conducted research with college students to develop the Academic Self-Regulation Scale. From an initial scale of 200 items completed by 340 undergraduate students, through a statistical analysis (factor analysis) and correlations of students' grade point averages with their scale scores, the Academic Self-Regulation Scale emerged as being highly predictive of which students would get high GPAs and graduate within five years (Rollins, 2003). The Academic Self-Regulation Scale appears in Table 4. You may want to take the scale to see how you compare with the men and women who were academic high achievers. If you don't score as well as you might hope, you can look at the items on which you received a low score to try to improve in that area.

It is apparent from looking at the items which lead to a high score on the scale, that those students who schedule their time, have goals and work hard toward achieving them, try to work to the best of their ability, and do not procrastinate are the most successful students. They also say they have self-discipline, not only regarding academic work but also in managing their money, which removes what could otherwise be a major worry.

Some researchers discuss self-regulation in terms of the use of cognitive and metacognitive strategies (strategies for improving learning and memory). A comparison of 94 low achieving with 49 high achieving university students found that high achieving students used more cognitive and metacognitive strategies such as elaboration, organization, and critical thinking as well as resource management strategies—time and study environment management, effort regulation, peer learning, and help seeking (Van Zile-Tamsen & Livingston, 1999). Elaboration is a memory strategy that involves forming of associations among objects. Organization is a memory strategy that involves clustering of information into groups of similar objects or into meaningful categories. Critical thinking involves examining one's assumptions and biases, gathering and evaluating evidence, and assessing one's tentative conclusions before making a final conclusion or decision.

Motivational factors such as self-efficacy for learning and achievement and intrinsic goal orientation were also found to play a role in achievement. Self-efficacy for learning and achievement involves having the belief that you are capable of learning and doing well in your courses. Intrinsic goal orientation involves recognizing that the goal is one you want to achieve, that you can control your learning, and that the task has value to you. Students who had these motivations were more likely to be self-regulated learners (Van Zile-Tamsen & Livingston, 1999).

Table 4.
Academic Self-Regulation Scale

Below is a list of statements that may describe your thoughts, feelings, and behaviors. This questionnaire is designed to tell you something about how you see yourself and the way you lead your life. Please indicate for each statement whether that thought, feeling, or behavior is characteristic of you:

a) Always b) Frequently c) Sometimes d) Rarely e) Never

_____ 1. I try to do things perfectly.

_____ 2. I put things off that I don't feel like doing.

_____ 3. I am disorganized.

_____ 4. I have self-discipline.

_____ 5. I schedule my time.

_____ 6. I organize my time around my life priorities.

_____ 7. I try to do things to the best of my ability.

_____ 8. I prioritize items on my to-do list in accordance with my own values.

_____ 9. I feel capable of handling money.

_____ 10. I have difficulty managing money.

_____ 11. I usually achieve the goals I set for myself.

_____ 12. I schedule and organize my weekly activities.

_____ 13. I make a habit of doing the most important things first, rather than putting them off.

_____ 14. I budget my resources to achieve my goals.

_____ 15. I put off doing homework until the last minute.

_____ 16. I could get better grades if I tried harder.

_____ 17. I work hard at pursuing my goals.

_____ 18. I turn in assignments late.

Scoring key: For the positive items # 1, 4, 5, 6, 7, 8, 9, 11, 12, 13, 14, 17 score your answers as follows: a = 5, b = 4, c = 3, d = 2, e = 1. Your subscore is: _____. For the negative items # 2, 3, 10, 15, 16, 18 score as follows: a = 1, b = 2, c = 3, d = 4, e = 5. Your subscore is: _____. Your total score is: _____. Divide your score by 18 (the number of items in the scale) to get your mean (average) score for the items in the scale. Your mean score is: _____. How does your score compare with other college students? The mean (average) score of students who graduated within five years with a baccalaureate degree was 3.60. The mean score of students who were still enrolled after five years was 3.41. The mean score of students who never graduated was 3.33. Review the items for which you had a score below 3 and see if you can identify the skills you may need to learn to be successful in college. The higher your mean score the more skills you have to successfully complete your college degree. If your mean score was 3.33 or lower, you should go to your college counseling center to ask about workshops they may offer in skills such as time management, money management, self-esteem and other areas that may be of benefit to you in developing your potential as a student.

Many of the strategies we suggest in this book could come under the heading of self-regulation. It means that to achieve your goal of a college education, you must be in control of your behavior and have the self-discipline to work hard toward your goals, schedule your time, organize your studying, and manage your money.

We have observed, however, that many college students who seem to be highly motivated find it difficult to maintain self-discipline in all of these areas for an entire semester, particularly when they are feeling tired or stressed out. For example, some students say that they begin to procrastinate or go shopping instead of studying for scheduled exams because they feel "burned out"; others say that they cannot control their smoking, drinking, or eating behavior when they feel exhausted. Why would students find it so difficult to maintain self-control during these times? The results of recent studies suggest that one reason might be due to the fact that the resources available for all acts that require active control by the self may be limited (Schmeichel, Vohs, & Baumeister, 2003).

Researchers have found evidence that many different types of activities that require active control by the self—including self-regulation or self-control, decision making, and complex information processing tasks—have a limited supply of some resource that resembles energy or strength and that this resource may be susceptible to depletion after strenuous use (Muraven & Baumeister, 2000; Schmeichel, Vohs, & Baumeister, 2003). Students in an experimental group engage in an initial act that involves some form of active control by the self whereas students in a control group engage in an initial act that did not involve active control by the self. Next, both groups of students perform a different act that involves active control by the self. Typically, the behavior of students in the experimental group is impaired on the second task involving active control by the self after performing the initial behavior involving active control by the self. In contrast, the behavior of students in the control group is not degraded on the task involving active control by the self after performing the initial behavior that did not involve active control by the self (Baumeister, Bratslavsky, Muraven, & Tice, 1998; Muraven, Tice, & Baumeister, 1998; Muraven & Baumeister, 2000; Schmeichel, Vohs, & Baumeister, 2003).

Researchers conducting these experiments have used a variety of tasks for both the initial and second tasks involving active control by the self in order to demonstrate that many different types of behaviors that involve active control by the self depend on and deplete the self's limited available resources for active control. For example, the tasks involving active control by the self that the college students in the experimental groups performed in the first part of these studies have included eating radishes while resisting the temptation to eat chocolate, making a meaningful personal choice of behavior, controlling their emotions when viewing a segment of an upsetting video, performing a tedious word editing task, suppressing thoughts about a white bear after being instructed not to think about one, writing about events in which they were or were not successful in controlling their emotions, and focusing their attention on watching a woman being interviewed in a video while irrelevant words are flashed on the screen. Students in the control groups performed the same or similar tasks in the first part of these studies but were not given any instructions that required them to use processes involving active control by the self. The acts requiring active control by the self that both the college students in both the experimental groups and the control groups performed in the second part of these studies have included persisting at a task when frustrated from working on unsolvable puzzles, making an active choice to stop watching a boring movie, sustaining physical stamina in squeezing a handgrip, controlling facial signs of amusement while watching a humorous video, or engaging in complex mental activity by taking a test of logical reasoning (Baumeister, et al., 1998; Muraven et al., 1998; Muraven & Baumeister, 2000; Schmeichel, et al., 2003).

Muraven and Baumeister (2000, p. 253) have noted that if it turns out to be true that self-regulation behaviors requiring control by the self involve a strength or energy that resembles a muscle, then "...it could be possible to increase strength gradually through exercise, provided the exercise is suitable and is interspersed with periods allowing for recovery." They pointed out that additional research is needed to determine the types of exercise that would be suitable for increasing this strength or energy and how much rest would be needed to replenish the depleted resources available for performing acts requiring active control by the self after strenuous exertion.

What are the implications of this research for you? First, these studies demonstrating degradation of performance on a variety of tasks involving active control by the self after prior completion of another unrelated task involving active control by the self suggest that you have a limited resource available for performing behaviors that involve self-regulation and cognition. Therefore, you would probably be more successful trying to change one habit or behavior involving self-regulation such as giving up smoking or starting a diet at a time (Muraven & Baumeister, 2000). You would also be wise to monitor how you use your self's limited self-regulation and cognitive resources and to learn how to manage or conserve them in order to be able to produce your highest quality academic work and to remain in control of your behaviors. Be sure to rest and replenish this resource after periods of exertion in order to be able to sustain a high level of performance in course work involving complex information processing and to avoid losing self-control and engaging in self-defeating behaviors such as procrastinating instead of being self-disciplined and working on a research paper, loosing your temper, starting to smoke cigarettes after a period of abstinence, or binge eating after being on a diet.

Remove Distractions from Your Study Environment

As you are reading this book, we're sure many other stimuli are likely to be bombarding you in addition to the words from the printed page. Stimuli that are external to you, such as the barking of your next door neighbor's dog, a truck going down the street outside, and your girlfriend's fingers running through your hair are bombarding you. Internal stimuli are also competing for your attention. You may feel hunger pains if you haven't eaten for a few hours, you may have a headache, and you may be distracted by worries about how you will pay your bills. What determines if you will remember the concepts you are reading?

Selective attention is the necessary first step in information processing and learning. Most of the stimuli in our environment are not consciously perceived, and only those that we attend to are *encoded*, that is, put in a form that can be transferred from our sensory memory store to our short-term memory stores in working memory. Whether or not we consciously record a stimulus is due to both the characteristics of the stimulus and what we are motivated to pay attention to at the time. When one stimulus in the environment is very compelling, others may be ignored. For example, research on eyewitness testimony shows that when a criminal is carrying a gun, eyewitnesses are less able to identify the culprit than when there is no gun (Steblay, 1992). This is because the eyes fixate on the gun and pay less attention to the face. In a demonstration of this effect, Elizabeth Loftus and her colleagues (Loftus, E. F., Loftus, G. R., & Messo, 1987) recorded eye movements of research participants who viewed slides of a customer who walked up to a bank teller and pulled out either a gun or a checkbook. The research participants spent more time looking at the gun than the checkbook. These studies tell us that if there is a very compelling stimulus in your environment, you will focus on that and spend a lot of time looking at it. The moral of the story is that it is better to study in a quiet environment without a lot of distracting stimuli present.

Photo courtesy of Bristol Community College.

It is better to read and study in a location where there are no other people present. Research has been conducted in social psychology for many decades that has shown that learning new tasks take longer in the presence of other people. This finding has held true for animals (i.e., rats, goldfinch, ants) as well as humans (Zajonc, 1965). This is true only when the other people present are not involved in your learning process, such as their teaching you the material or you teaching them. The research is clear, when studying new material or working on a complex problem, you will learn more rapidly if no one else is present and there are fewer distractions in the environment. On the other hand, the research has shown that learning a simple task or performing a well-learned task is better in the presence of others. In his research Zajonc found that students who tried to memorize simple word associations (mother-father) learned more rapidly in the presence of others than alone, whereas those who were given difficult associations to learn (mother-algebra) learned more slowly in the presence of others than alone. What are the implications of this research for you?

The results of this research indicate that the characteristics of the physical setting in which you study complex new material for your college exams is very important. Pick a place with few distractions. If you live at home with your family or share an apartment with other students, study alone in your room. If you live in an on-campus residence, it may be better to go to the library and find a quiet cubicle, as did Denise who is featured in the Success Profile below. That way you will not hear the loud talking of others in your suite or in the corridor, and others will not be coming into your room trying to convince you to go out somewhere with them.

Success Profile—Denise

Denise is very self-disciplined. When she was a child her parents were heavy smokers. She had frequent ear infections. The doctor told her parents that their smoking at home was the cause of her ear infections. Within two weeks they quit smoking. Her mother started going to the YMCA every day to work out. Both of her parents began running. Denise also began running a mile every day. The running was increased to two miles every day in high school. Her parents told her they would not pay for the gymnastics lessons she wanted unless she ran two miles every day.

During her senior year in high school she enrolled in an early enrollment college class taught in her high school. The teacher gave her an application for an Early Enrollment Scholarship. She won a half-tuition scholarship for four years of college. She also received an Honors Scholarship, which paid half of her room and board at college for four years.

Denise lived in an on-campus residence for three years in a suite that had two women to a room, with six women sharing a bathroom. It was coed by floor, half of the rooms occupied by men and half of the rooms occupied by women. The women had to lock the door right after walking into the suite because a guy would walk right in without knocking.

Denise was a member of the varsity gymnastics team beginning in her freshman year. Athletes at the college are required to do eight hours a week of supervised study hall. They had to sign in and sign out of the study hall. Many days she could not eat dinner because the only time she had to practice gymnastics was two to six p.m. five days a week. Freshman year was Denise's most difficult year.

Denise realized early in her freshman year that she could not study in the on-campus residence suite. There was too much noise and too many distractions. She would go to the library or to the study center for athletes. She did not work while on the varsity gymnastics team because of the hours required for practice and meets. From September through March they had one meet during the week and one meet on weekends requiring an overnight trip.

During her junior year she injured her shoulder and had to have surgery. The doctors would not allow her to participate in gymnastics any more. Since she was no longer able to do gymnastics, Denise runs six to eight miles each day for three days a week and she runs 4 miles each day for three days a week. Denise said "After I run, I can sit and study for hours." In addition, Denise works out on the Nautilus machines and the Stairmaster four days a week in the college recreation center. Denise carries a daily calendar and blocks out the time to do her studying, running and other tasks. She has a boyfriend in Los Angeles who comes to Rhode Island once a month. He runs and works out with her when he visits her.

Denise was a 22-year-old senior psychology major when interviewed. She had her own apartment off-campus. She said that when she studies, she studies for 45 minutes and then takes a five-minute break. She studies three to four hours a day, plus the time she spends in class. Class time is relaxation time. She reads the assigned text and other material before she goes to class, and takes notes on the reading. She gets up early every morning. Two days before an exam she begins reviewing class notes and notes she has taken on the book. The night before the exam she makes flash cards.

During her freshman year, Denise joined the Psychological Society, and in her junior year was elected to Psi Chi, the national honor society in psychology. These organizations sponsor many activities of interest to psychology majors such as inviting psychologists to speak about careers in psychology and attending psychology conferences in the area. Denise was accepted to a doctoral program in psychology at a university in California, where she also received free tuition and a stipend because she received a research assistantship.

Use Metacognitive Strategies for Improved Learning and Transfer

Metacognition is defined as an individual's monitoring of his or her thought processes and taking control over them. The individual who uses metacognition determines when he or she is having problems and adjusts the learning process accordingly. A student who develops learning strategies is using metacognitive skills. A number of studies have shown a relationship between self-reported metacognitive activities and achievement outcomes. In the beginning of the semester, students who use metacognition may not do as well, but by the end of the semester have higher achievement (Pokay & Blumenfeld, 1990).

In an experiment that studied metacognitive activity by allowing students to select the complexity of exercises to practice, individuals with a mastery orientation (an interest in learning the task) showed greater use of learning strategies than did individuals with a performance orientation (getting a good grade) (Ford, Smith, Weissbein, Gully, & Salas, 1998). Students using metacognitive strategies had greater knowledge acquisition, more skilled performance at the end of training, and greater self-efficacy. These training outcomes were related to better performance on a transfer task. What this means for the student is that using metacognitive strategies improves learning and performance and increases self-efficacy for the task. Students who use more complex learning strategies also perform similar tasks better.

Researchers have found that many adult students, including those with learning disabilities, benefit from instruction in identifying and using metacognitive strategies. For example, the Strategic Content Learning (SCL) approach is an instructional model developed to help students learn how to analyze the steps needed to accomplish specific academic tasks; monitor, record, and evaluate their task performance; and identify and use more effective metacognitive strategies to improve their performance. Butler (1998) used a pre-test/post-test design in three studies to assess the effectiveness of the SCL approach to promoting self-regulated learning. The participants in Butler's studies were adult students ranging in age from 19 to 48 years. At the beginning of the studies, each student selected the specific tasks and course work they desired to work on improving (e.g., reading, writing, note taking, math). Then, they were assessed on measures of metacognitive knowledge, strategies, and self-regulated processing; task specific self-efficacy; pattern of attributions for task performance; and their strategic approaches to a specific task. Following these pre-test assessments, students were provided with individualized SCL tutoring focusing on the specific task that they had selected to work on improving. The tutoring sessions were for two to three hours per week for either one or two semesters. In the tutoring session, students were encouraged to discuss the metacognitive strategies they used to accomplish their specific tasks and to think about how they might create new strategies for improving their task performance. For example, students who reported having difficulties accomplishing writing assignments were encouraged to break down the assignment into various tasks such as reading, researching, writing, revising, and editing and then to break down these tasks into subtasks.

At the completion of the tutoring sessions, students were reassessed on the measures used at pre-test. Butler (1998) reported that the post-test results indicated that the SCL instructional method was effective for improving students' metacognitive knowledge about key self-regulated processes, perceptions of task specific efficacy, attributions for successful performance, task performance, and strategic approaches to tasks. At pre-test, students included an average of 4.82 steps in describing how they would complete a task; at post-test they used an average of 35.97 steps. Some students were also found to transfer strategic approaches across contexts and tasks. Strategies that a student learned to improve reading, such as paying closer attention to key points and details, were also used spontaneously to assess how to solve math problems.

The results of this research show that if you lack knowledge of effective metacognitive strategies, training in using them can improve your performance in your course work even if you have a learning deficit or disability. If you need help in identifying and using metacognitive strategies to accomplish your course assignments, get help from the learning specialists at your college's center for developmental education or tutoring center. Knowledge of metacognitive strategies is a skill that you will need to master in order to achieve success in college and in your professional life.

Joan H. Rollins, Ph.D. and Mary Zahm, Ph.D.

Use Chunking, Mnemonic Devices, and Imagery to Improve Your Short-Term Memory Span

Typically people can store about seven or so items from a list of letters, words, names or numbers in their short-term memory stores. Psychologist George Miller wrote a well-known article about this phenomenon titled "The Magical Number Seven, Plus or Minus Two" (1956). Try this for yourself. Ask a friend or try yourself to remember the table of chemical elements. If you try to remember more than seven or eight at one time, you will begin to forget the first ones on the list as the later ones "push out" the memory of the first ones. But when you group the elements into groups or chunks of elements, then you are able to use your storage capacity more efficiently. Chess masters are able to look at a chess board and quickly remember the location of all of the pieces on the board by chunking the individual pieces into patterns familiar to chess players (Gobet & Simon, 1996). It is estimated that chess masters can store up to 50,000 chunks of chess patterns in memory. So when you are trying to remember individual items, chunk them into meaningful groups and you will quickly and dramatically improve your short-term memory.

There are several mnemonic devices that can be used to aid in the memorization of specific items. *Acronyms* are a type of memory device in which a set of letters forms a word. For example, ask a friend to memorize the following 12 letters: FB ITW AC IAIB M. How long did it take him/her to correctly repeat the letters? Now ask another friend to memorize the same 12 letters chunked this way: FBI TWA CIA IBM. Which list was learned more quickly? Although both lists contain the same 12 letters, when they are chunked in familiar combinations, they become a more manageable four stimulus units rather than 12 (Bower, 1970).

In *categorical clustering*, items are grouped into meaningful categories. For example, if you are going to the supermarket, you might group what you need into type of food items, such as grouping fruit together—grapes, apples, oranges—then grouping milk products—yogurt, milk, ice cream—and so on (Sternberg, 1998).

You might use *acrostics*, which is taking the initial letters of a series of items that can be used in forming a sentence. Many children taking music lessons learn to memorize the notes on lines of the treble clef by learning the phrase "**E**very **G**ood **B**oy **D**oes **F**ine." So one way of memorizing more quickly is to make up a phrase in which the first letter of every word stands for a word you have to memorize (Sternberg, 1998).

Relating new information to what you already know is a good way to remember. For example, if you just met Joe who is tall and has a hearty laugh like your uncle Charlie, you can make the association between Joe and your uncle Charlie to remember Joe. Of course, the most important person in the world is you, and if you can relate something to yourself, you will remember it better. The *self-reference effect* refers to the phenomenon that when information is relevant to our self-concepts we process the information more quickly and remember it better (Symons & Johnson, 1997). Many college professors, however, prefer that students understand the concepts rather than memorize definitions. You can think of how this concept applies to your everyday life. On the multiple-choice tests the students take in some classes, they are not asked for the definitions, but given examples and asked what concept that example illustrates.

You can also use *interactive images* to enhance your memory. Suppose you had to learn a list of unrelated words such as frog, box, car and snow. You could imagine a frog in a box riding in a car driving through the snow. In a series of experiments with college students, it was demonstrated that both elaborative interrogation (students were asked "Why" questions about the statements about animals they were asked to remember) and imagery conditions (students were shown pictures of the animals along with the statements about the animals they were asked to remember) facilitated learning of material from a familiar domain (Willoughby, Wood, & Khan, 1994). When pictures were not provided, however, students asked to create an image in their minds of the animal had significantly greater memory for the facts about the unfamiliar animals than did students in the elaborative interrogation condition. Similarly, students provided with key words outperformed elaborative interrogation students and students who used simple repetition in learning information about the unfamiliar animals.

When you have subject matter to study that involves a lot of memorization, such as anatomy, chunking and mnemonic devices can save a lot of time and improve your recall of the items. The research also suggests that when presented with new material from an unfamiliar domain, using imagery may encourage remembering to a greater extent than using elaborative interrogation and simple repetition strategies. So studying effectively does not necessarily mean studying longer, it also means studying smarter. By studying smarter, you can learn the same material in a lot less time.

Reread and Rehearse Material Right Away to Move it From Short-Term to Long-Term Memory Stores

Information in the short-term memory stores vanishes quickly, as noted above. That is good because we do not want to clutter up our minds with every bit of information to which we attend. If we read the newspaper every day or watch the news on TV, we certainly would not want to remember all of the robberies, weddings, car accidents, and other information we read about in the paper or see and hear on a news program. We don't want to clutter our mind with everything we just saw or heard. Short-term memory obliges us by holding unrehearsed material in memory only about 30 seconds. In a classic study, L. R. Peterson and M. J. Peterson (1959) prevented students from rehearsing three consonants they had just been shown by requiring students to count backwards from three from the time the consonants were shown to them until they saw a light that signaled the recall test. The recall test began at 3, 6, 9, 12, 15, or 18 seconds after the students began counting. The students recall accuracy declined sharply from 3 to 18 seconds. The Petersons' experiment supports the interference theory, that the individual forgets information because of new information that competes with the memory, thereby causing the individual to forget the information. Research also supports a theory of proactive interference, that material previously learned can interfere with short-term memory storage. People show almost no forgetting of a nonsense syllable when they had no previous syllables to learn (Keppel & Underwood, 1962).

Suppose you are studying for a course and you want to remember the material at least until the exam. Hermann Ebbinghaus (1885), who holds an important place in the history of psychology, demonstrated in the nineteenth century that when learning nonsense syllables (i.e., tuh, har, qel) the greater the number of repetitions of lists, the greater the retention. Thus, the more we repeat the information, the greater our memory of it. Without repetition, according to the decay theory, forgetting occurs quickly with the passage of time. The implications of this research for students is that you should chunk the material you want to learn and reread the material and repeat it to yourself a number of times before you go on to what you want to learn next.

Rehearsing the information can be used to keep material in short-term memory, such as when you don't have a pencil and paper and want to remember a phone number until you can put your money in a pay phone and dial the number. Repetition also gradually moves a memory from short-term to long-term memory. When learning lists of items, the serial position effect occurs, which is that the learner has better recall for items at the beginning and end of a list than for items in the middle. This is a well-established phenomenon in memory research. The reason appears to be that the beginning and the end items in a series are distinctive (Reisberg, 1997).

When Crowder (1993) asked participants to list the Presidents of the United States in correct order, typically the earliest and latest, were best recalled, with the exception of Lincoln. The practical implication of this research is that the learner must rehearse the middle of the list more if he or she wants to learn it as well as the beginning or end of the list. The other approach would be to note something distinctive about the mid-list items.

Distribute Your Time Studying over More Episodes of Shorter Duration

Suppose you have your first psychology exam in two weeks and a cumulative final at the end of the semester. You will do better on both exams if you study psychology one hour every other day for two weeks for a total of seven hours rather than study all day for seven hours the day before the exam. You will also remember that material better for the final exam if you had spaced your learning. Cramming is an ineffective study strategy.

In one experiment, postmen, who claimed to have neither used a typewriter nor played a keyboard instrument, were trained to type code material using a conventional typewriter keyboard (Baddeley & Longman, 1978). The men were divided into four groups, each group given a different pattern of training. Learning was most efficient in the group given the most spaced pattern (one session of one hour/day), and least efficient in the group given the most massed pattern (trained for two two-hour sessions). When tested for retention after one, three, or nine months, the group trained for two daily sessions of two hours continued to perform most poorly. This research supports the principle that training should be distributed over time rather than massed. Studies of other more cognitive skills have also found distributed practice to improve learning of French vocabulary (Bloom, & Shuell 1981) and to improve performance on a reading comprehension task (Krug, Davis, & Glover, 1990). The reason that spaced, distributed practice leads to improved learning is that it allows the individual to have time for deep or elaborative information processing.

Even if you go over material briefly and don't remember any of it when someone quizzes you, the next time you study the material you will learn it more quickly than if you had not previously read it. That is called relearning. Each time we relearn the material, it is more quickly learned than if we had not previously looked at it. Research reveals that higher scoring students on factual, conceptual, and essay tests in a college course were those who actually spent significantly less time studying, but distributed (spaced) their study time over more periods of shorter duration of time, than low scoring students (Dickinson, O'Connell, & Dunn, 1996). Improve your grades by distributing your learning. Read the chapters when they are assigned rather than waiting until the day or two before the exam. Review the notes you took that day before you go to bed that night and again on a weekly basis rather than waiting until just before the exam.

Overlearn to Aid Retention and Performance

It has been known for years in psychology that overlearning, which is continuing to relearn the information even after you are able to remember it correctly, enhances performance. After reviewing the literature and statistically combining the data from all the experiments on the effect of overlearning on memory and performance, it was concluded that overlearning produces a significant effect on retention (Driskell, Willis, & Copper, 1992). In other words, people will remember material longer if they continue to rehearse it even after they have learned it. Thus, if you want to remember the information in order to pass a cumulative final exam, overlearning during the course of the semester will lead to better final exam results.

One overlearns by continuing to repeat the information even after being able to pass a test on it (Driskell et al., 1992). Semb, Ellis, and Araujo (1993) found that college students who were tutors retained more after four months than the students they tutored. Tutoring is a type of overlearning. If you want to really learn and remember the material, teach it to someone else. In order to do that you have to think about the information and outline its main points, which help you retain the material.

Understand and Make Meaningful Associations with Information You Want to Learn and Remember

Deliberately attending to the information and trying to understand it, moves the information from the short-term to the long-term memory store. Trying to make connections and associations between the new information and your existing store of information will greatly enhance your ability to move the new information into your long-term memory stores. If you can associate new information with concepts you already have in memory, you can improve your retention of the new information. Short-term memory storage is also a dynamic process, however, and emotion, motivation, and meaning also play a role in how long we remember something. We are more likely to remember material that was emotionally dramatic. If you are old enough, do you remember what you were doing when you heard that the Challenger space shuttle had exploded or that the World Trade Center in New York had been destroyed by terrorists who had hijacked American commercial airplanes? Very dramatic events are more likely to remain easily recalled.

The self-concept also affects the way people perceive the world and integrate information, selecting out information that is relevant to the self and ignoring what is not. Research in social psychology has found that people spend more time thinking about and better remember information that is relevant to the self (Klein & Loftus, 1988). The practical application of this finding is that if we want to remember information, we are best able to do so if we can relate it to ourselves in some way. Another implication is that if we show others the relevance of information to themselves they will pay more attention to it and better remember it.

Long-term memory stores have unlimited capacity and can store materials for long periods of time, even a lifetime. The more deeply the material is processed, the more likely it is to stay in long term memory. In a study with 9th grade students, Spires and Donley (1998) asked one group of students to make spontaneous connections between personal knowledge and their textbook reading. The students who made personal links with the text material outperformed other students on application level questions. Students who were told to read the text for the main ideas, and also those not given any instruction for reading, did not perform as well as those making personal connection with the material. Combining instructions for making personal knowledge connections and looking for the main ideas in the text increased both their application level comprehension and improved their attitudes toward reading.

Recent research has shown a linking between knowledge, interest, and recall—an interrelationship of cognitive and affective (emotional, motivational) dimensions (Alexander, Jetton, & Kulikowich, 1995). During the first of the stages of knowledge acquisition in a subject area, *acclimatization*, learners have very little knowledge of the topic and deep-seated individual interest is also quite low. Interest is more situational, and they may have to get through the task for reasons such as a course requirement. Understanding and recall of the information is more difficult in this stage. We find more personally involving information of greater interest to us during this stage. With continued exposure to the subject over time, many learners will move to the next stage, the stage of *competence*. More knowledge about the area helps in organizing the information around basic principles of the field, which aids the student in distinguishing between important and unimportant information. There is an increase in understanding and recall in this stage, and motivation to learn becomes stronger as a consequence. The final stage is *proficiency*, a stage that is reached by only certain learners because it is characterized not only by extensive and highly integrated bodies of knowledge of the subject area but also deep interest and involvement in the field. This research illustrates that all of your efforts to memorize new information and accumulate knowledge in a subject area in which you are interested will be rewarded in the long run as you achieve competency and then proficiency in that area.

Don't Drink or Use Marijuana While Studying, Performing, or Being Tested.

In an early demonstration of state-dependent effects on learning, 48 medical students performed four memory tasks either while sober or under the effects of alcohol. In tasks measuring recall, learning was better when the student was intoxicated during both sessions than when under the influence of alcohol only during the learning session (Goodwin, 1969). This study shows that learning is state dependent, or that if you are drinking alcohol while studying, you should also be drinking alcohol while taking the test.

Learning has been shown to be impaired when either drinking alcohol or smoking marijuana. In a recent experiment students were given alcohol, marijuana, or placebo. Students under the influence of either alcohol or marijuana had impairment in digit symbol substitution and word recall tests as compared with students who took only the placebo when performing or remembering what they had learned (Heishman, Arasteh, & Stitzer, 1997). Since you want to learn efficiently, that is to spend the least amount of time to learn the most material, it is unwise to either drink alcohol or smoke marijuana while studying.

Success Recommendations

This section contains a summary of the main points in this chapter to help you reflect on and recall what you have learned.

- **Understand How the Information Processing Model of Memory Explains How You Process and Learn Information.** The three types of memory stores include the sensory memory stores, short-term memory stores located in working memory, and long-term (permanent) memory stores. These memory stores differ in the types of control processing that can occur, the amount of information that can be retained, and the duration of time over which information can be retained in them.

- **Plan Your Search When Seeking Specific Information.** Use a systematic approach to search for information. Before you begin to search, make a search plan. Look in your text for key words for your topic. Determine what source of information (e.g., journals on reserve in the library, databases, or books) and key words you will use to conduct your search.

- **Be a Self-Regulated Learner.** Strive to learn and use cognitive and metacognitive strategies for effective learning such as elaboration, organization and critical thinking. Develop the habit of continually monitoring and evaluating your studying and test preparation strategies to see which ones are effective or ineffective for you in various learning or testing situations. Believe that you can succeed in your college courses, and that you are in control of your academic fate. Focus on the value and joy of learning and achieving your educational goals.

- **Remove Distractions From Your Study Area.** Study alone in your room. Keep your desk clear of everything other than the material you are currently working on. If your residence is noisy, go to the library to study, but pick a spot that is relatively isolated.

- **Use Metacognitive Strategies for Improved Learning and Transfer.** Develop the habit of monitoring your thought processes and taking control over them by learning effective metacognitive skills. Learning metacognitive skills may increase your study time in the beginning but by the end of the semester you should have acquired more knowledge.

- **Use Chunking, Mnemonic Devices, and Imagery to Improve Your Short-Term Memory Span.** Group material you have to learn into meaningful units. Use mnemonics, rhymes, or other similar devices to remember material. When presented with new material from an unfamiliar domain that you will later be asked to recall from memory, form a mental image of it to help you remember it.

- **Reread and Rehearse Material Right Away to Move it From Short-term to Long-term Memory Stores.** After reading a chapter, go over the summary and main points. Every night spend fifteen minutes reviewing the lecture notes for each class you had that day. Review the middle of the chapter or of a list you are memorizing more frequently than the beginning and the end.

- **Space Your Learning.** You will better learn new material if you space your study sessions rather than cramming all at once. The more times you review that information in spaced study sessions, the better you will retain it and be able to recall it for an exam.

You will also remember that material better for the final exam if you had spaced your learning.

- **Overlearn Important Class Material.** Teach what you have just learned to someone else. This forces you to organize the key points and gain a deeper understanding of them.

- **Make Important Course Material Personally Meaningful.** Pay attention to material you want to remember. Make associations between the new material and your own personal experiences. Think of examples from your own life that illustrate the principles you are learning.

- **Don't Drink or Use Marijuana While Studying, Performing, or Being Tested.** Do not self-handicap and waste your time by drinking alcohol or taking drugs while studying because you will not recall the material as well when tested.

Chapter Six
Attend Class, Read and Write Effectively, Overcome Test Anxiety, and Ace Your Exams

Researchers from the Heldrich Center for Workforce Development at Rutgers University recently surveyed 1,015 American workers about their educational background and what type of college education they believed was the best preparation for the workforce. Of the workers surveyed, 63% had participated in some education or training beyond high school or attended college. The results of the survey revealed that most of the workers rated "general skills, such as the ability to communicate and think critically, as being more important…" than other job-specific skills (as cited in Hebel, 2000, p.4). Of the workers surveyed, 87% said that good communication skills were very important for performing their jobs; 81% said critical thinking skills and basic literacy were very important; and 50% said that computer skills were very important. A total of 66% of the respondents indicated that on-the-job training was the best preparation for their current job. Even though the majority (64%) of the workers believed that the primary purpose of college should be to prepare students for specific careers, workers with higher levels of education were more likely to state that colleges should teach general skills as well as specific knowledge.

Why do educated American workers feel that learning general skills in college is so important? American workers are continually forced to learn new technologies and adapt to changing work structures, so it makes sense that they would rate possessing general skills, which facilitate life long learning and adaptation to change, and on-the-job training as being very important preparation for the workforce.

Based on the results of this research, we recommend that you make sure to develop your basic academic skills, especially in communications, critical thinking, basic literacy, and computers in addition to gaining the specific area knowledge presented in your classes. We present strategies to help you gain proficiency in reading, note-taking, writing, and test-taking skills in this chapter. We recommend that you save evidence of your growing proficiency in both basic academic skills and knowledge areas so that you will be able to construct a portfolio to demonstrate your skills to prospective employers and others, when needed. We discuss the details of how to construct customized job portfolios in a later chapter.

Read and Follow the Instructions on Your Course Syllabus

In order to be successful in college, you must understand and follow the rules for successful performance within the specific college program and class. Even though students who attend classes receive better grades than those who do not, attendance does not guarantee that you'll always be prepared for assignment deadlines. Many students who attend classes regularly still come to class unprepared for an exam or miss deadlines for assignments because they didn't know when they were due. Some of these students don't check the syllabus, or course outline, provided to them by the instructor because they are used to receiving directions and repeated reminders from their high school teachers. They are surprised to find that their college professors expect them to know and follow the class schedule by themselves.

Photo courtesy of Bristol Community College.

Don't get caught short. Read your syllabi outlining your instructors' requirements for all of your classes and make sure you refer to them often. Understand and follow the requirements and deadlines for the exams and assignments for each course. Evaluate the teaching and testing style of the professor so that you will know what information to focus on when preparing for class and studying for exams.

Mark test dates and assignment due dates from each course syllabus in your personal calendar. As the semester progresses, record any changes the professor makes to the course requirements or test and assignment due dates on both the course syllabus and your personal calendar. If you don't understand what is required on an assignment for your class, visit your professor during his or her office hours and ask for guidance and/or a referral for a source of tutoring assistance. As soon as possible, find out about sources of help that are available to you at your school. Many colleges have free tutoring centers in which students can receive help in learning how to read and study more efficiently. Complete all assignments on time. Follow specific directions for written assignments and make them look good. Always bear in mind that you may want to ask your professor for a letter of recommendation for a special college program, scholarship, award, or job someday.

Be an Active Learner. Attend Class, Ask Questions.

Research conducted by Lindgren (1969) compared the college students who had B averages or better with students who had grades of C– averages or below. He found a clear association between poor attendance and poor grades. Among successful students, 84% attended class always or almost always, whereas among unsuccessful students only 47% attended class always or almost always. Only 8% of successful students were often absent in contrast to 45% of unsuccessful students. Thus, the first step in doing well in college is to always go to class. When Heather began attending the state university, her mother, a college professor, told her that the most important aspect in doing well in college would be for her to go to every class. Although Heather was a student who liked to engage in many activities and did not spend long hours studying, she did attend almost all of her classes and it paid off in her making five honor societies in her senior year.

To really benefit from the lecture, be familiar with and prepared to discuss the material when you come to class. How can you do this? Read the assigned text for that day before you go to class. Be aware that reading a textbook is not like reading a novel. When reading a novel, we want to start with the beginning and read straight through to the end. With a textbook, however, we want to read the summary at the end of the chapter first, next review the illustrations and any definitions of key terms before reading the chapter. Why? Because the summary, key terms, and illustrations help us organize our thinking about the material. Use a dictionary to look up words that are not familiar to you. Begin to make associations and think about how what you are reading relates to your own experiences. If you don't have time to read the complete assignment, at least look at the illustrations, read the summary of the chapter, review key terms that may be in the text, and try to skim the chapter. That way you will have a better idea of the important points. You will then also have some familiarity with the information.

Even if the lectures seem boring, you still learn material and gain a clearer understanding of how the professor thinks, which can be of help on the exams. Of course, the student must pay attention to benefit from the class. Students who are checking their pagers for messages or surfing the web on their laptops instead of taking notes while the professor is talking are not learning very much. One of our colleagues had the experience of a couple sitting in the last row of her large lecture class and passionately kissing and caressing each other during the class. She did not call attention to them, but at the end of class went up to them and suggested that they find a more appropriate place to make out if they were unable to restrain themselves during class.

Photo courtesy of Rhode Island College.

Actively listen to what the professor is saying so that you will be able to ask relevant questions and make comments. Active learning helps you process the information and remember it better. Asking questions in class will also provide you with valuable experience for your future career when you will attend meetings and be expected to comment on the task at hand or speak in front of groups. Actively participating in class will also make the class more interesting for you. Other ways for students to make a class livelier and the information presented in it more meaningful are to ask questions and to provide examples of what the professor is talking about from their own experiences. Most professors welcome questions and comments. They don't want to do all of the work of the class. Professors realize that students sometimes understand the material better after hearing examples provided by their peers. Some professors even give extra credit for class participation to encourage students to read the text before class, attend the class, and practice critical thinking and public speaking skills.

Organize Your Lecture and Study Notes

Learning to take good lecture notes can help you pay attention and can provide a good review for your exams. A proven method for taking effective and efficient notes, the Cornell Note-Taking Method (Pauk, 2000; Pauk & Fiore, 2000), is described below. You should *not* try to write down everything the professor says. Instead, you should try to make an outline of the important points. You can determine what is important to the professor by noting how much time he or she spends lecturing on a specific topic as well as from comments the professor makes in class. For example, your professor might say that a certain problem or research study will be covered on the exam. Some faculty use an overhead projector or Power Point presentation to outline important topics of the lecture, and taking these down in your notebook can also give you a written record of the main points of the lecture. Some professors frequently lecture from the book and stress the key points to remember in it. Sometimes what professors say first when introducing a topic or what they say last when summarizing the topic will tell you what's important for you to know. In addition to taking notes, you could highlight in your book the key concepts, studies, and points the professor stresses as being important for future reference.

Some of the freshmen students enrolled in classes do not do well on their first tests in college because they do not have good note-taking skills. Many of them are surprised and say that they "did very well" in high school. However, college classes proceed at a faster pace and some students can quickly become overwhelmed and fall behind. Once students learn how to take efficient notes, their grades improve. Researchers have also found a positive relationship between effective note-taking and GPA (e.g., Cohn, Cohn, & Bradley, 1995). If you have a note-taking strategy that is working well for you, continue to use it. However, if you find that your old system isn't working in college, we recommend that you learn and use the Cornell Note-Taking Method, (Pauk, 2000; Pauk & Fiore, 2000) described below. Feel free to modify the method to suit your own preferred cognitive learning style.

Use a loose leaf binder with a section divider for each class to keep your notes. This allows you to insert pages when needed. Put your name, address, and phone number on the cover in case you lose it. Include your course syllabi, handouts, and a spiral-bound assignment planner to help you keep track of classes, assignment deadlines, and exam dates.

To use the Cornell Note-Taking Method, draw an inverted "T" on each sheet of loose leaf paper to divide it into three distinct sections: Ideas and Questions, Notes, and Summary. Tailor the size of the three spaces divided with the inverted "T," as shown in Figure 5 below, to meet your own course requirements and to suit your own cognitive learning style.

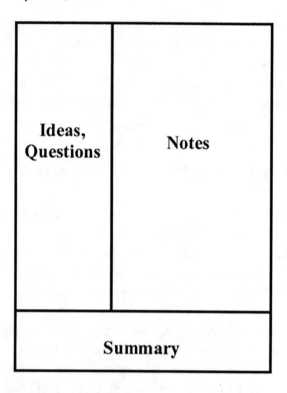

Figure 5.
Sample Page for Cornell Note-Taking Method

Source: Adapted from Pauk (2000). *How to Study in college*, 7th ed. Boston, MA: Houghton
   Mifflin Company.

Ideas and Questions. Enter ideas and questions you have while reading and outlining the material before class in the Ideas and Question section. Write clarifying ideas and questions taken from your detailed lecture notes in the narrow left-hand margin. During class, ask the instructor to clarify your remaining questions not covered in the lecture if they still seem to be relevant to the lecture and important to you. During or after class, write out any questions concerning the key names and concepts included in the text, lecture, films, or overhead presentations that you think could be covered in tests in the Ideas and Question sections so you'll have them readily available when reviewing for exams.

Notes. Write the class topic, date of lesson, and page number at the top of the Notes section on each page. Write your detailed lecture notes in the wide right-hand margin of the page. To improve your efficiency and information organization, consider using the Notes section to outline the chapter before class, leaving large blank spaces in each subsection to write-in relevant class notes. Doing this in advance may reduce the amount of notes you need to write during class and will help you better organize your notes (Pauk & Fiore, 2000). This may be an especially useful technique to use in classes taught by instructors who talk fast, digress, or do not present the material in an organized manner. Write the key concepts presented in the lecture notes in your own words and abbreviate, as needed, to keep up with the professor. Put all names of key people, key terms, diagrams, and other information presented in the lecture, on the board, or on the overhead screen in your Notes section (Kiewra, 1991).

Pay attention from the beginning to the end of the class. Don't be like some students who arrive late or start to pack their bags and put their notebooks away during the last ten minutes of class because they are mentally preparing to run to their next class or to work. Instead, pay very close attention to what the professor is saying during the first and last ten minutes of each lecture. Those are the times during which he or she will introduce the topics to be covered, sum up and reiterate the key points of the lecture, and remind the class of upcoming deadlines. You'll want to include this important information in your notes. If you miss a lecture or have difficulty taking complete notes in class, repeat the lecture using an audio or videotape, if possible (Kiewra, 1991). If not, ask to borrow the notes of someone in your class who takes good notes and clarify any questions you have with your professor. If you miss a movie shown in class, ask the professor how you can access it to view it on your own.

Summary. After class, write a brief summary of the key concepts and points in the ideas, questions, and notes sections at the bottom of the page. Be sure to go back and briefly organize and summarize the key points in the lecture soon after your class. Make a brief textual outline of the most important material. If you are like most people, you probably find it easier to understand and remember complex information presented in a visually organized format than lengthy textual material. Therefore, we recommend that you include visual presentations such as outlines, graphs, flow diagrams, and concept maps of important processes, principles, theories, and concepts in your Summary sections to enhance encoding and recall of important material. Your lists of key concepts, sample questions, and concise textual and graphic summaries will be very useful for you to use as streamlined study guides when preparing for tests.

Using the Cornell Note-Taking Method will help you prepare for classes as well as to be actively engaged in and pay attention to your professors during classes. It will also help you to organize material in a format that you can readily use to review and process information more deeply when preparing for exams. Learning and using efficient note-taking and information organizational skills will not only increase your academic performance (Kiewra, 1991) but will also increase your self-efficacy as a learner (Hatcher & Pond, 1998). Since psychologists have found that people remember information more easily if it is organized rather than unorganized, learning effective note taking and information organizational skills are important prerequisites to your success in college.

Summarize the Text in Your Own Words

Reading for pleasure is different from reading a textbook. You have to first understand and then remember the material you read in a textbook. Typically, students will underline the material and go over it again. Students often conceptualize memory as a collection of discrete facts. This is not an optimal way to learn because the more cognitive links we have to a concept, the better we remember it. Phrasing the section in your own words and providing yourself with examples, where possible, will begin making links to your own experience.

Learn to recognize repeated arguments or references that the author is making. Is there a concept that the author keeps talking about?

Rosalie Friend (2000) conducted an experiment with 147 freshman students who had failed the university writing placement test. The students were randomly assigned to one of three groups: those given instruction in summarization using argument repetition, those given instruction in summarization using generalization, and a control group instructed to use their own personal judgments of importance. Students who were taught to summarize by either argument repetition or generalization did significantly better than those in the control condition on tasks requiring judging the importance of content such as excluding unimportant material. Instruction in generalization led to more effective performance on constructing the thesis of the article.

Friend (2000/2001) has developed guidelines for writing a summary of an article or section of text, summarized as follows.

- Read the whole section for understanding.
- Figure out the central idea or thesis the author is making.
- What are the supporting ideas for the main thesis?
- Write the summary in your own words.

In these suggestions we are linking reading with writing. Most studies conclude that reading and writing are fundamentally connected (Pugh & Pawan, 1991). A number of writing activities have been found to improve reading including dictation, paragraph paraphrasing, and sentence combining. Analytic writing improves short story reading test scores (Marshall 1987, as cited in Pugh & Pawan, 1991). Thus, one way of improving your reading is to write analytic summaries of what you are reading. Switching back and forth between the reader's and writer's roles helps students conceptualize the meaning of the text (Dahl, 1984, as cited in Pugh & Pawan, 1991)

Obviously, you are not going to have time to write a summary of all of the text material that you have to read in college. But, this may be a good approach to use with texts that you have particular difficulty in understanding. If you do this initially in your college career, you will find that reading a text becomes easier as you are able to grasp the author's main points. You will need to listen carefully as your professor explains the objectives of the course and read your syllabus carefully in order to understand how much of the details of the text material you will need to learn as well. On material for which you only have to learn the important arguments, try to increase your reading speed, because research finds that college students who are fast and slow readers do not differ in text recall (Ehrlich & Tardieu, 1991).

Do not highlight or underline the text. Although it may help you to select what is important, students may be fooled into thinking that because they have highlighted the material they have learned it. But highlighting or underlining does not increase recall of the information because it does not involve deep mental processing of the information (Wade & Trathen, 1989). Besides, if you want to resell your text at the end of the semester, underlining and highlighting large areas of text may reduce its resale value.

Pre-reading main idea questions reduces the amount of unimportant information students in all ability groups highlight or summarize. Lower-ability students who receive pre-reading questions recall significantly more important information than those who did not receive pre-reading questions (Wade & Trathen, 1989). If there are pre-reading questions in your text, use them to help you focus on the key points you are reading. If not, ask your professor for questions that you will be able to answer from reading each chapter. Keeping those questions in mind while reading the text will help you recall more of the important information, especially if you are a student who tends to get lower scores on standardized tests of verbal ability.

Use the "Hamburger" Method of Essay Construction, with Particular Attention to the Introduction

Students are taught to write essays using the "hamburger" method of construction, which consists of an introduction, a main part, and a conclusion. According to a review of writing guides by Townsend et al. (1993) a good introduction for an essay should

- discuss the importance or timeliness of the topic,
- state the problem to be addressed,
- indicate the scope of the essay,
- define the terms to be used, and
- delineate the argument to be presented

In the introduction, you need to draw the reader's attention to the importance of the topic as well as to the problem that you perceive to be central to it and what your argument will be.

The meat of the essay goes in the middle and includes all of the supporting material for your argument. Here is where you put the factual information that substantiates the case you are making. You may cite other authors here as well, providing their supporting evidence and what their conclusions are.

Finally, a good conclusion should summarize the main ideas of the essay, provide an answer to the question posed, and discuss the broader implications of the topic (Townsend et al., 1993). Writers can also use various rhetorical structures such as definitions, examples, illustrations, and figures of speech to draw attention to important concepts.

Improvement in the introduction and conclusion of an essay has been shown to improve the grade it is awarded (Townsend et al., 1993). Student essays that had introductions or conclusions revised by professors or were in the original form were graded by college students, teachers, and student teachers. The grade of the essay was influenced by the nature of the introduction. There was some evidence for a better grade with an improved conclusion, but not as marked as for an improved introduction. Pay special attention to writing your introduction. Rivet the reader's interest in the beginning with an organized, logical statement of what the essay is all about. You will get a higher grade on your papers and essay exams if you do this.

What makes a good writer? Research with Canadian junior-college students who were given 50 minutes to write a text comparing Montreal where they lived with a city of their choice showed that poor writers were no less self-regulated or linear in their arguments. However, good writers did wait longer before beginning to write and made more comparisons

(Ferrari, Bouffard, & Rainville, 1998). Good writers also had fewer errors in their texts and wrote longer essays of better quality.

When writing an essay, take time to think about what you want to say before you begin. Have an introduction, middle, and conclusion. Make sure your introduction organizes your essay, providing the reader with the reasons for writing about the topic and what your argument will be. Write as much as you can about the topic, and go back to revise (see next section). End with a conclusion that summarizes the important points you have made.

Revise Your Written Work

Writing is thinking on paper. But just as our thinking is not exactly precise and needs further refining, our writing needs revision. Research points out that while expert writers engage in reflective revision, student writers tend to revise very little. "Revision is the process of returning to our thoughts, evaluating and clarifying them, sometimes restructuring or even reconceptualizing them within a text" (McCutchen, Francis, & Kerr, 1997, p. 667). In a series of experiments with college students, it was found that knowledge of the topic helped with meaning-level revising but was not necessary when surface level editing such as for grammar, spelling, and punctuation was the goal. Knowledge of error location helped college students to better revise as well as edit their papers. It is a good idea to have someone go over your paper and point out the location of grammar, spelling, and punctuation errors as well as to discuss the meaning and concepts of your essay with you before you revise.

How can students learn to improve their revision skills? In one experiment undergraduates in entry-level English courses, who were given eight minutes of instruction on how to make global revisions on the essays they had written, improved the quality of their revisions compared to students asked only to make revisions. The students instructed in global revision (making large scale changes such as adding new paragraphs, etc.) were also shown how global revision differs from local revision (making word and phrase level changes) (Wallace et al., 1996). College students in remedial writing classes, however, did not show an improvement in quality with global revision instructions. If you have some basic writing skills, when you revise your essay think not only about spelling, grammar, and sentence structure but also about how you might improve the essay by adding new ideas and information that support your arguments and deleting unimportant information.

Your own involvement in the writing task is another key ingredient for effective writing to occur. Being involved in the writing task requires cognitive processes such as comprehension and concentration as well as motivational/affective factors such as current goals and emotions (Reed & Shallert, 1993). Students who report being more involved in the task report more positive emotion and less anxiety than less involved writers.

Reading and writing is a single dimension, one that is primarily influenced by reading (Shell, Murphy, and Bruning, 1989). The implication of this research is that if you are having difficulty with writing assignments, it is probable that you also have reading difficulties for which you should seek help from the tutoring center at your college. If your writing skills need some polishing, visit your college's writing center and have a faculty or peer tutor read and help you edit your papers before you turn them in to your professors. Don't wait until you get a poor grade to get help. Your professor will notice your efforts to do your best work and will begin to perceive you to be an enthusiastic, motivated student. Who knows, you may end up discovering that you have a talent for writing and become a peer tutor yourself and/or go on to write for publication.

Master Writing Styles for Courses across the Curriculum

A cartoon about college teaching shows a student complaining that his history professor gave him a "D" grade on a paper for which his psychology professor had given him an "A" grade. Why do so many students seem confused at the end of the semester about their grades on papers? Is there a special way to write an assignment that will guarantee that you will receive an "A" from any professor in any subject? No! In fact, the reason that this cartoon about writing strikes college professors as humorous is that it is obvious to them that people in different academic areas think and write in very divergent styles. Therefore, professors realize that the required paper for a history course would probably be very different from the one required for a psychology course.

Professors and students who work as volunteer tutors in the writing center at one community college have a two-week training workshop in which writing styles across the curriculum are a chief topic of discussion. The faculty attending the workshop are asked to bring in an article from their area of expertise, which is representative of one that a typical student might be assigned to read. They are also asked to bring in a sample writing assignment they require of their students. Professors find out, first hand, that students in general education courses are assigned many different kinds of reading and writing assignments. The reading assignments are written in all kinds of styles, which make them hard for students to read in one night. The articles that faculty members bring to the workshop include terse computer science reports filled with technical jargon, formal scientific reports, and essays on writing and literature. It is enlightening for faculty to realize that students who are enrolled in general education classes could have such a wide range of readings and writing assignments to complete in one week. The student tutors agree that they are challenged with that type of diversity in thinking and writing styles all the time. Each of the reading assignments have the same general purpose, to help students learn how to think and write like a professional specializing in the specific discipline. Many of the writing assignments have very different types of requirements, however, depending on the academic discipline of the professor and the specific purposes of the assignment.

If thinking and writing assignments vary across the curriculum, what does it mean to learn to think and write well? How can a student know the differences? These are not easy questions to answer but we will attempt to provide some general information and guidelines concerning the various types of writing assignments that you will be required to complete during your college career and how you should complete them. Your professor who assigns the writing will most likely provide specific directions for completing it. Here we just want to provide an overview of the types of writing assignments you will be asked to complete.

The most common types of assignments include:

- Journal or workbook entry
- Essay
- Brief essay answers on an exam
- Technical report
- Review paper
- Research study report

Journals and Workbooks. Many of your professors may require you to write a journal, but the requirements for them may vary from class to class. For example, one writing instructor requires students to *free write,* or enter whatever ideas come into their minds, in their journal and instructs them to use their creative ideas as a basis for their essays and papers. An instructor of literature requires students to keep a reading journal into which they write formal essays about the ideas they have when reading each of their assignments. An astronomy professor requires students to make several observations of the night sky and describe what they saw in their observation log. The assignment for this observation log consists of a series of probing questions that the students must include in their answers. A psychology professor requires students in her psychology of personal adjustment class to keep a workbook into which they write the answers to exercises in the text concerned with holistic life planning. Students are instructed to refer to these answers when writing their essays for exams, preparing required collages depicting their life goals, and writing their final paper for the course. These instructors all provide students with detailed directions in their course syllabi on how to complete these journal assignments. Therefore, the key to earning an "A" on any of these assignments would be to faithfully follow the directions provided for them. If directions are not provided, ask the instructor to clarify his or her requirements for you. And, if you are still not sure how to proceed with your assignment or just want some help proof-reading it, visit the writing center at your college with your instructor's directions in hand.

Essays. In a beginning level college writing course, freshmen students are typically taught that an essay must have at least three sections, each containing a minimum of three sentences. The first section must present the *thesis statement,* which informs the reader of the position, opinion, argument, or question to be addressed in the essay. The second part is the *body of the essay,* which explains the thesis in detail. The third part is the *summary,* which presents the key points addressed in the essay as well as any conclusions the writer has drawn. Unless directed to do otherwise, you can follow this general format, which was described as the "hamburger method" in a previous section, whenever you are assigned an essay.

Essay Questions. Students who have just finished learning how to write a proper essay in a writing class can become confused when a professor assigns an essay question on an exam because they may not be using the term "essay" correctly. When a professor asks for a brief essay answer in response to an exam question, he or she may direct you to simply repeat the stem of the question and answer each part of it. Some instructors include short essay questions on exams. Since students are expected to write their answers from memory during an exam, the answers are typically brief. Other instructors provide students with the essay questions in advance to be completed as take home exams. These take home assignments are expected to be complete, formal, typed essays.

For example, a professor asks students in her psychology of child development class to "list the five characteristics of a high quality day care that *you* feel are most important and explain how each contributes to some aspect of child development (physical, cognitive, or psychosocial)." The professor instructs the students to

- Write a thesis statement by repeating the stem of the question (e.g., "Five characteristics of a high quality day care that I feel are most important include:...") then list the five characteristics, being sure to include one aspect from each category (e.g., safe environment, proper nutrition, age appropriate toys, responsive caregivers, outdoor play area),

- Write a brief paragraph about each of the five characteristics, describing the aspect(s) of child development involved, and why you think it is important, and

- Summarize the key points in the essay.

As you can see, the professor does require a formal essay and tells the students that it is very important for them to make sure they have answered each part of the question before handing it in because they will lose points for an incomplete answer.

Technical Reports. In applied courses in subjects such as computer science and engineering, you will be asked to write technical reports and memos like the ones used by professionals in the workplace. The purpose of this type of writing is to relate technical information to other professionals or to a customer. Mastering this type of writing will help you prepare for work in those fields. Therefore, your instructor will provide detailed directions for you to follow in producing them.

Review Paper. You will likely be expected to write many different types of literature review papers since they are a common teaching tool used in many fields of study including: history, psychology, sociology, chemistry, education, social work, criminal justice, nursing, and the humanities. These review papers will help you learn how to think and write across the curriculum, become more knowledgeable about a current topic of interest to you in the field, and learn skills you'll need to get a managerial or professional level job. The instructor will either provide directions for you or tell you which style guide to follow. In psychology, for example, we always use the most current style guide created by the American Psychological Association (APA). In humanities courses the Modern Language Association (MLA) style guide is used. Copies of these style guides are available in your college library and may even be accessible online from your library or writing center home page. They can also be purchased at book stores. In the review paper you will organize, integrate, and evaluate previously published material in order to clarify a particular problem (APA, 2001).

As a general rule, the format you use for a review paper in psychology will include the components below. Unless directed otherwise, you can use these tips as a guide to get your research report started.

- *Title Page.* Provide the title of your review paper, your name, the name of your college and the course, your instructor's name, and the date you turn in your paper. The title of the report should give the reader a strong clue about the main idea(s) included in your review of the literature. For example: "Does Spanking Cause Children to Become Aggressive?"

- *Introduction.* Briefly introduce the main idea of your study and provide a brief summary of the issue(s) addressed in it. For example: "This literature review examined the effects of physical punishment of children by parents on children's level of aggressive behaviors. It examines the effects of different types of physical punishment and level of severity." Provide a summary of the reason(s) why you selected the particular topic. For example: "I chose to study the effects of physical punishment of children because the topic is of interest to me as a future parent." Or, "I was inspired to conduct this study after reading a newspaper article on _____ (include the title) about a case in which a father was charged with child abuse for spanking his child in public." (cite the author and date of the source material in parentheses after it, as we have in this book) Most professors like the research paper to have a more formal, impersonal voice, such as: This paper addresses the pros and cons of using spanking to discipline children, which is a controversial topic in our society. Check the requirements for the level of formality required for your assignment with your professor. The review paper would be organized as follows:

- *Review of the Literature.* Review scholarly articles or books that you have selected to use for your research and present a summary of the key concepts in them that are concerned with issue(s) addressed in your paper. Do not use popular magazine articles or non-scholarly online sources. Be sure to cite all your sources in the text using the format specified in the assigned style guide.

- *Results and Conclusions.* Summarize your results and draw conclusions from them. Include any insights you may have gained while exploring your topic about how researchers could study your particular issue in the future or ways that the theory you used as a model might be changed to incorporate your findings.

- *References.* In this section, you must include a list of all of the references that you used for your report in the format specified in the assigned style guide. The required style guide should be available at your college's library or writing center, as noted above.

Research Study Report. The research study report consists of an abstract and four distinct sections: Introduction; Method; Results; and Discussion (APA, 1994). As you advance to higher level courses in disciplines such as psychology, you will be expected to design and conduct your own research study and to write a report describing it. You may also be asked to give an oral report describing it to your classmates. In addition to the material required for a research paper, you will also be expected to provide a detailed description of your own study. For example, a professor of a psychology of child development class provides students with the following directions.

> First, state the theory that you used as a model for your study, the hypothesis you are testing, and the operational definitions of all of your independent variables and dependent measures. Then compare the design of your study to those yours is based on or inspired by. Briefly describe your sample and all measuring instruments (e.g., tests, questionnaires, description of tasks, drawings to be evaluated, tables, etc.) that you used to collect data or record data. Be sure that your description is detailed enough for the reader to be able to replicate (repeat) your study. Make sure you follow the APA ethical guidelines

for research with children as participants and that you have a consent form for any study or experiment in which human subjects participate. (Put "Informed Consent" form and a copy of any materials used in your study in the Appendix to your report). When finished, write an abstract or brief summary of your research explaining how you conducted your study and the results.

Don't worry if you do not know how to complete all of these types of writing assignments at this time. You are not expected to have these skills at the start of your college career. You will be taught how to complete these various kinds of writing assignments in your classes. You can also get help from your college's writing center staff whenever needed. We provided an overview of the different types of writing assignments here to show you that it is very important for you to master each type of assignment as you progress through your college education. As you can see, the more complex writing assignments you'll be required to do in advanced college courses will build on the skills you learn in your entry level courses. If you do the best possible written work you can do at every level, you will later have the skills you need to succeed in advanced level college courses and in your career.

Always follow the style guide format and directions required by the professor who will grade it. Check before handing it in to make sure all the key parts are included and that you have followed all of the directions. Don't get yourself expelled from school or barred from graduation for *plagiarism* of any sources used, including those from the Internet, as some students recently did (Haffner, 2001). Revise, rework, and redo your paper before handing it to your professor. Check your grammar and language usage in a reference book such as the *Elements of style* (Strunk & White, 1979). Use a dictionary or thesaurus when choosing words to use in order to build your vocabulary. Use a dictionary or the spell check feature on your computer to make sure there are no spelling errors. Proofread your work to make sure that you are using the correct words. Remember that spell check can tell you if *there* is spelled correctly but not if you should have used *there* or *their*.

Be sure to optimize the chances of earning a high grade on all your work by handing in neat and clean looking papers. Type essays and papers. Make a copy of papers before handing them in so that you can replace them in case they get lost. Be sure that your papers are either stapled together or bound in a lightweight cover that doesn't fall apart. Every paper represents you and your abilities to your professor and can be saved and also used as a portfolio piece to document your developing thinking and writing abilities for prospective employers.

Improve Your Test Taking Techniques

Some students do not do well on tests containing multiple-choice questions even though they know the material fairly well, whereas others seem to be able to pass this type of test because they have excellent test taking skills. Are you test-wise or do you need to learn more efficient test taking strategies? When going over an exam in class, do you ever say to yourself "I knew that answer, why didn't I get it right?" only to discover that you had checked the wrong answer on a multiple-choice exam or did not provide the relevant material in an essay question? Here are 12 tips for improving your test taking techniques.

General Test Taking Tips

- Take a minute to look over the entire exam to estimate how much time you can spend on each item.

- Guess on items on which you do not have a clue and move on.

- Carefully read directions and questions so that your answers provide the information that is requested. Do you have to answer all of the items or are you permitted a choice?

- Ask the professor for clarification of a question when necessary. Professors (or secretaries who type exams) make an error on exam questions upon occasion. Most professors are glad that students ask about it so they can clarify the question for the whole class.

- When first given the exam, turn it over and write down some facts and formulas that you expect to be on the exam on the back, even before you start answering the questions, so that information will be readily available to you.

Test Taking Tips for Essay Exams

- For essay exams, jot down the main points you want to make in your answer to the question in outline form before you begin writing the essay so you do not forget to include them.

- On essay exams write in complete sentences, but do not include information that is not asked for in the question. If you do not think you know the answer, however, you should write something as close to what is asked as possible.

Test Taking Tips for Multiple-choice Exams

- On multiple-choice items, try to answer the question before reading the answers. Then look for the answer that most closely matches the one that you wrote down. If you are still not sure of the answer, cross out any answers that are obviously wrong or unfamiliar to you to narrow your choices.

- On multiple-choice items, read all of the alternatives before marking your answer. The right answer might be "All of the above."

- When absolute qualifiers are used on multiple-choice items, such as "always" or "never," they generally indicate a false statement.

- When stumped by a question, look for answers in other test questions. A name, date, or other information could remind you of the correct answer.

- When you get a paper or test back, don't throw it away. Review the feedback from the instructor on papers and tests so that you can understand how to improve your performance the next time. Some professors provide you with the correct answers whereas others do not. Whether or not your professor provides the correct answers, look up the information for your incorrect responses on tests in your text and notes. Try to determine why you selected the wrong answer. Doing so will improve your performance on future tests.

Do some students typically perform better than others on specific types of tests? Psychological researchers have found gender differences in performance in testing situations: Females tend to perform better on written exams than on multiple-choice tests (U.S. Department of Education, 1997, as cited in Halpern, 1997). Males tend to perform better on exams that require transforming information in visual-spatial short-term memory and in math (Robinson, Abbott, Berninger, & Busse, 1996, as cited in Halpern, 1997). Keep in mind that these gender differences are average differences that, although statistically significant, are small and do not apply to everybody. For example, many women are better than many men in taking multiple-choice tests and in doing math, and many men are better than many women in writing essay exams. These gender differences in test taking preferences can probably be attributed in part to differences in cultural conditioning of boys and girls. Test taking is a learned skill like any other and you can learn to budget your time, follow the directions, and organize your essays or eliminate the incorrect answers on a multiple-choice exam. Whether you are a man or a woman, if you find that you make factual and conceptual errors, revise your study strategies.

If you do not perform well on an exam, go back and review the right and wrong answers and determine as soon as possible why you put the answers that you did. Did you select the wrong answer on a multiple-choice exam because the terms all seemed equally familiar? Did you fail to include that specific term or concept in your notes? Did you misread the question? Were the answers you got right related to material that had been covered in class lectures or was the material from the book? The answers to these questions can help you in organizing your studying for the next exam in that course. Look for patterns of careless mistakes. Learn from what you did right as well as from your errors. If you find that you perform poorly because you do not understand the English language well enough, ask the professor if you could be allowed to use a dictionary to look up unfamiliar words during tests. One psychology professor allows the whole class to do that.

If you don't understand what you did wrong or how to perform better next time, ask your professor for assistance or for a referral to your college's tutoring center or other appropriate source of help. Even though you feel pressed for time, make the time to learn the test taking, research, writing, oral presentation, math, and computer skills you need to ensure success in college early in your college career. Doing so will help you get better grades sooner and will save you time, effort, and grief in the long run.

Vary Your Study Strategies for Different Types of Exam Questions

What is the best way to study for an exam? It all depends on the particular subject and type of exam question the professor asks. In his famous *Taxonomy of educational objectives*, Benjamin S. Bloom (as cited in Bloom, Englehart, Furst, Hill, & Krathwohl, 1956) categorized different types and levels of questions that require different types of teaching and study strategies because they assess different student thinking proficiencies. The categories in Bloom's taxonomy of educational objectives include several levels of both simple and complex types of thinking, with descriptions that suggest the different types of questions that would be used to assess them.

Simple Questions—require the student to demonstrate that he or she:

- Has amassed specific *knowledge*
- *Comprehends* or understands the meaning of that knowledge

Complex Questions—require the student to demonstrate that he or she can:

- *Apply* the principle underlying that knowledge
- *Analyze* that knowledge and perceive the relationship among the various parts of it
- *Synthesize* or combine knowledge from varied sources in order to generate new ideas
- *Evaluate* or judge the value of that knowledge based on specific criteria

Bloom (1956) pointed out that professors should demonstrate different levels of thinking in their examples when teaching and should include questions assessing mastery at each of the levels of thinking on their exams in order to allow the students to demonstrate proficiency. However, some students are not aware that different types of exam questions require different types of study methods. Consequently, when they perform poorly on their first exam, students may decide to continue to use the same study strategy (e.g., memorization of key words and concepts using cue cards) for longer periods of time in order to improve their test score. They do not realize that many of the exam questions require a different method rather than more time studying using a method that is ineffective for a specific type of question.

As a review of the types of thinking outlined in Bloom's taxonomy suggests, memorization of key words and concepts using cue cards is only suited for accumulating knowledge and demonstrating that you have learned it. This rote learning method will allow you to adequately answer questions asking you to recall or repeat facts, key concepts, or definitions of terms. However, it will not help you perform very well on questions that require a more analytical approach, such as questions that asks you to apply what you have learned by analyzing a case study, providing an example from your own life experience, or compare, assess, or interpret several theoretical approaches.

Be aware that most professors will incorporate a variety of thinking levels in lectures and tests, as Bloom has suggested, and that you will need to demonstrate proficiency at the more complex levels in order to earn an "A" in your courses. Analyze how your professors teach and test and use the study methods that are most appropriate for the types of questions they ask. Do they ask you to be able to recall key terms and theorists names? Do they discuss case examples to explain important points of a theory, and ask you to analyze case examples in relation to a particular theory when they test? Do they ask you in class and on exams to provide examples of how knowing a particular theory might be useful in your own life? Some professors will give you a copy of a previous exam to analyze if you ask for it. Other professors keep old exams on file in the library for students to review. Many publishers include with their textbook, a study guide that has similar test items to those in the test bank that many professors use to construct the exam.

Pay attention to your professor when he or she talks about what types of questions will be on the exams. If you feel that you need more help identifying the study methods that are appropriate for demonstrating proficiency in the different levels of thinking, ask your professor for help or get assistance from the staff at your college's tutoring center. One of the tutors working there may have previously taken that same class and, therefore, may have first hand knowledge about how that professor tests or insight about the requirements for essays and papers.

Overcome Test Anxiety

Several years ago a student, whom we shall call Anne, became so anxious before an exam that she suffered from headaches, nausea and vomiting. The young woman had begun college at 18, but her high anxiety about exams caused her to drop out. After working at boring clerical jobs for ten years she returned to college. During her first semester back she suffered from the same severe test anxiety as she had during her first college experience. Her professor suggested she go to the college Counseling Center. Anne took the advice and said that the Counseling Center had arranged funding for her to have ten visits with a psychiatrist. The psychiatrist pointed out that the root of her problem was low self-esteem, which resulted from her growing up in a home where she had been constantly criticized. Anne began to change her thinking about herself, to realize that she had the intelligence and ability to do her academic work in a step-by-step fashion, attending class and preparing for exams. She was able to take exams without suffering from debilitating anxiety and managed to go on to graduate from college Cum Laude.

One study evaluated several possible components of test anxiety among 338 students enrolled in graduate and undergraduate-level statistics courses (Bandalos, Yates, & Thorndike-Christ, 1995). Self-efficacy for statistics (agreement with the statement "I can do well in a statistics class") was found to be negatively related to the worry component of test anxiety. In other words, students with low self-efficacy in statistics worried more about the tests than students with high self-efficacy in this area. Attributions for success and failure (the perceived causes of success and failure) influenced both general test anxiety and statistics test anxiety. Both men and women who attributed failure to lack of effort had lower levels of test anxiety. Men who attributed failure to external causes (i.e., "The test was not fair") had higher levels of statistics test anxiety—worry. Women who attributed success to behavioral causes (i.e., "I construct graphs to help me understand the material") were found to have higher levels of math self-efficacy than women attributing success to external causes.

Is your goal only to get an "A" in the class or is it your goal to learn the subject? When the goal is a *performance goal* (i.e., the grade), the student is more likely to have test anxiety than when the student has a *learning goal* (i.e., learning statistics). The learning goal orientation is more likely to lead to changes in learning strategies and increased effort when the student encounters difficulty (Ames & Archer, 1988; Elliot & Dweck, 1988). The reason for this difference seems to be that students who have performance goals are more likely to attribute failure to external, uncontrollable causes such as bad luck or hard teachers. In one experiment, when the value of performance rather than learning was stressed, even children with high ability in the area responded to failure in a helpless kind of way, giving up, saying that their mistakes were due to lack of ability (Meece, Blumenfeld, & Hoyle, 1988). On the other hand, when the value of learning was highlighted, both high and low ability children sought to increase their competence when given negative feedback and responded in a mastery oriented manner, taking opportunities to increase their skill.

Three theoretical models have been developed to explain test anxiety and academic performance (Smith, Arnkoff, & Wright, 1990). The *Cognitive-Attentional Model* postulates that variables such as worry, task-irrelevant thinking, and negative self-preoccupation (I'm not smart; I never do well on tests; etc.) increase test anxiety and impair test performance. A more comprehensive model, the *Cognitive Skills Model* posits that both negative thoughts and underlying concerns and academic skills (e.g., study habits) are responsible for test anxiety and poorer performance. The third model, the *Social Learning Model* explains test anxiety by perceived self-efficacy, perceived outcome expectations (what grade the student expected) and goal-related motivation.

In research designed to test the three models by Smith et al. (1990), 178 undergraduate students completed both test and achievement anxiety measures, a measure of positive and negative thoughts that they have during an exam, and a measure of worrisome and task-irrelevant thoughts immediately before tests. Underlying concerns in relation to grades and exams were derived from an open-ended questionnaire about the tactics they use for taking tests. The researchers also constructed a self-efficacy scale for test taking skills. Six variables derived from social learning theory were assessed: test goal, course goal, test goal importance, course goal importance, self-efficacy for test-goal attainment, and academic satisfaction. Test grades and course grades were also included in the analysis. A comparison of the alternative models found that although cognitive-attentional processes of task-irrelevant thinking and negative self-preoccupation are relatively more important in explaining performance and test anxiety, cognitive skills and social learning also contribute to both course grades and test anxiety.

The implications of this research are that in order to overcome test anxiety you must use multiple approaches. Although the literature has shown that counseling that targets or focuses on the emotional component of test anxiety is effective in overcoming the anxiety, it is less often related to improvement in grades (Allen, 1972; Finger & Galassi, 1977; Tryon, 1980; as cited in Smith et al., 1990). Based on this research, we make the following recommendations for overcoming test anxiety:

- Perceive yourself as having the ability to succeed in challenging subject areas such as math (High math self-efficacy).

- Believe that you can do well in the course, as recommended by Michelle, a graduate student who is featured in the Success Profile below.

- Perceive the cause of success in the course to be how much effort you put into doing the work of the class.

- Focus on learning the subject matter of a course rather than on the grade. This type of learning goal orientation will lead to higher achievement and lower test anxiety.

- Practice relaxation techniques before an exam.

- Practice the study skills recommended elsewhere in this book, such as: spacing your learning, scheduling your time, and using mnemonic memory devices.

- Replace negative thoughts about your test taking ability with positive thoughts about your ability to succeed on the exam and in the course.

- Be motivated to do well on the exam and in the course.

- Create a positive affirmation about your performance on the test and repeat it often to help you relax and stay focused on your test answers rather than your fears. For example, affirmations you might use before a math test might include: "I will perform well on the test," "I have the ability to succeed in math," or "I will relax and perform to the best of my ability on my math test."

- If you find that you still cannot control your test anxiety, seek help from your college's counseling center.

Success Profile—Michelle

Michelle is completing her first year of a master's program in psychology. Michelle has been an excellent student throughout high school and college. She was a member of the National Honor Society for 3 years during high school. During her first two years of college, Michelle lived at home while attending college full-time and worked at a bakery 25 to 35 hours per week. She did a variety of jobs including prep cook (slicing, greasing pans, washing pans, cracking eggs, etc.) and cashier work. Her mother was a single mother who also had two younger children to support, so Michelle got Pell grants, college scholarships and earned money at the bakery to pay for college. At the end of Michelle's sophomore year of college, her mother married a man with 3 sons. All four of them moved into Michelle's mother's small ranch house. Michelle moved out and into a cottage with her boyfriend. Michelle continued working at the bakery and also got student loans to help pay for college. During the summer, Michelle taught horseback riding to Girl Scouts during the day, while working at the bakery nights and weekends. Michelle still rides in horse shows occasionally.

How did Michelle manage to graduate Cum Laude while working so many hours per week? Michelle says that she goes to every class. Her advice to incoming freshmen would be to go to every class, actively listen and take notes. Michelle says "It's not worth it to cut class because you'll miss whole topics and even assignments. Notes are definitely a key to doing well on exams. I put a heading in my notes about a topic—and then put the points under the heading. I summarize the points. I don't write every word. While sitting in class I try not to daydream, instead to listen and focus on the main points the professor is making to be able to outline my notes. I try to make connections between the lecture material from my other classes and that class. I also relate the material to my own life." Michelle also tries to review the lecture notes from each class that same evening, or at least once a week and more intensively the week of an exam.

When asked what advice she would give to a college freshman, Michelle says that in addition to her advice to definitely go to every class, she would say "Always think positively. Believe that you are capable of doing well in college. When you go to take an exam, tell yourself you know the material because you sat through every class and heard all of the lectures. You have to believe you are capable of doing well when you begin the course." She said she recently gave this advice to her little sister who is in junior high school and had a negative attitude about her schoolwork.

Michelle says that when she was in the 7th or 8th grade, she realized she was an auditory learner. Although Michelle admits that she skims the book rather than reading everything word for word, she says that she does study the key terms in textbooks.

When Michelle is assigned a term paper to write, she begins to gather the information soon after the assignment. She goes to the library and gets all of her books and articles for the paper, and that way if she needs materials that her library does not have, she has time to get them through the interlibrary loan office. Then a couple of weeks before the paper is due, she reads all of the materials she has gathered, and if she thinks she needs more information, she gets it at that time. Michelle does admit to some procrastination in that she does not actually begin writing the paper until a few days before it is due. She then sits down and puts all of the information together, writing the paper on the computer.

The spring of her senior year, Michelle got a job related to her psychology major. She assists developmentally disabled adults with cerebral palsy, retardation, or autism, who live in group homes and assisted living facilities. She helps them with grocery shopping, goes to the movies with them, drives some to work and helps supervise them on the job, and does a myriad of other tasks for which they need some assistance. She works 20 hours per week while working on her master's degree. She wants to finish her master's degree and go on to a doctoral program in neuropsychology.

Inoculate Yourself against Stereotype Threat in Order to Perform as well as Possible

Have you ever been in a test or performance situation in which you felt threatened and couldn't figure out why? Perhaps you couldn't recall anyone making particularly nasty remarks about you but, nevertheless, you felt threatened and, consequently, performed more poorly than you normally would. What caused you to feel threatened? According to Claude Steele (2003), individuals have a social identity formed in their reference groups such as race, religion, ethnicity, social class, etc. Society and people judge and treat others differently based on their social categorizations. These social contingencies can affect one's internal processes and shape one's behavior, such as performance on a test.

Based on years of experience working with and observing performance of college students, particularly minority students, Claude Steele (1997) hypothesized that their performance becomes impaired in test situations in which they are reminded of limiting stereotypes about the expected performance of members of their reference group on the particular task. To test his hypothesis, Claude Steele conducted a series of experiments investigating how stereotypes about one's own gender and race shape one's intellectual identity and performance on specific tasks.

In one experiment by Steele (1997), women and men college students with equivalent math preparation were given a difficult math exam and were either told that the test generally showed gender differences or the test generally showed no gender differences. The results supported Steele's hypothesis. Women performed worse than men did when they were told that the test produced gender differences, which apparently reminded them of the pervasive stereotype that men are superior to women in math. Women performed equal to men when the test was represented as insensitive to gender differences.

In another experiment, Black and White students took a test composed of the most difficult items on the verbal Graduate Record Exam (GRE). They were either told that it was a test of intellectual ability or a laboratory problem-solving task. In this experiment, students either were or were not asked to record their race on a questionnaire just before taking the test. Black participants performed more poorly than White participants when told it was a test of intellectual ability, which apparently reminded them of the common stereotype that Whites are superior to Blacks in intelligence. Blacks performed equal to Whites (with SAT test scores statistically controlled) when the test was represented as a specific problem-solving task. Whether or not they recorded their race on a questionnaire also influenced their score. Based on the results of his research, Steele concluded that invoking limiting stereotypes about one's reference group acts as a "threat in the air" that causes people who care about doing their best to become anxious about their performance on tasks that are stereotyped as atypical for their group (Steele & Aronson, 1995).

A number of other studies have illustrated stereotype threat. The academic performance of African American college students was found to be worse at colleges with small minority student populations (Cole et al., 2000, as cited in Steele, 2003). In another study, the underperformance of Black and Latino students was completely explained by the degree of stereotype threat they experienced as they began college (Massey & Fischer, 2002, as cited in Steele, 2003). Women do more poorly in math performance when greatly outnumbered by men in the class (Inzlicht & Ben-Zeev, 2000). Women who saw videos of women acting silly and brainless did less well in performing a math task afterwards (Davies & Spencer, 2001, as cited in Steele, 2003).

What are the implications of this research for you? Knowing the results of Steele's research is important because you will be able to understand why you might suddenly feel anxious or threatened for no apparent reason in situations in which your performance is being evaluated. Then, you will be able to take some quick, positive action to help you stop feeling threatened. If you were a woman taking a college math test, for example, you might find yourself engaging in negative *self-talk* (private messages), which undermines your self-confidence after a callous professor makes a remark about expecting men to earn higher grades than women. At other times, group stereotypes could be invoked about some aspect related to your ethnic or racial background. If you quickly realize that your anxiety was triggered by the group stereotype being evoked, you can stop the negative self-talk and start engaging in positive self-talk, which will restore your self-confidence. Another approach for minority group members is to seek out as mentors professors whom you believe do not perceive you in terms of stereotypes but instead respect you for your intelligence and ideas.

Enjoy Dance, Music, and Art to Help You Adjust to College

Dance, music, and art are ways of expressing our feelings and getting in touch with our inner selves. They can change our mood, help relieve test anxiety, and impact our ability to study and perform on a test. Dance movements can reduce test anxiety. That was the finding of an experiment conducted with graduate and undergraduate students at an urban university who were randomly assigned to either the control group or four dance movement sessions of 35 minutes in duration over a two-consecutive-week period (Erwin-Grabner, Goodill, Hill, & Von Neida, (1999). The dance movement interventions were structured around themes of test taking situations. The Test Attitude Inventory (TAI) was administered to participants in the study both before and after completing the dance movement sessions. Results indicated that the dance intervention group showed a significantly greater reduction in test anxiety as compared to the control group. What this research suggests is that engaging in dance movements related to the theme of test taking situations may be a way of reducing test anxiety. Thus, if you are feeling anxious about an upcoming test, express in dance movement your fears and anxieties as a way of relieving it.

Listening to music can influence academic performance. Do you listen to music when you study? If yes, what type of music do you prefer? If you listen to rock and roll music, you might want to reconsider listening to it while studying. Research with 151 college students found that student performance on mathematics, verbal, and reading comprehension problems declines while listening to rock and roll music played at 80 dB compared to performance in silence (Tucker & Bushman, 1991).

On the other hand, some research with college students has demonstrated small but significant improvement in spatial performance after listening to Mozart's music. That result was found by researchers who tested 22 college students on a pencil-and-paper maze task after a 10-minute presentation of each of three listening conditions: Mozart piano concerto, repetitive relaxation music, and silence (Wilson & Brown, 1997). In another experiment with male and female college students, small but statistically significant improvements were found on spatial tasks immediately following their listening to Mozart's Sonata for 2 pianos in D major (Rideout & Taylor, 2001).

Still a third study presented college students with a Mozart sonata (a pleasant and energetic piece) or an Albinoni adagio (a slow, sad piece), or silence, after which they completed a test of spatial abilities. Better performance on the spatial task was found only for the students listening to the Mozart music. The effect was due to improvement in enjoyment, arousal, and mood found when listening to the Mozart music (Thompson, Schellenberg, & Husain, 2001).

The combination of music and visual art can have a more powerful effect on mood than either alone. In one experiment, 226 college students were presented with either music or paintings, or music paired with paintings (Stratton & Zalanowski, 1989). The music and paintings were selected to reflect the mood states of depression, positive affect, and neutrality. It was only when music and painting were paired that they had a significant effect on pre and post measures of mood change.

Preferences for styles of painting vary by personality and sex. Paintings that had previously been rated for style and tension were shown to 372 undergraduates whose scores on a scale measuring sensation seeking (looking for thrills, taking risks) had been assessed (Zuckerman, Ulrich, & McLaughlin, 1993). Men showed a preference for complex, high-tension paintings to a greater extent than women did. Generally, high sensation seekers liked tension evoking paintings and expressionist paintings, whereas low sensation seekers showed a greater preference for realistic, pastoral scenes. Take a course in visual art and discover the type of painting you prefer so that you may enrich your environment by buying art that matches your personality style. The research summarized in this section suggests that certain types of dance, music, and art can help you relax before tests, improve your performance on spatial tasks, and enhance your mood while studying. Decorating with art that reflects your personality will make your study surroundings more pleasant.

Success Recommendations

This section contains a summary of the main points in this chapter to help you reflect on and recall what you have learned.

- **Read and Follow the Instructions on your Course Syllabi.** Mark important dates to remember on your calendar. Check each one of them often to make sure you know all of the important dates for upcoming exams and assignments as well as any changes the professor makes during the semester. If you have any questions of your professors concerning your course requirements, make sure you ask them either in class or privately.

- **Be an Active Learner. Attend Class, Ask Questions.** Read the assigned material before class. If you can't read all of the assigned readings before class, at least review the chapter summaries, list of key concepts, and illustrations. Attend class lectures, be an active listener, and take notes on the key points that are stressed. Demonstrate an interest in the class material by asking questions when you need to clarify a key point and by providing relevant examples when the professor asks for class participation.

- **Organize Your Lecture and Study Notes.** Use the Cornell Note-Taking Method to take efficient, well-organized lecture and study notes. Use a three-ring binder with loose-leaf paper and subject dividers to separate your course work. Put your name, address, and phone number on the cover in case you lose it. Include your course syllabi, handouts, and a spiral-bound assignment planner to help you keep track of classes, assignment deadlines, and exam dates.

- **Summarize the Text in Your Own Words.** When reading sections of a textbook that you have particular difficulty understanding, use strategies that help you form cognitive links to the concepts so that you can better remember them. Read each whole section for understanding. Figure out the central idea or thesis the author is making and identify the supporting ideas for the main thesis. Write a summary of the section of the text in your own words and provide yourself with examples, where possible, to begin making links to your own experience. Increase your reading speed if you only have to learn the main points of the material.

- **Use the Hamburger Method of Essay Construction, with Particular Attention to the Introduction.** Write essays using the "hamburger" method of construction, which consists of an introduction, a main part, and a conclusion. Take time to think about what you want to say before you begin. Make sure you provide the reader with the reasons for writing about the topic and what your argument will be in a way that captivates his or her attention. Write as much as you can about the topic in the body of the essay. End with a conclusion that summarizes the important points you have made.

- **Revise Your Written Work.** Go back to check your written work for completeness and clarity before handing it to your instructor. Did you follow instructions? Does it make sense? Do you need to improve the essay by adding new ideas and information that support your arguments or deleting unimportant information? Consider having a friend or someone at the writing center proofread it for you. As you learn strategies for improving your writing, you will increase your self-efficacy concerning your writing skills.

- **Master Writing Styles for Courses across the Curriculum.** Always follow the style guide format and directions required by the professor who will grade your written work. Don't get yourself expelled from school or barred from graduation for plagiarism of any sources used, including those from the Internet. Revise, rework, redo, and make a copy of your paper before handing it to your professor.

- **Improve Your Test Taking Techniques.** When taking tests, learn to budget your time, follow the directions, and organize your essays. Review each question you get wrong on every test you take and find out why it was marked incorrect. Look for patterns of careless mistakes. Learn from your errors. If you made factual and conceptual errors, revise your study strategies. If you are an ESL student, ask the professor if you could be allowed to use a dictionary to look up unfamiliar words during tests. If you need to learn better test taking strategies, get help from your college's tutoring center.

- **Match Your Study Strategies to the Different Types of Exam Questions.** Most professors choose exam questions that allow them to assess students' proficiency at a variety of thinking levels. Analyze how your professor teaches and tests and use the study methods that are most appropriate for the types of methods used in class and the types of questions he or she asks on exams. If you need help identifying the study methods that are appropriate for demonstrating proficiency in the different levels of thinking, ask your professor for help or get assistance from the staff at your college's tutoring center.

- **Overcome Test Anxiety.** In order to overcome test anxiety, use multiple approaches. If you are worrying more about specific tests because you have a fear of failure in that subject, overcome it by believing that you are capable of doing the work (high self-efficacy). If you need tutoring help to learn how to approach studying that subject, get some help. If you are worrying because you attribute your success or failure to external causes (i.e., "That professor's tests are not fair"), learn to attribute your successes and failures to temporary internal causes (i.e., "I will construct graphs to help me understand the material" or "I didn't spend enough time organizing my notes"). Develop a learning goal orientation. Focus your attention on learning metacognitive skills. Use these metacognitive skills to identify effective study and test taking strategies that work best for you rather than wasting time and energy worrying about your test grades. Create a positive affirmation about your performance on the test (e.g., "I have the ability to succeed in math") and repeat it often to help you relax and stay focused on your test answers rather than your fears.

- **Inoculate Yourself against Stereotype Threat.** Learn How to Diffuse Anxiety Caused by It. Form the habit of monitoring your cognitive self-talk to make sure that it is positive and self-affirming during situations in which your performance is being evaluated. If you find that you are undermining your self-confidence by engaging in negative self-talk about what "people like you" can or can not do, tell yourself to STOP. Then begin to engage in positive self-talk such as "I have performed very well on tests like this before, I can do this now" to restore your self-confidence. Realize that stereotypes are unfair and unreasonable and that you should not allow them to define you and your abilities.

- **Enjoy Dance, Music and Art to Help Adjust to College.** When feeling anxious about exams, dance to relieve your fears and anxieties. Listen to music such as a Mozart sonata (a pleasant and energetic piece) to improve your performance and mood. Take a course in visual art and discover the type of painting you prefer so that you may enrich your life by buying art that matches your personality style. Decorate your study area with art that reflects your personality to make your surroundings more pleasant.

Chapter Seven
Improve Your Creativity, Critical Thinking, and Decision Making Skills

What are your basic beliefs about the world? What evidence and reasoning support these beliefs? How do you gather and evaluate your information? What are the implications and consequences of your beliefs? What is your frame of reference? Are you looking at the world through the perceptual lens of Christianity, of capitalism, of racism or of a particular discipline such as biology, sociology, psychology, or economics (Paul, 1995)? We all interpret the world in ways that contain many systematic biases. We are not conscious of these influences in our thinking. We may not have clear, specific criteria for judgment. We observe reality through the prism of our perceptions and thoughts about reality.

Of what relevance is critical thinking in your life? When we judge without knowing what the bases for our judgments are, we can make decisions that are devastating to us. Did you buy the car you bought because the salesman was adept at the low balling tactic? Using this tactic, he first offers you a sale price that you agree to, then he comes back after supposedly speaking with the manager and says that the manager would not allow him to sell the car at that price with air conditioning. The price will be a few hundred dollars higher than what you agreed to pay. If you are like many people, you will still buy the car at the higher price. Once people have committed to doing something such as buying a car, even when the terms are altered to be less favorable to them, they still follow through.

Although we can't eliminate all of the biases in our thinking, we can better understand what some of them are, learn to be more objective in our thought processes, and make more effective decisions that better facilitate goal achievement. Strategies to help you learn to be a critical thinker as well as an effective decision maker and problem solver are outlined in this chapter.

Don't Believe Everything You See and Hear

According to recent research and theory by Daniel Gilbert and his colleagues (Gilbert, Krull, & Malone, 1990), a distinction can be made between *automatic believing* and *controlled unbelieving*. Gilbert argues that people have a predisposition to believe everything they see and hear. They then assess the information and unaccept it if, based on their deliberation, they find a reason not to believe it. If we hear a candidate for governor say, "If elected I will lower your taxes, balance the budget, reduce crime, and wash your car every Sunday afternoon," we may then stop and think about what is being said. Then we begin to doubt it if we think we have reason to do so. If people are tired, preoccupied, or unmotivated to consciously think about what is being said, they will accept it without further cognitive processing.

In one experiment, Gilbert, Tafarodi, and Malone (1993) asked participants to read crime reports on a computer and then to recommend a prison sentence for the criminal. The participants were told that some of the statements from the reports had been accidentally typed from other criminal cases and these false statements would appear in red, whereas the true statements pertaining to the case would appear in black. The false statements given to some participants made the crime appear worse, whereas the false statements given to others made the crime seem less severe. Because people were clearly able to see which statements were false and which were true, they were not influenced by the false statements printed in red. The prison sentences they gave to the "criminal" were the same for people who had or had not read the false statements. When the experimenters increased the work some of the participants were doing while reading (they had to push a button every time some numbers appeared on the computer screen), they were more likely to believe the false information. For example, people in the condition where they had to push the button in response to certain numbers on the screen, were more likely to be influenced by the false information in the sentence they recommended for the criminal. Thus when the false information printed in red was extenuating, the people who also had to push the button in response to the numbers on the screen, gave shorter sentences than people not performing this task while reading the crime report.

The moral of the result of this experiment is that when you have to make an important decision, such as deciding which car to purchase, do not do so when you are tired or distracted by other concerns. Making poor decisions about major purchases can be costly and can jeopardize your goal achievement. For example, you may end up having to work extra hours to pay for an expensive car and have less time to study for exams.

Consider the Possibility that You Might Be Wrong

Human thinking can use faulty reasoning processes and have unfair, unpleasant, and/or tragic consequences. People tend to use mental shortcuts in their reasoning. Several of these mental shortcuts that lead to biased thinking have been pointed out by social psychologists.

Anchoring People may use an arbitrary value or standard or be influenced by an irrelevant value or standard. For example, a college professor reading a student term paper may be influenced by the student's grades on the exams in grading the paper. One strategy to avoid biasing their paper grades would be for the professors to grade the papers without looking at who wrote them.

Base Rate Information People are less likely to use statistical information than they are to use individual case information. People will buy lottery tickets week after week even though their chances of winning may be one in 100 million because the few people who do win the jackpots receive a great deal of money.

Biased Sampling People make generalizations from samples that are known to be biased. For example, if you talk to people who belong to a particular political party about an issue, you can't generalize their position on the issue to everyone in the population.

Availability Heuristic Some information can easily be recalled from memory and, therefore, influence our thinking. For example, many more people have a fear of flying than a fear of riding in cars. The data show that far fewer people are killed per mile traveled in airplanes than are killed in automobiles. Airplane crashes, however, receive much more widespread and repeated publicity than do car crashes.

False Consensus Effect We have a tendency to believe that others share our views to a much greater extent than they do. Before jumping to the conclusion that friends or relatives agree with your position, ask about their thoughts on the issue.

Be consciously mindful of these mental shortcuts when you are making important decisions so that you will not be caught off guard and end up making unfair or costly errors in judgment.

Develop Critical Thinking Skills

Naive and flawed reasoning practices can derail you from achieving your goals. The world is changing at an accelerating rate. If you have poor cognitive skills, the jobs available to you will pay poorly and provide little security. There is at the same time demand for the worker who can manipulate abstract and complex symbols and ideas. The wealth of information provided by the Internet has to be selected, integrated, and applied to the issues confronting both the individual and society.

Diane Halpern (1998) has developed a model for teaching thinking skills that will transfer across a number of domains and contexts. The first step in Halpern's thinking skills instructional model involves an *attitudinal component*, which involves the willingness to generate alternatives and generate probabilities. The individual must be willing to exert the effort to think critically about the issue, choice, or problem. The critical thinker has to rely on plans rather than impulsive behaviors. At the same time he or she must be willing to give up on nonproductive strategies and be flexible and open-minded. There is also a necessity for awareness of social realities such as seeking consensus or compromise in implementing ideas. Halpern notes that parents and teachers should provide children with instruction in and practice with critical-thinking skills, using activities designed to facilitate transfer across contexts.

The second step involves learning about *structural aspects of concepts* in order to transfer them to different situations. An example used by Halpern (1998) is teaching about "sunk costs." The idea is that decisions about future costs should be made without regard to prior investments (see the next strategy).

Finally, the third step in Halpern's model involves evaluating one's thinking process when engaged in critical thinking. This is called *meta-cognitive monitoring*, which means to have knowledge or awareness of monitoring your own cognitive processes or thinking. How do you know when you have reached your goal? What critical thinking skills are useful in solving this problem? Are you moving toward a solution? How well was the problem solved? Ask yourself questions such as these as you engage in problem solving in college and every day life.

Develop critical thinking skills and use them for effective problem solving. Generate creative alternative solutions to your problems and proactively assess the probable outcomes of each one. Make decisions about your future without regard to prior investments. Monitor your own thinking process.

Try to Avoid "Sunk Costs"

Although we are taught that persistence pays off, things may not always go as planned and we must then decide whether to continue a course of action or jump ship and change our behavior and allocate our time, energy, and/or money differently. For example, if your friend says that she is going to spend $500 to repair her beat-up old car because she has already spent hundreds on its repair, she is engaging in thinking that is not relevant to the problem. The decision should be based on whether the car is now worth a $500 repair. Should Congress spend millions of dollars on a missile system because they have already spent millions on the missile system in the past? That decision should be based on the role of the missile system in the future defense of the country and what other alternative defensive systems would cost in relation to their effectiveness. Why do people consider time, energy, or money previously invested when making decisions?

In an experiment giving varying descriptions to participants of the conditions under which decisions about resources were being made, participants were more likely to continue to invest in the current project if they had already invested considerable resources (Bornstein & Chapman, 1995). The more that has already been put into a project, the less likely are people to "jump ship" and get out. They follow the principle of "throwing good money after bad," which is usually perceived as irrational thinking. The researchers found that the main reason for sunk costs is the desire to avoid wastefulness, not wanting to waste the money or time that has already been spent. When a relatively small amount of resources had been invested, people are more likely to get out.

Sunk costs appear in a variety of situations such as personal decisions, decisions about interpersonal relationships, business financial decisions, evaluations of employees' performance, and competitive behavior. It is considered to be a sunk cost when future resources could be used more effectively in some other way.

For example, Ron invested in commercial real estate just before a market downturn. Ron was not getting sufficient rent to pay the mortgage, taxes, and insurance on the property, so each month he kept losing money. After a year, his friend suggested that he sell the property. He told her that he couldn't sell it because he would lose money at the current market price since he could only sell it for less than he had paid for it. Plus he would lose all of the money he had paid in expenses (i.e., taxes, insurance, etc.) that was greater than his total rental income had been. Ron said he could not afford to sell the property. So he held the property and kept losing more money every month until he finally had to file bankruptcy. He lost everything he owned!

Avoid making new decisions based on "sunk costs" to reduce the likelihood of making costly mistakes. Don't be afraid to protect your assets by cutting your losses or choosing a new direction or goal when that course of action is most desirable.

Overcome Your Stereotypes.
Learn to Appreciate Diversity.

We live in a world in which the populations of many countries are growing more culturally diverse and more accepting of individual differences. The same is true of the populations of many colleges and universities (Gose, 1996). The diversity of the students and faculty enriches the college atmosphere and enables students to learn first hand about different cultural beliefs and practices from each other and from professors. The accepting atmosphere at many colleges and universities affords students with varying religious and cultural beliefs and practices and sexual orientations an opportunity to openly express their ideas. Some students who may not have had opportunities to experience and learn to appreciate living in a diverse environment before entering college may feel that their beliefs are being challenged in their new living and learning environments.

As students interact with and get to know people who are different from themselves, they may begin to examine negative stereotypes (oversimplified ideas) and prejudices they learned during childhood about people of a certain gender, sexual orientation, physical and mental ability, religion, ethnic or racial group, or nationality. Students' beliefs are also challenged in many classes because a goal of a college education is to help students examine their old belief system and form their own philosophy of life based on their new knowledge of world. Researchers have found that students who have diverse experiences improve their critical thinking skills during their college years (Pascarella, Palmer, Moye, & Pierson, 2001).

Seek out college courses, activities, and diverse experiences in which you have an opportunity to learn about and interact with people from all types of backgrounds. Use your critical thinking skills to examine negative group stereotypes and prejudices. Learn to respect and accept others and embrace diversity. Understand that an attitude of respect and acceptance of others will be essential for your future success in a diverse workplace.

Learn How to Critically Evaluate Information
on the Internet

You will be required to write many research papers during your college career. These research papers will require you to include a review of literature on a specific topic and area of study, as noted in a previous chapter. The Internet allows everyone to gain quick access day or night to a burgeoning wealth of information on almost any topic by simply entering the key words ("critical thinking" for example) for any subject into a search engine such as Google (http://www.google.com) or Ask Jeeves (http://www.ask.com). Therefore, students like to use it to gather information for their research projects. Can you use the Internet to conduct your required search of the literature in an efficient and productive manner?

The first place you should go when looking for information for a review paper on the Internet is to your college or university library website. Many colleges and universities have paid subscriptions to online databases of many disciplines and the media. The Rhode Island College library website, for example, has an option called paid Online Resources which lists over 60 different databases that the library pays for with yearly subscription fees and that can be accessed by students, faculty, and staff by using their ID number online. One such database is Psyc Articles, which has full text articles of journals published by the American Psychological Association, and Psyc Info which provides a search of hundreds of journals, books, dissertations, and manuscripts from which can be printed abstracts and references. Other such databases accessible through the college website include Medline, Historical Abstracts, American Humanities Index, and Biological Sciences. Articles in professional journals are reviewed by other respected professionals in the field. You can have confidence in the scholarly merit of the research reported in these professional journals and books.

If you are looking for information about the people of the United States, there are many United States government websites to which you can go. Some of the information in this book was found online from government websites such as the U.S. Census Bureau. These are also highly reliable sources.

If you need more personal instruction about how to critically evaluate information on the Internet for a discipline-specific review paper, ask the reference librarian at your college or your professor to assist you. Students will still have to go to the college library to find full text of articles for which they were only able to access abstracts through the Internet. If the book or article is not available at your library, college libraries provide interlibrary loan services where they will borrow the book for you from another library. This is another reason to begin your paper early, so that you will have the time to get books and copies of articles you need from interlibrary loan.

Photo courtesy of Bristol Community College.

How can one know what websites to use as sources of reliable information in research papers? Follow the steps below to critically evaluate Internet sites and help you reach a good decision.

Refine Your Search. First, make your key word search as specific as possible to limit the number of sources referenced to only the ones that are most relevant.

Evaluate the Source of the Information. Since anyone can post information on the Wide World Web, critical thinking skills must be used to evaluate information found on it. Look at the copyright and contact information. Who developed the website and wrote the information? What academic credentials and subject area expertise does the writer have? Does he or she have a degree that signifies expertise in the topic such as M.D. for a topic relating to physical health or medicine or Ph.D. for a topic about psychology or history, for example? Some websites do not say who developed it or wrote the information. These should definitely not be used as sources of information, especially for academic work.

Check out the web address. Does the website address end in "edu" if in the United States or one that indicates that it is associated with a college or university in another country? Is it accessed from or linked to a college or university home page? Does the site contain an article from a magazine or a professional scholarly journal? You should not use information from non-scholarly sources such as popular magazines or newspapers in a college review paper unless you are specifically told that you may do so by your professor. For most college review papers, your professor will require you to use information from scholarly articles and books in the course discipline.

Develop Constructive Thinking Skills

Constructive thinking has been defined as "the ability to think and to solve problems in everyday living with a minimum cost in stress" (Park, Moore, Turner, & Adler, 1997, p. 584). The need for a scale to measure constructive thinking was based on the observation that people with high intellectual ability are not necessarily able to use their ability for solving everyday problems in living, such as successfully raising their children and/or successfully performing a job (Epstein & Meier, 1989). A Constructive Thinking Inventory (CTI) was developed to measure people's everyday automatic thinking. Statistical analyses revealed a global (comprehensive) scale of coping and five interrelated specific factors. People who score high on the global scale are accepting of self and others and are biased in the direction of positive thinking. Their optimism, however, is realistic and not naive.

In this research, four specific CTI scales were found to be particularly important to constructive thinking. What are those four specific scales and what do they measure?

- *Emotional coping*—a tendency not to take things personally, not to be sensitive to disapproval, and not to worry excessively about failure and disapproval. People high in emotional coping are self-accepting and do not over generalize from, or overreact to, unfavorable experiences. They do not dwell on unpleasant past experiences or worry about future ones over which they have little control.

- *Behavioral coping*—a tendency to release past hurts and focus on goals for the future. "People with high scores on behavioral coping are action oriented, optimistic, and do not hold grudges or dwell on past injuries, but let bygones be bygones and focus their energy on planning and carrying out effective action" (Epstein & Meier, 1989, p. 339).

- *Categorical thinking*—refers to a tendency to think in extreme or rigid ways. People with high scores in categorical thinking tend to classify others as good or bad, as either for or against them, and to believe that there is only one right way to do anything.

- *Superstitious thinking*—refers to a tendency to engage in superstitious thinking and behaviors. People who engage in superstitious thinking have many personal superstitions, such as a belief that if they talk about anticipated success it will keep it from happening. They also engage in conventional superstitious behaviors, such as to "knock on wood" to protect themselves from bad luck. They are also likely to believe in questionable phenomena such as astrology and ghosts.

Emotional coping and behavioral coping accounted for half of the content and processes in the specific CTI scales, which indicates that coping can largely be divided into coping with the inner world of emotions and thoughts and the outer world of events. Do emotional and behavioral coping skills directly impact academic achievement?

Global scores of the CTI were significantly related to success in work, love, social relationships, and in maintaining emotional and physical well being, but not academic achievement, according to studies with a total of 379 undergraduate participants. It appears that the CTI is measuring emotional and behavioral coping, but not IQ or non-cognitive hard work and time management skills related to academic success. However, these skills are related to success in areas that can indirectly affect college and life success such as emotional problems due to excessive worry about events that may never happen in the future or inability to learn to trust others and begin to form satisfying interpersonal relationships.

Success Profile—Kimberly

Kimberly is going into her senior year. She just switched majors from social work to psychology. She has decided that her career goal is to become a school psychologist. Her mother had been a social worker for 16 years and discouraged her from going into the field because of burnout. Actually, the pastor of the church where Kimberly attends is a part-time minister and a full-time school psychologist who absolutely loves the job. She has also obtained information from the National Association of School Psychologists and found the information provided to her to further her interest in the field.

Kimberly moved to Rhode Island from Pennsylvania when she graduated from high school because her sister was there and her boyfriend was moving there. Although Kimberly graduated 3rd in her high school class, she worked as a part-time waitress while in high school and did not spend the money but saved it for college. Her mother was widowed and a pastor for a small church so she could not afford to send her to college.

When Kimberly moved to Rhode Island, she got an apartment with a roommate. She attended the community college because it was less expensive and paid for her first year out of her savings and working part-time (about 30 hours per week) as a waitress and also received a scholarship. She also worked as a work-study student at the community college.

When she moved to Rhode Island, Kimberly's boyfriend proposed. She planned her wedding for two years and had a big wedding with 250 people. After two years at the community college, Kimberly transferred to a four-year college.

Kimberly says that she over prepares for her classes. She studies every day. She never goes out at night unless she thinks that she has her schoolwork done. After getting a 4.0 average in her first year of college, Kimberly decided to set the goal of getting a 4.0 average for her four years of college. Her most important advice to freshmen students is to never miss class. She comes to class even when she is ill. She says she doesn't trust other people's notes. She rewrites her notes right after the class if she can or as soon after as possible. She finds the examples professors give in class are very helpful in understanding the material. She says if the professor is very boring and doesn't give examples, she will read the book. Otherwise, she skims the book. A few days before the exam she begins reading her notes out loud. She also calls her mother and tells her what she is learning. "I'm not one to memorize. I try to apply the concepts to my own life. I make up mnemonic devices of very silly things when I have to memorize material such as in Biology 101. But everything has to fit together. You can't just memorize."

For the past year Kimberly has worked at a hospital for emotionally disturbed children. "I love the kids, perhaps too much. I cry when they leave. I want to have children of my own, but I plan to get my Ph.D. before I have children. I can't do school half-heartedly. So, I don't plan to have children for eight more years. I love my psychology courses. It is easier to learn something you enjoy."

Learn and Use the Rules of Formal Logic to Solve Problems

Formal logic is critical thinking that solves problems in an organized way. Reasoning occurs when one uses facts or evidence from which to draw conclusions. It is often divided into two types, inductive and deductive reasoning. "Whereas induction is concerned with inferences from specific instances to more general principles or constructs, deduction can be defined as the opposite process in which predictions are derived about specific instances, starting from general principles or constructs" (Maas, Colombo, Sherman, & Colombo, 2001, p. 391).

Inductive reasoning is being used when we gather specific information relating to a problem, then draw a conclusion. Inductive reasoning is the first step in science. Scientists observe some phenomena. Then they develop general statements that they think are true and test their hypotheses or predictions by the experimental method, where they control some variables while systematically varying others. Psychology is a science that studies the experience and behavior of people. A psychologist might observe that children who watch aggressive television programs are more aggressive than children who do not watch aggressive television programs. It is still possible for the conclusion to be false because the conclusion from observation does not allow us to infer what is causing the behavior. For example, the children who prefer to watch violent television programs may come from homes where there is more aggression toward one another. The aggression in the home rather

145

than what they watch on television may be the cause of their aggression. Thus, in inductive reasoning the conclusion may be false. Scientists are always making new observations that may conflict with old observations or add new facts that change the conclusion. This does not mean that we should not use inductive reasoning, but only that we should stay open to the possibility that new information can change our conclusions.

Deductive reasoning is being used when one starts with certain premises or information and then proceeds to a specific, logical, conclusion. Provided the premises are true, the conclusion will be true. One reasons from what is known to reach a new conclusion. Logical syllogisms are a common form of deductive reasoning. A classic syllogism is:

1. All persons are mortal.

2. Socrates is a person.

3. Therefore, Socrates is mortal.

The premises in this syllogism are sentences 1 and 2. The conclusion in sentence 3 is true, if the premises are true. You are most likely to have encountered deductive reasoning problems on tests of intelligence or on college entrance exams. You have to draw conclusions given certain premises or information and there is only one correct answer. In everyday life, logic is a useful tool to have but is not sufficient to solve the major moral dilemmas of the day, such as whether a state should have capital punishment for the crime of murder. We think in syllogisms in everyday life without explicitly stating those syllogisms. For example, we might remember that on Mondays we have a quiz in biology, today is Monday, therefore we will have a quiz.

In order to draw cause and effect conclusions, however, it is necessary for the scientist to use the scientific method, which takes some important steps beyond drawing logical conclusions from premises derived from observations. Using the experimental method, the scientist isolates and manipulates some of the variables while controlling others in order to draw causal conclusions. He or she then collects data under these controlled conditions allowing causal conclusions to be made.

In everyday life, in perceiving other people, we are more likely to use inductive processes, inferring traits (characteristics) on the basis of behavioral information, than we are to use deductive processes, inferring behavior from traits (Maas et al., 2001). You might have a friend who helps out at a soup kitchen once a week. You are likely to draw the conclusion that he is an altruistic person. On the other hand, if you learn that someone is altruistic, you are less likely to draw conclusions such as he helps out in a soup kitchen, volunteers for Big Brothers, etc. Thus, when perceiving other people, there tends to be an induction bias of quickly drawing conclusions about a person's traits based on observations of behavior.

This research shows that using the method that scientists use to test hypotheses and draw conclusions is helpful in everyday life. Be aware that we are prone to make snap decisions from limited information unless we make a conscious effort not to do so. Be mindful that a person's behavior may be attributable to characteristics of a given situation rather than their personality. If possible, try to suspend drawing conclusions about a person until you have observed his or her behavior several times in a variety of situations.

Use A Rational Approach to Making Decisions

Intuitive processing of information is automatic. It is based on self-evident beliefs and often uses stereotypes. "By contrast rational processing is conscious, effortful, analytical, slower, utilizes context-independent principles, and requires logical justification and empirical verification for decision-making" (Klaczynski, Gordon & Fauth, 1997, p. 473). Those who rely on intuitive processing are more likely to drop out of college, and to advocate less effective coping strategies. Two components underlie critical thinking processes:

- Students must possess the intelligence to detect logical flaws in their own and others' reasoning.

- Students must be able to metacognitively evaluate evidence independent of their own beliefs and goals. Metacognition refers to the ability to be aware of one's own thought processes and strategies in thinking, as noted in a previous chapter. For example, if you have to solve a problem, metacognition would involve a systematic plan such as hypothesis testing rather than just trial and error.

When making an important decision, ask yourself the following questions, and any others you can think of, and record your answers to help you clarify the issues involved.

- What is the decision you have to make?
- What are your values relating to this decision?
- What do you want the outcome of your decision to be?
- Who else will be affected by your decision. How will it affect each of them?
- What information do you need in order to make the decision?
- Is any information that you need missing? If yes, what is it?
- Where could you get the missing information needed to make the decision?
- What are all the possible alternative decisions you could make?
- What are all the possible outcomes of each of the alternative decisions?
- What is the probability of each of these outcomes happening?
- What is the desirability of each of these possible outcomes?
- What are the consequences of leaving the problem alone?
- What are the possible alternative courses of action you could decide to take?
- What resources do you need in order to take each of the possible courses of action?
- Do you have the necessary resources? If not, what are the ones you do not have? How could you get them?
- What are the likely outcomes of each course of action? What are the pros and cons of each course of action?
- What alternative makes the most sense in view of your goals and available resources?
- What decision will you make?
- What actions will you take to implement your decision?

At first glance you may think that it would take too much time and be too much bother to ask yourself these questions and write down your answer for all of the important decisions you need to make. Be assured that it is well worth the time and effort, however, because getting yourself out of trouble after making bad decisions is usually far more time consuming.

There may be times when making a split second decision is important and you don't have time for elaborate decision making. An intuitive decision may be best in that circumstance. For example, you may be walking to your car in a parking lot at night and don't feel comfortable about seeing a man sitting in a van parked next to your car. Follow you intuitive thought and don't unlock your car. Instead go quickly out of the lot and toward a building or place where other people are present. Call a security guard or the police to walk you to your car. In situations where we don't have much time to make a decision, going with our intuitive feeling, particularly with regard to safety, may be our best response.

Don't Self-Handicap, It Lowers Your Grades

Self-handicapping is the erection of obstacles to successful performance as a way of protecting self-esteem. Why would someone want to put obstacles in the way of their own success? If they fail, the person can claim that the reason they failed was not because of their poor ability, but because of the obstacle. If they succeed, they can take extra credit because they succeeded despite having the odds against them. For example, if you have an exam the next day, and you go to a movie with your friends, if you fail the exam you can say it was because you didn't study because your friends dragged you to the movie. If you do well anyway, you can say how smart you are because you did well despite having gone to a movie the night before the exam. "The various forms of self-handicaps were classified by Arkin and Baumgardner (1985) into *acquired obstacles* (obstacles that actually lower the likelihood of success) and *claimed obstacles* (obstacles that people claim to have)" (Zuckerman, Kieffer & Knee, 1998, p. 1619). The acquired obstacles "I got bombed the night before the exam" have a more detrimental effect on performance than the claimed obstacles "I have test anxiety."

Self-handicapping can also become habitual such as the case with the chronic procrastinator and the constantly ill hypochondriac. In a study of 262 undergraduate students, high self-handicapping scale scores were related to coping strategies implying withdrawal and focus on negative thoughts (Zuckerman et al., 1998). The researchers found that high self-handicappers also had lower grade point averages (GPAs), and GPA was mediated by their poorer study habits. Students with high self-handicapping scores also had more visits to the university health service during fall semester (although not during spring semester) to receive treatment for an illness than students who were low in self-handicapping. The result of self-handicapping is poorer adjustment and poorer health, which in turn elicits more self-handicapping. It is thus not hard to understand why the person who self-handicaps gets poorer grades.

Do you tend to self-handicap? Be honest with yourself. If you think that you have that problem, consider visiting your college's counseling center for help in breaking this habit before it stops you from achieving the success you desire in college and in your career.

Avoid Making Important Decisions when You Are in a Bad Mood

You have all heard the phrase "He is his own worst enemy." What this is referring to is what psychologists call self-defeating behavior (also known as self-destructive behavior). Why do people often behave in ways that are self-destructive? It is not rational for "normal" people to behave in a way that is contrary to one's own self-interest. According to a theory developed by Karen Leith and Roy Baumeister (1996), it is because people who are in a bad mood take risks that they hope will lead to a highly positive outcome. But, such a choice is also usually a high-risk option that carries with it the possibility of substantial costs. "They presumably choose these options in the hope of gaining the high payoff, but in many cases the risk will materialize, leading to an aversive and costly outcome" (p. 1250).

In a series of six experiments designed to test their theory, the researchers deliberately induced bad moods in some people and neutral or good moods in others and then observed whether participants would select a long-shot (high-risk, high-payoff) lottery over a low-risk, low-payoff one. Moods of participants were manipulated by activities such as:

- having them engage in personal recollections of self-defeating actions,

- leading them to expect a highly embarrassing, anxiety-provoking experience,

- exposing them to an unpleasant experiences, such as loud noise to induce stress or by angering them, or

- putting them in a good mood by exposing them to videos of comedy shows.

Results of these experiments supported the theory that being in a negative mood leads participants to choose high-risk, high-payoff options over low-risk, low-payoff options. Thus, people in negative moods will appear to engage in self-defeating behavior because the high-risk options are more likely to produce costly or harmful outcomes. "Emotionally distraught people may bring failure or misfortune on themselves by making poor, non-optimal choices and by taking unwise risks" (Leith & Baumeister, 1996, p. 1263). These self-destructive costs may come about because the person in a bad mood is seeking a "quick fix" for his or her bad mood and is willing to take high risks, which often end in disaster rather than in the joy they seek. This research demonstrates that when in a bad mood individuals are likely to make less rational and riskier decisions.

In another experiment in this series, however, a quick choice decision condition was compared with a condition in which the experimenter stressed the need to make a careful choice and participants were given a worksheet on which they were to list the advantages and disadvantages for each of the options. Even when in a bad mood, participants who analyzed the lotteries rationally no longer made the riskier decisions. This result demonstrates that it is possible for you to make wise decisions even when in a bad mood if you carefully weigh the pros and cons of the choice to be made. These experiments tell us that we are more likely to avoid disastrous decisions if we wait until our mood improves, engage in a pleasurable activity before making an important decision, or go through the steps of decision making by listing the pros and cons of each decision (as suggested in a previous section). Can you avoid misfortune and suffering in life? Unfortunately, you can not avoid all of it. But, you can go a long way toward preventing suffering in your life by making rational, thoughtful decisions that are in your best interest rather than impulsive, high-risk self-destructive ones.

Be Aware that Decisions You Make in Groups Are More Extreme than Decisions You Would Make By Yourself

Frequently, the activities we engage in are done in groups. Many times decisions are made by groups, to which we belong, that have a major impact on our lives. Are two heads really better than one? Do groups make better decisions than individuals? Most people believe that by pooling their knowledge and by avoiding extreme courses of action, groups make better decisions than individuals. In fact, experiments have shown that groups are likely to make more extreme decisions than individuals. Apparently, this is the result of individuals comparing their views with those of others during discussion and learning that they may not have as strong a view in the "desired" direction as some others in the group (Zuber, Crott, & Werner, 1992).

In addition, a process known as "groupthink" can lead groups to make disastrous decisions. According to the social psychologist Irving Janis (1982), groups exert strong pressures of conformity to accept the opinion of the group leaders and not examine alternative courses of action. A number of decisions in U.S. history provide illustrations of groupthink situations. Some examples are the failure of the U.S. military commanders in Pearl Harbor to send the ships to sea to remove them from the possibility of a Japanese attack; the decision by President Kennedy's cabinet to go ahead with the Bay of Pigs Invasion of Cuba; and more recently, the launching of the space shuttle Challenger, ignoring the warnings of possible equipment defects by the engineers. The likelihood of groupthink decisions occurring increases in highly cohesive groups under threat (Turner, Pratkanis, Probasco, & Leve, 1992).

How can we avoid groupthink in the groups to which we belong? To avoid groupthink, the leader should refrain from presenting at the outset what he or she thinks the decision should be. The group should be encouraged to come up with alternative decisions by using a number of techniques such as appointing a "devil's advocate" who will try to find fault with any argument that the group is offering to support a decision. Members can be asked to meet separately in subgroups, each arriving at a decision. Then the whole group can come together to select the better decision. Outside expert opinions can be sought out. The most important lesson for groups to learn is that minority opinions should be heard and carefully considered before making a group decision.

Groupthink does not just operate in high level groups such as the U.S. Cabinet. Groupthink also operates in groups in everyday life, such as when college students engage in fraternity hazing that can lead to injury or death, as in the case of making pledges chug-a-lug a large quantity of alcohol in a short period of time or fraternity gang rape of naïve freshman women (Sanday, 1990). When you are in such a situation, stop and think if you would behave the same way if you were not in the group. Is what you are doing consistent with your own values? Have the courage not to be involved or to try to change the direction of the action if the group is making a decision to behave in ways that are illegal or harmful to you or others.

Jumpstart Your Creativity

What is creativity and how can you become more creative? Creativity is certainly important to our everyday lives. The car you drive, the television you watch, the music you listen to, the computer on which you search the web, the paintings you admire, are all different manifestations of creativity. "A consensual definition of a creative contribution is of something that is (a) relatively original and (b) high in quality vis-à-vis some purpose" (Sternberg, 1999, p. 84). Originality per se is not a sufficient criterion for creativity. It must also be task appropriate, socially useful, or adaptive because otherwise there would be no way to distinguish schizophrenic thought from creative thought (Feist, 1998). Psychologists have identified attributes of people who display more creativity than others do (Simonton, 2000). Two categories of these differences have primarily been studied, intelligence and personality. Early research found that a certain level of intelligence was necessary for creativity.

Recent researchers have compiled a creative personality profile. "In particular, such persons are disposed to be independent, nonconformist, unconventional, even bohemian, and they are likely to have wide interests, greater openness to new experiences, a more conspicuous behavioral and cognitive flexibility, and more risk-taking boldness" (Simonton, 2000, p. 153). A comparison of personality characteristics of people considered creative in scientific and artistic realms, by means of a quantitative review of the literature, revealed that the largest differences between scientists and nonscientists and artists and non-artists are that the scientists and artists are open to experience, lower in conscientiousness, and higher in self-acceptance, hostility, and impulsivity. Some of these characteristics are opposite to those we have been telling you to develop in this book. Although conscientiousness has been demonstrated to be highly related to getting good grades, it is negatively related to scientific and artistic creativity. The traits required to make the most creative contributions to society are only in part (openness to experience) those required to get good grades.

Whether or not someone is creative, however, depends on the personality of the person in interaction with the situation in which he or she is working. In a job environment, it was found that conscientiousness results in low levels of creative behavior if supervisors engage in close monitoring and coworkers are unsupportive (George & Zhou, 2001). Interpersonal expectations can also contribute to creativity. For example, a teacher may expect the student to display creativity in a term paper or on an essay exam.

According to Robert J. Sternberg (2001), creativity is of two types: that which is "crowd defying" and reinvents or redirects a field and that which is more incremental and adds to an existing body of knowledge in a stepwise fashion. Intelligence is necessary to creativity in order to analyze and discriminate among the ideas generated. However, many creative people and many intelligent people are not wise. "Wise individuals balance the need for change (creativity) with the need for stability and continuity (intelligence) in human affairs" (Sternberg, 2001, p. 362).

Photo courtesy of Bristol Community College.

What are the components of creativity? Teresa M. Amabile (2001), who has studied creativity extensively, proposes three basic components:

- *Domain-Relevant Skills*—competencies and talents applicable to the domain or domains in which the individual is working;

- *Creativity-Relevant Processes*—personality characteristics, cognitive styles, and work habits that promote creativity in any domain; and

- *Intrinsic Task Motivation*—an internally driven involvement in the task at hand, which can be influenced significantly by the social environment (Amabile, 2001, p. 333).

What this tells you is that if you want to make a creative contribution, choose an area in which you are passionately interested, acquire the knowledge and skills that are necessary to develop proficiency in that area (whether it be art, chemistry, business, etc.), and practice work habits that develop creativity. What are these work habits? Working hard on the task is one of them. People will be most creative when their hard work is motivated by interest, enjoyment, satisfaction, and challenge of the work itself.

An irreverent book by Roger von Oech (1983) called *A Whack on the Side of the Head,* contains mental locks that people have on their minds that keep them from being creative such as:

- The Right Answer
- That's Not Logical
- Follow the Rules
- Be Practical
- Avoid Ambiguity
- To Err is Wrong
- Play is Frivolous
- That's Not My Area
- Don't be Foolish
- I'm Not Creative

In school we have been trained to get the right answer, so we neglect to seek the creative answer. Creativity may be based on intuition and insight rather than logic. By following the rules, we may miss an opportunity to create a better way. Earlier in this book we have told you to follow the rules at college, because it is important to your achieving a degree. A foundation of expertise in an area is necessary before you can use your creativity to develop new insights in discovering a more efficient or effective way of doing something. When you have taken a few courses in a science, for example, and get a position as a research assistant to a professor, you can use your creativity to make new discoveries.

By avoiding ambiguity, we miss the possibility of combining ideas in new ways. Sometimes we can learn a great deal from our mistakes, which may take us in a new direction. Play can give us an opportunity to let our subconscious minds work on a problem and allow us to gain new insights. A great many ideas can be gained from interdisciplinary thinking. Knowledge is not naturally subdivided into disciplines. Interdisciplinary approaches can provide novel thinking and solutions. Sometimes we are afraid to appear foolish and stifle our wilder ideas. Who would have thought it was possible to place a man on the moon? By labeling yourself as not creative you are shutting down your creativity. But if you practice creative exercises and begin to learn to think outside of the box, you will soon see that you have many creative ideas. Try developing your creativity.

Psychologist Mihaly Csikszentmihalyi studied the lives of very creative people to learn how creativity works. Csikszentmilalyi discovered that creative people experience a state he calls "flow." Flow describes activity so engrossing and enjoyable that it is worth doing for its own sake. "Creative activities, music, sports, games, and religious rituals are typical sources for this kind of experience" (Csikszentmihalyi, 1999, p. 824). We have frequently experienced flow when writing this book. When you become interested in something, follow it, learn all you can about it, play with it, and be open to the creative ideas that will come to you.

Joan H. Rollins, Ph.D. and Mary Zahm, Ph.D.

Brainstorm to Think of Creative Solutions to Problems

Suppose your concern is increasing your creativity in daily life now rather than making a major creative contribution during your career. Can you do certain things to increase your creativity? Yes, another approach to creativity has been to have people look at problems in novel ways and generate ideas. One such approach has been to introduce brainstorming rules.

In 1957, an advertising man, Alex F. Osborn, claimed that with brainstorming rules, groups could be more productive than individuals (Osborn, 1957, as cited in Diehl & Stroebe, 1987). Brainstorming rules are:

1. The more ideas the better.

2. The wilder the ideas the better.

3. Improve or combine ideas already suggested.

4. Do not be critical of the ideas.

Brainstorming groups became very popular in business and industry. Research by social psychologists found, in fact, that brainstorming rules can increase the creative production of both individuals and groups. Reviews of the literature, however, of research that assessed the total quality and quantity of ideas produced by individuals working alone versus working in groups, found that individuals working alone were more creative than when working in groups (Dugosh, Paulus, Roland, & Yang, 2000; Taylor, Berry, & Block, 1958). It makes sense that individuals are more creative than groups when one reflects on great artistic contributions. Has there ever been a great symphony, art masterpiece, or novel created by a group? So when you want to come up with creative ideas, write them down following brainstorming rules. Then you can have others whose judgments you trust help you select the best ideas.

Muzafer Sherif, a famous social psychologist, frequently said, "Ideas are the most important thing in the world." A good practice is to follow brainstorming rules and come up with as many ideas as possible to solve a problem such as how you could earn extra money. Following the brainstorming rules summarized above, write down all the legal ways you could earn money while still attending school full-time (or a topic you choose). Write down at least 10 ideas, more if you can think of them, about how you could earn money while still attending school full-time. Don't censor your ideas. The wilder the idea, the better.

When finished listing as many ideas as you can think of, review them and combine your ideas to form 10 better ones. Do not be critical of the ideas. Something wild you come up with may help you think of a truly creative solution to your problem. Practice brainstorming whenever you have a problem to solve. It can help to generate creative ideas whether you have a personal problem, a problem related to one of your courses, or a problem on your job to solve.

You can also practice brainstorming and increase your ability to creatively solve problems by asking yourself "What if" questions like "What job could I get if I chose this specific college major?" or "What if I were required to have a second major in college. What would I choose? Why?" Doing so will help you make more creative decisions.

Take a Stitch in Time—Proactively Avoid and Offset Potential Problems

Most of the psychological research literature focuses on how to cope with stress, pain, and misfortune in life after it has occurred. However, it is a better strategy to avoid future problems or to proactively seek to minimize the impact they may have on you. Folk wisdom has many sayings for avoiding future problems such as "Read the handwriting on the wall," or "A stitch in time saves nine." To a degree, automobile accidents, financial problems, academic failure, inability to land a desired high paying job or professional level career, interpersonal conflict, and even illness are preventable occurrences. That is not to say that we can prevent all misfortune. You may have learned skills, worked diligently, and been laid off from your job due to a merger, downsizing, or other event over which you had no control. If you spent every cent, however, and had not saved for a rainy day, you would be in a worse position than if you had put some money in the bank, or in investments that could cushion your unemployment while you sought another job.

Psychologists Lisa G. Aspinwall and Shelly E. Taylor (1997) have developed a conceptual framework derived from research that specifies five stages in proactive coping:

- *Recognition of Potential Stressors* is a necessary preliminary step leading to mental simulations of what could happen if the threat were not dealt with ahead of time. After recognizing a potential threat, it is then important to be able to project into the future and assess the potential impact of the threat on one's life as well as to determine how to prevent or minimize it. There may be the liability of being hyper vigilant, however, which means that the individual attends to so many potential threats that he or she is constantly in a state of emotional turmoil. It becomes more difficult in a high stress environment such as living in a situation of domestic conflict, a noisy, high crime neighborhood, or under financial pressures to be able to detect and prevent the potential threat. That is why resource accumulation is an important first step in proactive coping, as noted below.

- *Resource Accumulation* includes the acquiring of many different types of resources such as time, money, a support network, organizational and planning skills, as well as other more individualized resources. For example, lack of time because of working 70 hours a week at two jobs can prevent the individual from having sufficient reflective time to recognize potential problems or to acquire new job skills which could lead to a higher paying job. People without a support network, for example, will have trouble meeting emergencies such as getting a ride to school or work when their car is broken down. The individual must take steps to accumulate and preserve resources such as a support network, money, time, and skills in order to be able to engage in proactive coping.

- *Initial Appraisal* consists of two central tasks: definition of the problem and regulation of arousal. Definition of the problem involves calling on past experience and the use of mental simulations to project how the danger is likely to unfold. People with high levels of optimism and self-efficacy see stressful events as less threatening, which may enable them to better cope with them. High anxiety and high arousal to the threat often lead to less ability to process the information pertaining to the threat and inability to be proactive. One's social network can have profound influence on appraisal of the threat by comparing one's reaction with theirs in a similar situation and testing our understanding of the situation by using others as a sounding board.

- *Preliminary Coping Efforts* depend on one's appraisal of the problem and one's perception of his or her ability to cope with it. A person's appraisal of his or her problem solving ability is an important determinant of the action that the person will take. Depression has been linked with one's perception that the individual could do nothing about the threat. Optimism, on the other hand, has been linked with the appraisal that one is able to cope with the situation among people facing a variety of dangers. Among patients who have had coronary bypass surgery, women awaiting an abortion, and men at risk for AIDS, optimists appraise their ability to cope much more favorably than do those who are less optimistic. People typically respond to small signs of danger with small initial steps, which do not deplete coping resources. For example, if your grades take a small drop, rather than going out and hiring an expensive tutor or counselor, one might first try to structure homework time and learn better study skills. If the low grades continue, then one might move to the next step such as having a conference with the professor to seek advice. Another approach to analyzing coping efforts is to examine whether the individual uses active or avoidant forms of coping.

  Active coping is making an effort to prevent or solve the problem.

  Avoidant coping such as self blame and wishful thinking or using drugs or alcohol, puts the individual at greater risk for negative outcomes in the long run (Bolger, 1990, as cited in Aspinwall & Taylor, 1997).

- *Elicitation and Use of Feedback* concerning the success of one's initial efforts to cope with a problem or solve problems is an important step in proactive coping. Modification of preliminary coping efforts will be made as the individual gains information about how successful their initial coping efforts are. In psychological laboratory situations, participants who were first asked to solve a series of problems that were, in fact, insoluble showed poorer problem solving skills than others not first given insoluble problems. They did not gather information that would have provided them information about alternatives and did not gather the most important information first. This research points to the importance of the individual having a belief in one's sense of ability to control outcomes in order to try to cope and solve problems.

The wisdom of psychology is in this instance the same as folk wisdom "A stitch in time" or "An ounce of prevention" as important ways of preventing stressors in the first place rather than having to respond to the threat once it has created the dangerous situation. Learn to be proactive in identifying festering problematic situations that might turn out to be major sources of stress later on. For example, do you need to learn a new skill but do not seek help in learning it? Which skill is it? Do you procrastinate about gathering the information you need to make informed life choices and decisions? Are you letting a small problem fester so that it might become a major life crisis later?

Use meditation and creative visualization to identify current problems or areas of your life in which you might profit from acting in a more proactive manner, to minimize or avoid stress. As you evaluate your current life challenges or problems, try to determine how you can proactively take steps to solve them following the rules of brainstorming presented in the previous section of this chapter and record your insights in your success journal for future reference. For example, if you are failing a class, you might consider going to your college's tutoring center for help. If your parents treat you like a child, think of some things you can do to convince them that you are a responsible adult. If you have trouble communicating with a particular professor, you might ask your advisor for help in doing this. If you are in a violent intimate relationship, you might think about calling your local women's shelter and asking for help.

Success Recommendations

This section contains a summary of the main points in this chapter to help you reflect on and recall what you have learned.

- **Don't Believe Everything Your See and Hear.** Pay attention and listen carefully to what is being said by someone when the information is important to your making a decision. Do not engage in distracting activities while listening or making important decisions because you may not take into account crucial aspects related to your decisions.

- **Consider the Possibility that You Might Be Wrong.** Be consciously mindful of the following mental shortcuts when you are making important decisions so that you will not be caught off guard and end up making unfair or costly errors in judgment: anchoring, base rate fallacy, biased sampling, availability heuristic, and false consensus effect.

- **Develop Critical Thinking Skills.** The critical thinker must be willing to exert the effort to think critically about the issue, choice, or problem. Examine your beliefs when you are making a decision and the evidence that supports your beliefs. Use meta-cognitive monitoring, which means to have knowledge or awareness of monitoring your own cognitive processes or thinking.

- **Try to Avoid Sunk Costs.** People consider time, energy, or money previously invested when making decisions. Rather than putting more resources into a failing course of action, it may be better to go in a new direction that would be more likely to cut losses and be more promising for future rewards.

- **Overcome your Stereotypes.** Learn to Appreciate Diversity. Examine your negative stereotypes about people from groups other than your own and the evidence that supports or negates your beliefs. Learn to appreciate and embrace diversity.

- **Learn how to Critically Evaluate Information on the Internet.** Use critical thinking skills to evaluate the source and quality of the information on the Internet before relying on it in a research paper.

- **Develop Constructive Thinking Skills.** To achieve success in work, love, and social relationships as well as to optimize your emotional and physical well-being, develop adequate emotional and behavioral coping skills.

- **Learn and Use the Rules of Formal Logic to Solve Problems.** Develop deductive and inductive reasoning skills and use them to solve problems. Think about the approach you are taking to solving a specific problem and consider whether there are other more efficient systematic approaches to solving it.

- **Use A Rational Approach to Making Decisions.** Develop the habit of writing out the steps to making a decision and following those steps in making your decision so that it is a rational one. Consider creative alternative courses of action to the plans you are making. Weigh the pros and cons of following each course of action before making a decision.

- **Don't Self-Handicap, It Lowers your Grades.** Self-handicapping is the erection of obstacles to successful performance as a way of protecting self-esteem because you are afraid of failing and looking stupid. Be aware of any tendency you have toward self-handicapping, and avoid doing it. If you feel that you have that problem, consider visiting your college's counseling center for help in breaking this habit before it stops you from achieving the success you desire in college and in your career.

- **Make Important Decisions When You Are in a Good Mood.** Be aware that decisions people make when in a bad mood may be more risky because they hope that they will lead to a highly positive outcome. If you must make a decision when in a bad mood, be especially careful to weigh the pros and cons of following each course of action before making it.

- **Avoid Groupthink.** When making a decision in a group, ask if anyone has any doubts about the direction in which the group is going. Play "devil's advocate." Think of reasons why the group decision might not be a good one and express them in the group meeting.

- **Jumpstart Your Creativity.** Learn the required knowledge and skills to be creative in an area in which you are interested in working. Tell yourself that you can make creative contributions and work hard at doing so. Seek out classes and other opportunities to learn to think more creatively and to practice using creative problem solving skills.

- **Brainstorm to Find Creative Ways to Solve Problems.** Develop the habit of following the rules of brainstorming whenever you need to think of creative solutions to a problem at work, at school, or in your personal life.

- **Take a Stitch in Time—Proactively Avoid and Offset Potential Problems.** Use meditation and creative visualization to identify current challenges or areas of your life in which you might profit from acting in a more proactive manner, by using proactive coping strategies to minimize or avoid stress. Brainstorm about how you can strengthen your social support and friendship network at college. Be sure to consider ways you can identify and gain access to mentors who can help you achieve career success, such as joining and becoming active in a college club and regional and national professional organizations.

Chapter Eight
Achieve Your Most Important Life Goals

In *Escape From Freedom* (1965), Erich Fromm warned that the cultural and political climate of the entire world was evolving at a very rapid pace and would continue to present everyone with very different options and challenges from the ones with which people were familiar. He pointed out that many people who feared change should learn to embrace it. More recently, Alvin Toffler (1991) predicted that we will continue to experience life challenges and crises due to global breakdowns in traditional family and work structures well into the new millennium. These changes are currently happening. It is becoming obvious that people who refuse to go with the flow and change with the times will definitely miss out on many wonderful new opportunities for living a productive and happy life.

How can you learn to set and achieve challenging goals and cope with the life changes that will inevitably come your way rather than being fearful of them? Do you have dreams about how you would like your future life to be? Do you know how you can consciously and deliberately begin to turn your dreams into your reality? How can you learn to create and control your own life by anticipating, preparing for, and embracing change? Psychological researchers have identified some of the steps that you can follow to accomplish this feat. Strategies for setting and achieving your most important life goals that are based on this research are outlined in this chapter.

Set Personally Meaningful Goals in Order to Achieve Them

As the old saying goes, "Be careful what you wish for because you might get it." Goal setting is a very powerful motivating force, which acts as a servo mechanism keeping an individual moving in the direction of the goal. It is important to select goals that are in harmony with one's moral values, conscience, and priorities as to what is really important in one's life. Goals are in themselves neither good nor bad; it depends on what the goals are and how much you must sacrifice to achieve them. You might have a goal of earning $500,000 per year. But if you lie, cheat, and steal to achieve the goal, or have to travel extensively and are not able to spend time with your children and spouse, achieving the goal will be detrimental to you and your family. Thus, you must carefully select your goals to be in accordance with your moral values and not in conflict with other priorities in your life. The power of the goal for transforming your life increases when you write down the goal, in explicit detail, and read the goal on a daily or weekly basis.

The initial reason for selecting a goal can influence the likelihood of achieving it (Sheldon & Elliot 1998). In a study designed to test the hypothesis that goals caused by external incentives will lose appeal with time, Sheldon and Elliot (1998) asked 128 undergraduate students enrolled in psychology classes to generate a list of 10 personal strivings (such as "trying to be physically attractive" and "trying to seek new and exciting experiences") and to rate how much they pursue each striving on a scale from 1 "not at all because of this reason" to 9 "completely because of this reason" for each of four reasons:

- *Extrinsic/Controlled*—Striving because somebody else wants you to do so or thinks you should.

- *Introjected/Controlled*—Striving because you would feel ashamed, guilty, or anxious if you didn't.

- *Identified/Autonomous*—Striving because you really believe that it's an important goal to have.

- *Intrinsic/Autonomous*—Striving because of the fun and enjoyment that the goal provides you.

The students were asked to indicate how successful they had been in attaining their goals within the past month or so using a scale ranging from 0 (0–9% successful) to 10 (90–100% successful). The results of this study indicated that students who had Autonomous goals were more likely to attain them than students who had Controlled goals. Goals that we ourselves choose and are self integrated will be the ones on which we continue to work hard over time and that we are more likely to achieve.

In a follow-up study of goal attainment, 141 undergraduate students enrolled in psychology classes were asked at the beginning of the semester to first select a set of eight achievement goals from either the 51 items listed on the Achievement Goals Questionnaire (which included strivings commonly reported by college students in previous studies such as "Try new and challenging activities," "Avoid procrastination," and "Fulfill my potential") or to fill in their own goals. They were then asked to rate both the reasons they would pursue their goals and the amount of effort they intended to invest in the goals. The same four reasons listed above were used in this study. The students rated their intended effort on a scale ranging from 1 (not at all hard) to 9 (very hard). Eight weeks later, the students rated the amount of effort they were actually investing in each goal. At the end of the 15-week semester, the students rated how well they had attained each goal. The researchers concluded that achievement goals pursued for more autonomous (i.e., identified and/or intrinsic) reasons were better attained over a 15-week period (Sheldon & Elliot, 1998, p. 550). They attribute this goal achievement, in part, to the students working harder on their autonomous goals eight weeks into the study. In contrast, although participants intended to work hard in their highly controlled goals, their efforts declined during the first eight weeks of the semester.

A second study tested alternative explanations, such as perceived self-efficacy, for the autonomy effect observed in the studies summarized above. The results of this second study also found that autonomous motivation for personal goals was positively related to attaining those goals, whereas controlled motivation was not related to achieving them. Autonomous goals were apparently attained by engendering sustained effort. Notably, both the intrinsic interest in the goal and a goal consistent with one's enduring values and beliefs independently predicted effort and attainment, indicating that both provide motivation to continue toward the goal. Controlledness was found to be associated with intended effort but not actual hard work (Sheldon & Elliot, 1998).

What are the implications of Sheldon's and Elliot's research for you? This research clearly demonstrates that in order to optimize your successful goal attainment, you should only pursue goals that are personally meaningful and truly important to you as well as harmonious with your core values and essential beliefs. When you pursue goals that either engage your natural interests or express your authentic personal values, you are most likely to be effective because you will have the stamina to continue to expend the effort required to achieve your goals in the long run. This stamina will help sustain your efforts even in the face of inevitable obstacles or hardships that everyone experiences in their lives.

What are you passionate about? What work would you love to do? Begin your college career by exploring a variety of academic subjects and working in community organizations. These experiences will help you to find out your special talents and academic interests (such as computer science, history, mathematics, medicine, law, psychology, political science, science, sociology), the type of cultural activities that excite you (such as art, music, or theater), and the type of life work that interests you. Then you will be able to identify personally meaningful long- and short-term goals for yourself and you will be motivated to achieve them and work hard to do so.

Focus on the Goal You Want to Achieve Rather Than the Failure You Want to Avoid

There is an emerging consensus among psychologists that two types of primary achievement goals are important determinants of motivation and performance: mastery goals and performance goals, as noted in a previous chapter.

> Mastery goals concern the desire to develop competence (e.g., 'I want to learn as much as I can about psychology this semester'), whereas performance goals concern demonstrating competence relative to others (e.g., 'I want to be the best student in my class this semester') (Harackiewicz, Barron, Carter, Lehto, & Elliot, 1997, p. 1284).

In a study with college students, Harackiewicz et al. (1997) investigated personality predictors of achievement goals as well as the consequences of those goals for motivation and performance in an introductory psychology course. In addition to mastery and performance goals, the researchers also investigated work avoidance goals (i.e., to pass the course doing as little work as possible). Students who were mastery oriented were less likely to adopt work avoidance goals than were students who were performance oriented. Both mastery and performance goals, however, were independently and positively related to interest in and grades achieved in the course. Thus, students are just as likely to get good grades in a course if they have either intrinsic interest in mastering the course material or a competitive performance orientation to achievement. This research reveals that it is important for you to set goals for academic success whether those goals are determined by mastery motivation or by competitive performance motivation.

Psychologists have pointed out that the other side of the need to achieve is the fear of failure that is really a general desire to avoid failure. Fear of failure is the underlying motivation for avoidance of achievement goals. Experimental research (Roney, Higgins, &

163

Shah, 1995) has demonstrated that participants who were instructed on a precise number of problems they were to try to solve performed better and were more persistent at the task than those whose attention was focused on the number of problems they were to avoid not solving. In other words, those individuals whose motivation is to avoid doing poorly performed worse and were less persistent at the task than participants whose motivation was to attain task mastery. For success, focus needs to be on the outcome one wants to achieve rather than on the failure one wishes to avoid. To be a successful student, one needs to focus on getting good grades rather than avoiding bad grades.

In a study at the University of Rochester (Elliot & Sheldon, 1997), students' motive to avoid failure was assessed by means of self-report questionnaires and projective tests. Participants also reported their current perceptions of competence for each of their goals and their feelings of well-being during the course of the semester. The findings of the study were as predicted. Participants who had a greater number of avoidance goals expected to do worse during the semester, had a high fear of failure, and were more likely to report a decrease in self-esteem. They perceived the pursuit of their goals to have been less enjoyable, had low perceived competence during the semester, and reported that the semester had been less enjoyable.

Similarly, research with students at the University of Missouri found that students with mastery goals, those who wanted to learn and develop the skills taught in the course or had performance goals of wanting to do well had greater mental focus, enjoyed the tasks more and performed better than students who had performance-avoiding goals, who wanted to prevent negative outcomes. "The performance-avoiding goal pattern tends to promote worry, self-criticism, and anxiety, making it difficult for people to concentrate fully on the task at hand" (Lee, Sheldon, & Turban, 2003, p. 260).

This research is clear in showing that the student who keeps her or his eye on learning the material and doing well in the course has a more satisfactory semester and feels better about herself or himself than the student who focuses on avoiding low grades. This research shows that if you focus on mastery of your goal, you will have more success in achieving the goal and better feelings about yourself than if you focus on avoiding failure. As the folk wisdom saying goes, "Keep your eye on the doughnut and not on the hole."

Success Profile—Len

An African-American university student, Len, discovered the power of pursuing personally meaningful goals first hand. When he first enrolled in college, he did so primarily to please his parents. His older sister was enrolled in college and his parents wanted him to go too. He had no goal for his future except to become a college graduate. He didn't know what he wanted to study in college or what career he wanted to pursue. During his first year, he found himself hanging around with the party crowd at school and with his old neighborhood friends. His friends from his old neighborhood were high school dropouts who devalued education and ridiculed him for going to college. Len said he found his classes to be boring and the course work to be tough. He didn't spend much time studying and, consequently, he did so poorly during his freshman year that he was put on academic probation. Near the end of the second year, he left college and went to work at a group home for delinquent boys.

Len loved this work at the group home and soon found that he had a passion for helping delinquent boys as well as the personality strengths and talents with which to do so. After an absence of three years, Len returned to college and was earning high grades in a demanding human services program while continuing to work at the group home. He was determined to earn his college degree and pursue advanced study in social work. Len was proud to be a positive role model for the boys, especially those who were minority group members from poor neighborhoods like himself. He confessed that most of his former friends from his old neighborhood were either in jail or dead. He realized he couldn't help them but decided to become a social worker and devote his work life to helping teenage boys who might follow a path to destruction without adequate social support and intervention.

Achieve Meaning in Your Life by Selecting Goals that Are Consistent With Your Values, Beliefs, and Talents

There are differences in the types of goals people select and in the happiness and meaning resulting from their achievement. Happiness and meaning do not necessarily coincide. For example, researchers consistently find that couples with children living at home score lower in happiness than couples that are childless. However, couples with children have a greater sense of meaning in their lives. (Baumeister, 1992, as cited in McGregor and Little, 1998; Russell, & Wells, 1994).

To what extent are your personal projects consistent with your values, beliefs, commitments, and other important aspects of your self-identity? To the degree that they are consistent, you will achieve *meaning* (a sense of integrity) when you complete the projects. In two studies, McGregor and Little (1998) found that "participants whose personal projects were consistent with core elements of their self-identity reported higher levels of meaning than did those whose projects were less reflective of self-identity" (p. 505). *Goal self-efficacy*, the expectation of success of one's projects, was associated with happiness. Personality differences were also found for happiness.

> Agentic participants, whose identities were primarily oriented toward self-enhancement, were happier if their projects were supported by others. Communal participants, whose identities were primarily oriented toward fun and pleasure, were happier if they were getting things done. Achievement-oriented participants, however, did not conform to this compensatory pattern, being happiest when engaged in identity-consistent, efficacious projects. (p. 502)

Have you identified and set long-term life goals that will enable you to live the life you desire after you graduate from college? Write down your long-term 5-year and 10-year personal, career, and relationship goals in your success journal. For example, a 5-year personal goal might be to stop smoking. A 10-year personal goal might be to improve your public speaking ability. A 5-year career goal might be to earn a college degree and/or land a professional job in your chosen field. A 10-year career goal might be to establish your own business. A 5-year relationship goal might be to find a mate. A 10-year relationship goal might be to have children.

As you identify your 5-year and 10-year goals, be sure to select goals that are consistent with your values, beliefs, personality, and previous commitments as well as other important aspects of your self-identity to optimize your chances of achieving meaning in your life. Defining your 5-year and 10-year goals is important because they will clearly show you the direction of your life course for the next decade. When your goals are specific, clear, and personally meaningful, you will be motivated to identify and accomplish the steps you need to achieve them. If, after trying to define them, you feel that you do not know how to identify your goals, seek help. Consider asking one of your professors, your advisor, a friend, or an acquaintance that is living the type of life style you desire to act as your mentor or guide. If you do not know anyone to ask, consider seeking help from your college's counseling center or a licensed professional counselor who is a specialist in the area in which you need assistance (personal, relationship, or career goals).

Set Challenging Goals If You Want to Have Higher Earnings in the Future

Is a preference for challenge a good predictor of future wages? A sample of men who were in their twenties in 1972 were followed for 24 years (Dunifon & Duncan, 1998). They were part of the Panel Study of Income Dynamics, which has interviewed annually a nationally representative sample of about 5,000 families. Analyses of the data found that individuals professing an orientation toward challenge earned considerably higher wages 20 to 25 years after the initial interview. The effects of motivation persisted after controlling for differences in completed schooling, parental background, and cognitive skills. The effects of motivation on wages were stronger on 1988–1992 earnings than they were on 1973–1977 earnings. This indicates that much time seems to be required for the effects of motivation on earnings to become apparent.

What this study shows is that men, who have a motivation toward challenge when they are in their twenties, have higher earnings 20–25 years later. Men who are oriented toward challenge also are more likely to engage in more on-the-job training. Orientation toward challenge was measured by asking respondents to make forced choices on the following items: "Would you like to have more friends, or would you like to do better at what you try?" and "Would you prefer a job where you had to think for yourself, or one where you work with a nice group of people?" These items measure challenge versus affiliation. Those making the challenge choices were the ones with higher earnings twenty-five years later.

One of the more consistent findings from industrial organizational psychology is that difficult, challenging goals lead to higher performance than easy, unclear, and "do your best" goals (Locke & Latham, 1990). Be willing to challenge yourself. Identify a specific challenging goal that you intend to achieve in college and the tentative date by which you desire to accomplish it. Set difficult goals but make them specific so you will be able to clearly describe the steps to achieving those goals and the dates by which you will do so. Once you have identified the challenging complex goal you want to pursue, review it to make sure that it is stated in a way that makes it specific and clear rather than ambiguous and vague. For example, it is better to say "I need to complete my required psychology course report by the date due in order to get a high grade" than it is to say "I want to do well in my course work."

Illustrate Your Vision for Success

Create drawings or use photos, pictures from magazines, and inspirational quotes that motivate, stimulate, excite, or seem personally meaningful to you to illustrate your vision for your success and your goals. Your future life will seem much more real and achievable when you see it in living color. Include pictures depicting your college and educational goals, tentative career goals, family, and friends. Set tentative dates by which you intend to achieve your goals as well as the dates by which you intend to achieve major milestones along the way. You will learn more about your self and your goals for the future in your college courses. Add ideas and pictures to your collage often as you learn more about yourself and your goals for the future in your college courses. Doing this will keep your mind focused on your life goals and the steps you need to take to achieve them.

Display your mind map or collage illustrating your vision for your success in a prominent location in your bedroom or study area in order to keep your brain focused on achieving your dreams and goals concerning your college education and future life. Your personalized collage will be an inspirational visual tool that will be especially useful on dreary or stressful days when you need to motivate yourself to continue to make progress toward your goals. As your goals evolve, update your vision for your success and collage so that it accurately reflects your current vision of your future life. Doing this will help you clarify your college, career, relationship, and personal life goals as you progress through your college career.

At the same time, you need to plan the steps to achieving your dreams and goals and work to make them your reality. Middle school teachers enrolled in graduate courses at Rhode Island College say that they have a number of pupils choosing "medicine" as a career goal. But those same students are not doing well in their math and science classes and not taking steps to remedy the situation. To be successful in college, you must focus on the steps toward achieving your dreams and work hard to achieve them as well as focusing on the big picture.

Have High Hopes of Achieving Your Goals

Hope is defined by *Webster's New World Dictionary* (Neufeldt & Guralnik, 1994) as "a feeling that what is wanted will happen; desire accompanied by expectation." Hope is a motivating force that keeps one going despite setbacks. Psychologists have defined hope in terms of

- *Pathways Thinking* which is the person's planning of ways to achieve a goal, and
- *Agentic Thinking* which involves thoughts that get the person to initiate action and sustain movement toward a desired goal (Snyder et al., 1996).

167

Hope reflects an adaptive, goal directed type of thinking. Recent research has explored the role of hope in academic and sport achievement of college students (Curry, Snyder, Cook, Ruby, & Rehm, 1997). Hope can be characterized as a personality trait and for research purposes was measured by four items:

- I energetically pursue my goals.
- I meet the goals that I set for myself.
- There are lots of ways around any problem.
- I can think of many ways to get the things in life that are most important to me.

(Curry et al., 1997, p. 1259)

Photo courtesy of Bristol Community College.

Student athletes who were members of a National Collegiate Athletic Association (NCAA) Division 1 team at a state university were found to be higher in hope, as measured by the Trait Hope scale, than non-athletes at the same university, but were not higher in global self-worth. Among the athletes, those with higher Trait Hope scale scores also had higher grade point averages in their academic work than athletes with lower Hope scores. Items reworded from the Trait Hope scale to be in the present tense (i.e., "There are lots of ways around any problem that I am facing now") constituted a State Hope scale. Female cross country runners who scored high on both the Trait and State Hope scales were found to be more successful in sport performance (Curry et al., 1997). In other words, the hope measures were good predictors of quicker running times. What this research tells us is that student athletes who have hope get better grades and also have better running times.

But hope is not a *wishy washy* concept like wishful thinking. Hope involves both planning how to achieve a desired goal—that is, identifying the steps that need to be taken to achieve one's goal—as well as taking action to begin those steps and sustaining that action until the goal is achieved.

> The advantages of higher hope are many. As research shows, as compared to lower-hope people high hope persons have a greater number of goals, have more difficult goals, have more success at achieving their goals, have greater happiness and less distress, have superior coping skills, recover better from physical injury, and report less burnout at work (Snyder, 1994, p. 14).

In one study, an eight-item Hope scale was administered to freshmen college students who indicated how they perceive themselves in situational contexts related to goals. Students scoring low or high on the Hope scale were followed up for six years. The results showed that having higher Hope Scale scores significantly predicted higher GPAs, graduation from college, and less likelihood of being dismissed from college (Snyder et al., 2002).

Research finds that hope is not synonymous with intelligence or other emotions such as optimism and positive or negative affect. Hope is available to all of us. We do not have to be geniuses to have hope in our hearts and achieve our goals. As you strive to create your future life, be hopeful that you can turn your future life dreams into your reality.

Experience Flow and Enjoy Your Work

Why do some people spend an enormous amount of time engaged in tasks and activities that do not seem to bring them financial gain or professional recognition? Why do we happily spend our summer vacations and holidays writing this book? The answer is simple. When we are working on this book, we get into flow and achieve a state of optimal experience. What is flow? How does one achieve a state of optimal experience?

Psychologist Mihaly Csikszentmihalyi has been studying how people find enjoyment in achieving their goals for the past three decades. In some of their early studies, Csikszentmihalyi and his colleagues conducted lengthy interviews and administered questionnaires to people who spent a great deal of time and effort in work or leisure activities that seemed to be done for their own sake, intrinsic rewards, rather than for external rewards such as money, medals, or public recognition. The types of activities in which these people spent a great deal of their time included: rock climbing, composing music, playing chess, and participating in amateur sports. More recently, they have been interviewing a wide range of people in many stages of life, professions, and countries asking them to "...describe how it felt when their lives were at their fullest, when what they did was most enjoyable." (1990, p. 48) Based on data collected in their studies, Csikszentmihalyi identified eight elements of task structure and personal attitude that lead to task enjoyment and experiencing the optimal state of flow during which people more readily accomplish their goals.

- One must choose an interesting and challenging task she or he is able to perform.

- One must concentrate on what she or he is doing.

- The task must have clear goals.

- The task must provide adequate feedback on one's performance.

- One must act with a deep and effortless involvement that removes from awareness the worries and frustrations of everyday life.

- One must be able to exercise a sense of control over her or his actions.

- Concern for the self must disappear during task performance even though the sense of self will emerge stronger after the flow experience is over.

- Concentration on the task must be deep enough so that the sense of the duration of time is altered. Hours can fly by like minutes and minutes can stretch out to seem like hours.

Photo courtesy of Rhode Island College.

Csikszentmihalyi and his colleagues have found that "The combination of all these elements causes a sense of deep enjoyment that is so rewarding people feel that expending a great deal of energy is worthwhile simply to feel it" (p. 49). Consequently, they believe that "With this knowledge, it is possible to achieve control of consciousness and turn the most humdrum moments of everyday lives into events that help us grow" (p. 49). The results of this research indicate that if you structure your work and adjust your attitude toward it to include the eight elements of enjoyment listed above, you will be able to achieve the optimal experience of flow and accomplish your personal and professional life goals.

If You Are Having Difficulty Achieving Your Goal, Reassess it to Make Sure It Is the Right Goal for You

A student we will call Kristen was in the nursing program at the college when she enrolled in a psychology course. One day Kristen stopped by to talk with her professor in her office. She said she was a nursing major. She was having a very difficult time, however, in the nursing program and was having difficulty in a chemistry course that she was taking for the third time because she had failed it twice. Her professor asked her what her eventual goal was. Kristen said she wanted to become a pediatric nurse because she loved children and wanted to work with them in a helping capacity. Kristen also remarked that she really enjoyed her psychology courses and had earned As in them. Her professor suggested to Kristen that she might change her major to psychology with the goal of perhaps working with children with emotional rather than physical problems. Kristen said she would feel like a failure if she did not complete the nursing program and achieve her long-term goal of becoming a nurse. Her professor suggested that Kristen's strengths, which included being a warm and caring person with a love of children, could be very useful in working with emotionally disturbed children. Kristen changed her major to psychology, did well in her courses, and before graduation was able to get a part-time job working as part of a treatment team at a hospital for emotionally disturbed children, a job which she loved. She said that when she graduated the hospital wanted her to stay on full-time. Kristen recently returned to see her professor. She said she had now earned a master's degree in special education and had a position in a public school as a special education teacher. She said she loved working with the special needs children and that they loved her in return.

Although persistence is a very desirable quality, sometimes we have to reassess our goals in light of our skills, abilities, and life circumstances. Develop the habit of periodically reviewing your progress toward your goals. These periodic reviews will enable you to observe areas of your life in which you desire to make changes as your future life vision evolves and as new opportunities become available to you. They will also help you to observe and appreciate the progress you have made toward creating your future life.

Even as you are striving to achieve your transitional life goals, you must also focus your attention on each moment of your present life so that you are truly enjoying living it. All too often, people who want to change their lives for the better become so engrossed in planning and achieving their future life goals that they forget to enjoy their present life. They neglect to share quality time with their loved ones. They fail to make time to rest or to appreciate the beauty of nature. In a sense then, their real life begins to feel like a dress rehearsal or preparation period that precedes their future life while their real life slips by—unenjoyed and unbalanced. At the same time, students need to maintain self-discipline and as we pointed out in earlier chapters, schedule time for enjoyment rather than giving way to impulsive actions.

Make time daily to consciously appreciate and express gratitude for the rewards that you are reaping due to your own proactive efforts to improve the quality of your life. Doing this will help you find the inner strength and enthusiasm needed to remain highly motivated to achieve your life goals and to continue to improve the quality of your life.

Learn When to Delay Gratification

The capacity to resist the impulsive action begins in childhood. That emerging self-control can predict later success in life. Psychologist Walter Mishel conducted a study at the Stanford University preschool in the 1960s on impulse control of 4-year olds (Shoda, Mishel, & Peake, 1990). A four-year old was seated at a table and was presented with one marshmallow. The experimenter told the child that if he/she did not eat the marshmallow and waited until the researcher ran an errand and returned, the child could have two marshmallows for a treat. If the child could not wait, the child was told he/she could eat the one marshmallow right away, but would not get another one. Some of the four-year olds were able to wait the 15–20 minutes until the experimenter returned and got two marshmallows. It was not easy for the children to wait and some covered their eyes so that they would not have to see the temptation. Others talked to themselves, sang, and even tried to go to sleep (Mishel, Ebbeson, & Zeiss, 1972).

The power of impulse control in the lives of these children was clearly demonstrated when researchers tracked down these children 12 to 14 years later when they were adolescents (Shoda, Mishel, & Peake, 1990). Those children who had delayed gratification, who had waited patiently at four for the experimenter to return to give them two marshmallows, had far higher grades and Scholastic Aptitude test (SAT) scores in high school. The one third of the children who ate the marshmallow right away, had an average verbal score of 524 and an average math score of 528; in contrast, those children who waited for the experimenter to return, had average scores of 610 and 652, respectively. Socially and emotionally, the children who delayed gratification were, as adolescents, more competent and personally effective. The adolescents, who had resisted temptation at four, were less likely to go to pieces or freeze under pressure. They pursued challenges rather than giving up when the going got tough. They were self-reliant, confident, trustworthy, and dependable. In contrast, the one third of the children who grabbed the marshmallow right away were more likely to overreact to minor provocations, to be stubborn and indecisive, to provoke arguments and fights, and to still be unable to delay gratification.

All of this is not to say that you should forego pleasure and fun in your life for the sake of future goals. In fact, it is important to learn how to balance your life so that you can have pleasures while at the same time pursuing your goals. But balance requires impulse control so that you don't dash off when friends invite you out to party the night before a big exam.

You can party after you have passed your exam. Balance requires establishing priorities, scheduling your time, and honoring your commitments to yourself and others.

Don't Cry Over "Spilt Milk."
Learn from Experience and Change Your Strategy

Do you spend a lot of time regretting what you have done in the past and thinking of what you wish you had done instead of what you did? Someone who had an auto accident might think, "If only I had stopped at the Stop sign, I wouldn't have gotten into that accident." Psychological researchers have found that people can improve their lives by developing the habit of engaging in *upward counterfactual thinking*, which involves focusing on what went wrong and determining the steps one could take to be more successful in achieving their goals and avoiding misfortune in the future (Roese, 1997). Although upward counterfactual thinking is often triggered by negative emotions (unhappiness, anger, and depression), it also fills one with hope concerning his or her ability to make changes and, the next time, to have a more successful outcome and to improve the quality of life. In a sample of midlife women, Landman and others (Landman, Vandewater, Stewart, & Malley, 1995) found that upward counterfactual thinking was associated with the envisioning of positive changes in the women's lives, which were reflected in their future career, relationship, and lifestyle goals.

Counterfactual thinking under some circumstances, however, can lead to self-blame and depression. The rape victim who says to herself, "It was my fault because I went out alone at night" may become depressed and suffer prolonged posttraumatic stress. Successful cognitive reappraisals need to redefine the rape as not being her fault, and provide the individual an opportunity to be guided into positive experiences and coping (Koss & Burkhart, 1989).

Overall, the results of this research indicate that the benefits of using counterfactual thinking outweigh the disadvantages. Be mindful to use counterfactual thinking to analyze what went wrong in a situation as a guide to making changes that will lead to a more favorable outcome in the future. Be on your guard, however, not to let counterfactual thinking degenerate into self-blame, rumination, and depression.

Visualize the Steps to Achieving Your Goals

Visualizing what you have to do in order to achieve your goal is more important than visualizing the goal itself. *Mental simulation* is the ability to imagine things not currently present. We imagine the future and regulate behavior and emotions to bring it about. Mental simulations make events seem possible and motivate the individual to engage in problem solving activities to bring them about (or in the case of mental simulation of possible negative events, to avoid them). Mental simulation allows people to problem solve by trying out several possible scenarios and to evaluate how effective they might be in achieving a goal. For example, you might think about what courses you can register for next year. You remember fondly the favorite course you had with Professor Whitcomb who has a great sense of humor and you imagine sitting in his class again laughing at his jokes. Then you check the schedule and discover that he is not teaching any of the courses you are required to take to complete the major, so you think that if you took his course you might have to go to summer school in order to complete the major. You imagine what it would be like to have to go to summer school, so you don't take Professor Whitcomb's course and take a course you need in order to graduate. Thus, mental simulation helps one to weigh the advantages and disadvantages of alternatives we might select.

Not all mental simulations are equally effective in regulating behavior and achieving goals. In one experiment, college students were randomly assigned to one of two simulation conditions, which provided participants training in mental simulations. They were then instructed to practice on their own five minutes a day for five to seven days prior to the midterm exam (Taylor, Pham, Rivkin, & Armor, 1998; Pham & Taylor, 1999). In the *process-simulation* condition, participants were told to visualize themselves studying for the exam in a place such as in the library, or at their desks at home, and going over the lecture notes and reading the text chapters with the goal of achieving a grade of A. In the *outcome-simulation* condition they were told to see themselves having received the grade of A, beaming with joy, and feeling proud of their accomplishment. A third group was a control group not given any mental simulation training or exercises to practice. All three groups were called the night before the exam, and asked about the number of hours they had studied, when they had started studying for the exam and their expected grade. The results indicated that the process-simulation group began studying for the exam earlier, spent more hours studying, and received significantly higher grades on the exam than students who were in the outcome-simulation or the control groups. Further refinements of the research led to the conclusion that process simulation improved examination performance by two routes.

> First, it reduced anxiety, the emotional regulation component, which in turn enhanced performance. Second, it facilitated planning, the problem-solving component, which maintained aspiration level, namely, the grade that the student strove for, which in turn enhanced exam performance (Taylor et al., 1998, p. 434).

These studies show us that it is important to focus on the process of achieving our goals rather than just on the goal. Planning the steps to goal achievement reduces anxiety and focuses us on problem solving the best way to achieve the goal. In contrast, the popular self-help literature typically focuses on outcome-simulation, which this research did not find to be effective in improving performance.

In another experiment dealing with how mental simulation can be effective in relieving stress and coping with stressful events, college students were asked to designate a stressful event in their lives. One group of students was then asked to visualize how the problem arose, and to give a step-by-step account of their actions, the circumstances surrounding the event, and their feelings about it. Another group of students only completed an outcome simulation in which they pictured the successful resolution of the problem. A third group completed a follow-up questionnaire but did not engage in any mental simulation. Both immediately after the mental simulation and one week later, the group that had focused on the ongoing stressful event in their simulation reported more positive affect and reported they had used more *emotion-focused coping*, such as positive reinterpretation and the use of social support for emotional solace, as compared to the outcome-simulation and the control groups.

From both of these lines of research it can be concluded that not all mental simulations are equally effective. Mental simulation that focuses on the steps to achieving a goal or a problem that arose in one's life, what happened, actions one took related to it, and the feelings one experienced will be successful in both goal achievement and in emotional coping. On the other hand, outcome focused coping is no more effective than doing nothing. That is a pretty strong statement considering that many self-help books and tapes advise us to mentally imagine ourselves as having achieved a goal, but do not tell us to mentally simulate the steps necessary to achieving that goal.

This research reveals that using process simulations is helpful for clarifying the steps needed for successful problem solving and goal achievement. Learn to use mental simulations to help you focus on the steps you need to take to solve your problems and outline your goals and sub-goals. These mental simulations will motivate you to take the action required for achieving your goals.

Create and Practice Affirmations

Affirmations are positive self-talk. Research is accumulating that indicates self-talk has a definite impact on performance. Affirmations can help you achieve self-direction and self-motivation. A number of studies from sports psychology illustrate the effectiveness of positive self-talk. For example, among 12 gymnasts competing for berths on the 1976 men's USA Olympic team, those who became members of the Olympic team practiced self-talk whereas those who did not practice self-talk did not make the team. Similarly members of a university racquetball team who practiced positive self-talk had better performance than their teammates who did not practice self-talk (Neck & Manz, 1992).

Positive self-talk has also been found to be an effective tool in changing behaviors in a diversity of areas including: performance on a perceptual motor task, quitting smoking, and modifying the behavior of a group of impulsive children. Research with counselor trainees indicated that the acquisition of facilitative self-talk led to higher levels of reflection, confrontation, and empathy in the trainees.

What are some affirmations that you could practice in your daily life? You can tailor your affirmations to your specific goals and tasks. Following are some more general affirmations that you might find helpful:

- I love myself.
- I am in control of my life.
- I am kind and loving toward others.
- I am learning, and developing my capabilities.
- My life is filled with joy and love.
- I am thankful for the prosperity in my life.
- I attract kind, loving people to me.

- I set clear goals.
- I am healthy.
- I am a competent person.
- I work hard on tasks that are important to me.
- I am thankful for the many blessings in my life.
- I exercise every day.
- I send love to my body.
- I help others as much as possible.
- I spend quality time with my family.
- My income is sufficient to meet my needs and those of my family.
- I greet each new day with joy and positive expectations.
- I am creative.
- I follow clear plans that bring me to achieving my goals.
- I move in the world with love and power.
- I challenge my mind through reading and learning.
- I enjoy taking nature walks.
- I meditate.
- I laugh easily and often.
- The divine spirit within me guides my thoughts, words and actions.

Create affirmations that are tailored to achieving your specific goals and tasks for college. Make sure your affirmation contains all of the most important information. Choose positive words and present tense that indicates that your goal is already accomplished, as in the above examples.

Make One Big Change in Your Life That Is Really Important to You Rather Than a Lot of Little Ones

When making decisions about life change, we are sometimes faced with difficult choices. How can you decide, for example, if you should make a change that would confer great benefits in one area, such as accepting a dream job in a distant city, rather than moderate benefits in a number of areas, such as a job that would offer a moderate pay increase, but allow you to have somewhat more time for family and friends? Which of these alternatives would bring greater happiness and satisfaction in your life? During a life transition that brings about changes in the environment and in the self, we may ask ourselves if we did the right thing and how we're doing in the new situation. To answer these questions, Caroline Schowers and Carol Ryff (1996) gave self-report questionnaires to and conducted in-home interviews with 120 older women aged 55 to 97 years, all of whom had relocated during the previous year. They measured self-change in five areas of life: health, friendships, family, economics, and daily activities.

Showers and Ryff (1996) found that "individuals in a life transition who experienced great improvement in one very important domain of the self appeared to have greater well-being in the year following the transition than those who experienced the same average improvement spread equally across all domains" (p. 457). On the other side of the coin, a very negative event in an important area of life was more devastating than smaller losses across a broader number of domains. It was the evaluation of perceived self-change, not current self-evaluations that mattered. In other words, it was the change that occurred in each of the areas of life, not the overall evaluation of that area, that mattered. If one makes a move for a reason that may not be terribly important to her such as to improve her financial status, and in the process suffers the loss of friends that are very important to her, the change may be overwhelming. Thus, the message to be gained from this research is to think about what is really important to you before you make a change, because you want to make a change that will improve the area of your life that is most important to you.

Would you have to sacrifice an area that is really important to you in order to make moderate improvements in several areas? If that is the scenario, don't make the change. However, if the change would greatly improve one area of your life that is very important to you, then make the change even if it means smaller sacrifices in other areas. If your career is the most important domain in your life and you have the opportunity for a dream job in a distant city, then take it. Try to maintain other areas such as relations with friends and family through e-mail, visits home, letters, and phone calls. Make an effort to make new friends. Overall, the satisfaction with yourself and your life should improve when you voluntarily begin a life transition.

In order to decide what changes in your life to make, you must gain self-insight. You are the only person who can decide what is really important to you in life. Your transitions should be in the direction of improving your life in that domain. And, you will be better able to persist in your efforts to achieve your goals over the long run if they are truly personally meaningful to you (Sheldon & Elliot, 1998).

Make sure that you do not act hastily! Before making important life transitions, be sure to do a great deal of soul-searching and gather as much information as possible about what the change will mean in your life. Mark and Diane are a married couple with three small children. Mark works for a large corporation that wanted to give him a promotion and a $20,000 increase in salary if he would move to another state about 200 miles from where they currently live. After going to be interviewed, looking at houses in the area where his new position would be and talking with their families, Mark turned down the new position. They would have moved away from grandparents who help out with babysitting, would have had to pay more money for the same type of home, and the children would have had to leave a school where they had a very small class size. Taking all of these factors into consideration, Mark turned down the job to stay in his current position. Contemplate upon your future life vision. Analyze the pros and cons of all of your possible life options. Make sure that your plan is morally right as well so that you will be able to achieve a truly satisfying life.

Success Recommendations

This section contains a summary of the main points in this chapter to help you reflect on and recall what you have learned.

- **Set Personally Meaningful Goals in Order to Achieve Them.** Identify your highest priority life goals based on your values, and your interests and abilities. Begin your college career by exploring a variety of academic subjects and participating in extra-curricular activities in order to find out what special talents and academic interests you have.

- **Focus on the Goal You Want to Achieve Rather Than the Failure You Want to Avoid.** If you focus on your goal of doing well rather than on avoiding failure, you will have greater mental focus, enjoy the tasks more and perform better than if you are striving to prevent negative outcomes.

- **Achieve Meaning and Happiness in Your Life by Selecting Goals that Are Consistent with Your Values, Beliefs, and Talents.** Identify and write down your tentative long term 10- and 5-year personal, relationship, and career goals. Select goals that are congruent with your true talents, interests, core values, essential beliefs, and personality. Review and revise your goals as you gain more life experience and self-insight and have a clearer direction for the upcoming decade.

- **Set Challenging Goals.** Identify a specific challenging goal that you intend to achieve in college to help you get thinking in that direction. Setting and achieving challenging goals for yourself while you are in college is especially important if you want to end up earning a high income in your career after graduation.

- **Illustrate Your Vision for Success.** Once you have a vision of how you want your life to be after you graduate from college, create a mind map or collage illustrating it. Display your completed collage in a prominent location in your bedroom or study area. This visual tool will serve to motivate you by keeping your brain focused on achieving your goals.

- **Be Hopeful that You Can Achieve Your Goals.** As you strive to create your future life, be hopeful in identifying the steps that need to be taken to achieve your goal. Then, take action to begin those steps and energetically sustain that action until the goal is achieved.

- **Experience Flow and Enjoy Your Work and Play.** To optimize your chances of achieving flow in your work and play, be sure to either select interesting and challenging tasks that you can do or make arrangements to learn the skills needed to do it. Structure your environment so that you will be free from distractions and able to really concentrate on what you are doing.

- **Periodically Reassess and Update Your Goals.** Be sure to review and revise your life goals and associated sub-goals and objectives as you gain more life experience and self-insight about your talent, interests, opportunities, and desired life plan. Be flexible. If you have goals that no longer seem to suit you, transform them into ones that do.

- **Learn When to Delay Gratification.** It is important to learn how to balance your life so that you can have pleasures while at the same time pursuing your goals. To achieve balance, learn to control your impulses, establish priorities, schedule your time, and honor your commitments to yourself and others.

- **Don't Cry Over "Spilt Milk." Learn from Experience and Change Your Strategy.** When things do not work out as you had hoped they would, analyze what went wrong in the situation as a guide to making changes that will lead to a more favorable outcome in the future. Be on your guard, however, not to let your thinking degenerate into self-blame, rumination, and depression.

- **Visualize the Steps to Achieving Your Goals.** The research studies show us that it is important to focus on the process of achieving our goals rather than just on the goal. Planning the steps to goal achievement reduces anxiety and focuses us on problem solving, which is the best way to achieve the goal.

- **Create and Practice Affirmations to Achieve Your Goals.** Repeating positive self-talk or affirmations on a daily basis can help you achieve self-direction and self-motivation. Positive self-talk is also an effective tool you can use to change behaviors such as improving performance on a perceptual motor task, quitting smoking, or controlling your impulses.

- **Make One Big Change in Your Life if it is Really Important to You Rather Than a Lot of Little Ones.** Before making an important life change, take time to think about whether it is congruent with your true talents, interests, core values, essential beliefs, personality, and desired lifestyle. Evaluate all of the pros and cons of making the life change. If you want to improve your feeling of life satisfaction, make a big change in an area of life that is really important to you rather than a lot of little ones.

Chapter Nine
Select and Prepare for
a Rewarding Career

In 1991, futurist Alvin Toffler predicted that nearly everyone will make several job or career changes during their lives. Today, that vision is being realized. Many workers are being laid-off due to the global trend toward merging and downsizing of large companies and many more workers will be forced to rethink their work options in the future. Some workers are finding that they need to continually receive advanced education or technical training in order to be able to perform the types of jobs available to them. Others periodically create a new vision for their future life career and proactively prepare for and pursue new and more exciting career options. It is anticipated that this trend toward career discontinuity and life long education and retraining will become even more common in the future. Events such as the terrorist incident that occurred at the Trade Towers in New York City on September 11, 2002 and the Iraqi War also affect job stability around the world in unpredictable ways.

How can you plan a career path in such an unstable work environment? As you are preparing for a particular career, it is important for you to learn the broader academic and leadership skills that will enable you to adapt to and take advantage of changing opportunities for employment and advancement in our evolving modern workplace and world. You will also need to become resilient so that you will not feel defeated by the inevitable disappointments that everyone faces in life. Researchers have identified skills you will need to possess in order to land a high paying professional or managerial job and to be ready to assume a position of leadership in your family, the workforce, and the community. The success strategies in this chapter outline these skills and explain how you can develop them.

Philosopher Joseph Campbell told his students that a secret of a happy life was to follow their bliss when making decisions about their life work (as cited in Moyers, 1988). How can you decide what your bliss is and how you might pursue it? What are the steps involved in identifying and following your bliss concerning a career?

First, you need to begin to create a vision of the lifestyle you desire to live after you graduate from college and gain insight concerning your unique talents, abilities, and interests. Second, you must identify potential careers that you are interested in pursuing in which you will be able to use your special talents and interests in a productive manner. Third, you must identify the educational requirements for those careers as well as the demands and rewards associated with them. Fourth, you must select a tentative career path that you believe will allow you to earn a good living while adding a sense of integrity or meaning to your life. Fifth, you must select a college major or training program that will allow you to achieve your career goals and find mentors who can act as role models and guides for you.

Psychological and vocational researchers have identified work preferences and career choices that interest people with different talents and abilities, psychological or temperament types, and personality types and strengths. The success recommendations in this chapter, which are based on this research, will help you explore your career preferences and related educational requirements. You will also learn strategies that you can use to select your college major and to rethink and redefine your career and college plans whenever you desire to do so.

Understand How Ability, Past Performance, Self-Efficacy, Outcome Expectations, and Performance Attainment Levels Affect Your Career Development Process

The Social Cognitive career choice model predicts that *self-efficacy* (your perception of your ability to perform well on a particular task such as learn math), and *outcome expectations* (that for example you will earn a grade of A in a math course), influence your interests and your goals. Interests do not pop out of nowhere. "If one perceives mastery of the skills necessary to an occupation area and believes that positive outcomes will result from engaging in that behavior, interests are predicted to develop in that occupational area" (Fouad, Smith, & Zao, 2002, p. 164). The interest follows if you have been able to learn relevant skills in an occupational area, and you think that you will enjoy the work, and it will have other benefits such as good pay and high status. Or perhaps you think that you can find employment in that occupation in a geographic area where you prefer to live, or you can balance that type of career with family obligations.

The social-cognitive career model was tested in a survey of 952 undergraduate students at two Midwestern universities across four subject areas of art, social science, math/science and English. Self-efficacy was related to grades in all four areas, but the relationship was strongest for math/science. Students who got high grades in math had the highest self-efficacy for math. However, the relationship between high grades in math and career intentions was less strong in the math and science area than in other areas. Students who got high grades in other areas were more likely to say they would take future courses and want to enter that career field (Fouad et al., 2002).

Self-efficacy in an area is related to getting good grades and to interest in that field which leads to intentions to enter a particular occupation, but you should also evaluate job outcomes in that field before intending to enter that career. Ability and interest in an area are moderated by what the student perceives the job opportunities to be in a field. At some community colleges in our area, there are waiting lists for qualified students to get into nursing programs because of the current shortage of and high hourly wages paid to nurses.

Take the Myers-Briggs Type Indicator and Identify Your Psychological and Temperament Types and Careers that are Compatible with Them

What is your psychological type and problem solving style? How can knowing them help you develop your career plan? The notion of psychological types is based on the work of Carl Jung (1923, as translated by Hull, 1971) who believed that although humans are internally driven by universal *archetypes*, or instincts, peoples' behavior preferences differ due to their general attitude toward their environment as well as their style of gathering and evaluating information from their environment.

Jung identified two biologically based temperamental dispositions or *attitude-types*, which he believed to be important aspects of the self that *determine how one approaches his or her environment*. These two basic attitude-types are processes of adaptation to one's environment that are distinguished by the direction of one's interest toward objects in the physical world:

- *Extraversion Type*—Have a tendency to be outgoing, to be energized by people or objects in the world outside one's self, and to make decisions based on objective facts and conditions.

- *Introversion Type*—Have a tendency to be reserved; to be energized by one's inner world of concepts, thoughts, and ideas; and to make decisions based on subjective factors.

Jung noted that:

> The two types are so different and present such a striking contrast that their existence becomes quite obvious ... once it has been pointed out. Everyone knows those reserved, inscrutable, rather shy people who form the strongest possible contrast to the open, sociable, jovial, or at least friendly and approachable characters who are on good terms with everybody, or quarrel with everybody, but always relate to them in some way and in turn are affected by them. (p. 179)

Jung also defined four psychological *function-types* that he believed are involved in one's style of information gathering concerning one's environment and evaluation of that data. How does the behavior and problem solving approach of people with these four psychological types differ? The two function-types describing *styles of gathering information* concerning one's environment are:

- *Sensation Type*—Relies on physical and psychic datum concerning one's physical environment or facts gathered using one's five senses

- *Intuition Type*—Relies on one's personal vision, psychological insights, and hunches

According to Jung, people have a tendency to gather information about the world by either sensation or intuition, but not both simultaneously. Sensation and intuition are extreme positions at opposite ends of a continuum, with balance of these psychological functions in the middle position.

The two function-types describing *styles of evaluating information* concerning one's environment that Jung defined are:

- *Thinking Type*—Relies on rational analysis and impersonal principles such as fairness
- *Feeling Type*—Relies on person-centered values and concern for the welfare of others

Jung believed that people evaluate information about the world by either thinking or feeling, but not both simultaneously. As with sensation and intuition, thinking and feeling are also extreme positions on a continuum, with balance of these psychological functions in the middle position.

People who have the same general approach to their environment and the same primary orientation tend to exhibit similar behaviors. While the primary orientation dominates an individual's behavior, Jung believed that each person may also have a *secondary style* for *"fine tuning"* his or her basic approach to perceiving and making judgments about the physical world:

- *Perceiving Style*—Have a supremacy of the perceiving function based on subjective data
- *Judging Style*—Have a supremacy of the reasoning or rational judgment function based on objective data

A career assessment inventory called the Myers-Briggs Type Indicator (MBTI) (Myers, 1992; Myers & McCaulley, 1985; McCaulley, 2000) is based in part on Jung's theory of eight psychological types and problem solving styles described above. The MBTI is popular among industrial organizational psychologists and career counselors who use it as a tool for predicting people's suitability for various types of jobs, careers, and leadership positions. It is also very popular among college students as a tool for selecting a tentative career and a college major. The MBTI consists of 125 statements assessing 16 psychological types, which are based on combinations of the two general approaches to the environment (extraversion, introversion), the two information gathering types (sensation, intuition), the two information evaluation types (thinking, feeling), and the two secondary "fine tuning" styles (perceiving, judging). The test taker indicates how closely the statements describing behaviors of the various psychological types describe her or him. A report defining one's psychological type and a description of how one approaches his or her environment and problem solving functions is prepared based on the self-reported answers of the test taker. One reason the MBTI may be so popular is because all of the personality types are described in flattering terms. Another reason may be that the results seem to "ring true" because the report summary is based on the answers selected by the test taker. If you want professional help selecting a college major and career, visit your college's counseling center. Ask to have an MBTI or another vocational assessment test administered to you.

Take David Keirsey's Temperament Sorter Type II Online and Discover Your Possible Career Options

David Keirsey (1998) developed another popular type theory that he believes simplifies the eight types of Carl Jung and the sixteen Myers-Briggs Psychological Types by specifying only four temperament types:

- *Rational*—Instinctively looks for technological ways and means of overcoming obstacles. Desires to understand how things work and how to build things. Investigates patterns of nature and society. Motivated to learn about science and technology.

- *Idealist*—Interested in personal growth and development in self and others. Motivated to remove the walls of conflict and selfishness that divide people.

- *Artisan*—Adventurous, impulsive, resourceful, unconventional, risk-takers. Prefer the external world of solid objects that can be made and manipulated, and real-life events that can be experienced in the here and now.

- *Guardian*—Sensible, down-to-earth, cautious, people who are respectful of traditions and rules. Solid citizens who establish and defend society's most important institutions such as homes and families, schools, churches, hospitals, businesses, neighborhoods, and communities.

From the description of these temperament types, it is clear that no one type is superior to another. People embodying each of these types and career orientations are necessary for the institutions of the world to function smoothly while its population realizes personal growth and benefits from advancements in technology. The four temperament types, associated talents, and career orientation that Keirsey suggests are associated with each of them are in the Table below along with a list of occupations that may be of interest to people exhibiting each type.

Do you recognize your interests in one of the four temperament descriptions? How can you find out more information about your temperament type? Keirsey has developed a Keirsey Temperament Sorter II (KTS–II), which he says scores results in a manner similar to the MBTI (Keirsey, 1998) and he provides a version of it online that anyone can take free of charge. If desired, find out more about your temperament type by going online to http://www.keirsey.com and taking the Keirsey Temperament Sorter II self-assessment test.

Remember that the results of the MBTI and the Keirsey Temperament Sorter II can be useful and informative, but they are not to be considered the Truth about you or your possible career options. Neither the MBTI nor the KTS–II are crystal balls. The results will describe your psychological or temperament type based on a summary of the answers you selected concerning the way you tend to approach your environment and career areas in which people with your self-defined temperament type are successful. Realize that the type of careers that interest you may change as you develop new talents and abilities in college and life. Use this information as one of many sources of information about yourself when making decisions about a career and college major.

Table 5.
Keirsey's Temperament Types and Associated Talents, Orientation, and Careers

Type	Talents	Orientation	Careers
Rational	Sources of technological expertise	Architect, Field Marshall, Inventor, Mastermind	Architect, Computer Science, Electronics, Engineering, Inventor, Research Scientist
Idealist	Sources of emotional wellness, spirituality, and personal diplomacy	Healer, Counselor, Champion, Teacher	Counselor, Mediator, Minister, Nurse, Psychologist, Teacher
Artisan	Sources of artistic creations and solutions to problems	Composer, Crafter, Performer, Promoter	Actor, Artist, Athlete, Fashion Designer, Financial Analyst, Interior Designer, Musician, Politician, Producer
Guardian	Sources of cultural stability. Upholders of established institutions and traditions	Inspector, Protector, Provider, Supervisor	Business Manager, Doctor, Judge, Lawyer, Police, Religious Leader, Security Officer, Social Worker

Source: Retrieved March 23, 2003, from http://www.keirsey.com.

Identify Your Personality Type, Strengths, and Work Preferences on the Strong Interest Inventory

Another popular career interest assessment tool that is widely used by vocational counselors is the Strong Interest Inventory (SII), which assesses personality type, personality strengths, and work preferences (Harmon, Hansen, Borgen, & Hammer, 1994, as cited in Lattimore & Borgen, 1999). The SII, which has scales to measure basic interest and general occupational themes, is also considered to be very useful for making a career choice and selecting a college major. The SII contains test items related to J. L. Holland's theory of careers, which defines six personality types with related personality strengths and interests (Holland, 1985; 1997). Many researchers have found that Holland's six personality types are related to satisfaction in specific vocational or career areas.

- *Realistic Type*—Prefers solving practical problems and performing skilled, physical labor. Possesses traditional values. Possible career paths might include those involving an electrical, mechanical, or technical skill.

- *Investigative Type*—Prefers observational activities as well as thinking about and solving abstract problems. Values scientific or scholarly activities as well as self-determination (independence). Possible career paths might include those involving mathematics and scientific research.

- *Artistic Type*—Prefers ambiguous, free, unsystematic activities and expressing oneself through some form of artistic medium. Values aesthetic experiences and open self-expression. Possible career paths might include art, acting, dance, drama, music, and creative writing.

- *Social Type*—Prefers interacting verbally with and helping, training, or teaching people. Holds the belief that all people are equal and values solving social problems. Possible career paths might include medical work, law, religious ministry, teaching, counseling, psychology, and social work.

- *Enterprising Type*—Prefers taking the leadership role and has the ability to interact well with and to persuade others. Values the opportunity to control others while being free of control. Possible career paths might include business management, investment management, politics, sales, and entrepreneurial activities.

- *Conventional Type*—Prefers structured systematic office work. Values achievement in business and finance. Possible career paths might include banking, accounting, and general office work.

Some people exhibit strong preference for work suited for a specific personality type whereas others might exhibit a personality type profile with a combination of equally preferred personality types. People with clearly defined personality types and strong interest preferences find it easier to make vocational choices using Holland's scheme than do people with less clearly defined types and preferences.

Holland notes that some combinations of personality types are more compatible and consistent than are others. He uses an octagon to show the distance between these types, as shown in Figure 6 below, and he suggests that the types that are closer to one another are more compatible. For example, Holland notes that *Realistic* and *Conventional* are more closely related than are *Realistic* and *Artistic, Realistic* and *Enterprising,* or *Realistic* and *Social.* Profile patterns such as Realistic–Conventional or Investigative–Artistic or Social–Enterprising are considered to be more consistent than are other profiles such as Realistic–Enterprising, Conventional–Artistic, or Investigative–Social.

Holland (1997) emphasizes that one should not focus exclusively on defining one's personality type and interests when making decisions concerning a vocational choice or college major but should also consider the type of environment in which she or he prefers to work. He notes that certain types of work environments attract certain types of people and reward certain types of employee personality styles and associated behaviors. Therefore, different personality types require different types of environments. People will be happier and more successful when they are working in environments that suit their personality type and in which they are most likely to find like-minded bosses and co-workers with whom they can relate.

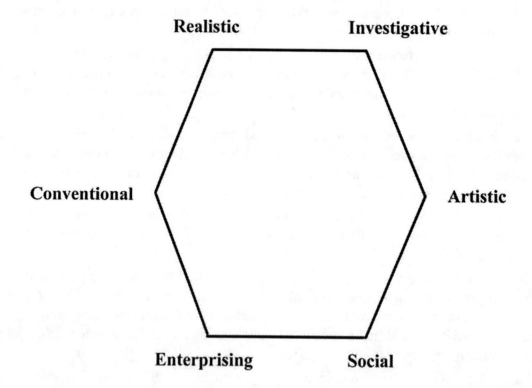

Figure 6.
Holland's Model of Personality and Environment Types

Source: Adapted from Holland, J. L. (1997). *Making vocational choices: A theory of vocational personalities and work environments* (3rd ed.). Odessa, FL: Psychological Assessment Resources.

In the past, the personality types in the SII and the related and career choices were viewed as more appropriate for either a man or a woman. For example, the realistic type was seen as more instrumental and "masculine," whereas the social type was seen as more expressive and "feminine." Since differential gender role socialization practices and life experiences influence one's vocational interests and choices, many women and men express gender-role stereotyped interests (Eccles, 1987). Vocational counselors used these traditionally stereotyped test results to track young men into college majors and careers with performance requirements that matched the practical or realistic personality type and to track young women into college majors and careers with performance requirements that matched the people-oriented or social personality type. This gender specific type of career tracking costs women a great deal of money over the course of their careers since many of the traditional female jobs pay much less than traditional male jobs.

The norms for the revised 1994 version of the SII were developed using both men and women in careers and, therefore, the recommendations are not stereotyped according to traditional gender roles. The revised SII norms were developed using 18,951 employed adults (9,467 women and 9,484 men) from over 50 occupations who indicated that they were satisfied with their job tasks and were successful in their current occupation (Harmon et al. as cited in Lattimore & Borgen, 1999). After analyzing data from a sub sample of that normative group (9,266 women and 9,266 men) who had indicated their racial-ethnic background, the researchers reported that the 1994 version of the SII is valid for counseling both majority and racial-ethnic minority group members in the United States who are seeking careers that require advanced education. They noted that more research is need to assess the validity of the 1994 version of the Strong Interest Inventory (SII) for people from other cultures and for occupations for women and men that require less education.

If you want to learn more about your personality type and career preferences, you can go online to http://www.nycareerzone.org/ to access the career exploration website of the City of New York, New York, USA. This site provides a free online self-assessment test based on J. L. Holland's theory of careers and matches the personality types you choose to describe yourself with a long list of careers. This site also has information on portfolio assessment, jobs, and college financial aid. Or, you can make an appointment with a vocational counselor at your college's counseling center and ask to have the Strong Interest Inventory (SII) administered to you. Some colleges may charge students a small fee to have this test administered and scored.

Remember to treat the results of the Strong Interest Inventory (SII) as one of many sources of data when making your career decisions. Avoid locking yourself into a gender role stereotyped college major or career if you have the personality type, strengths, talents, interests, and desire to pursue nontraditional options. Recent research finds that career interest positively predicted career choice of both male and female college students (Morgan, Isaac, & Sansone, 2001). Women report interpersonal work goals more frequently than men. That is one of the reasons women select the more traditional gender role careers in social service/ education. Men more frequently value high pay and status work goals than do women. College men and women perceive physical/mathematical science careers as less likely to provide interpersonal work goals, but more likely to afford high pay and status.

Success Profile—Kelley

When Kelley enrolled at the community college she began her "new life and new adventure." Kelley admits that she was not sure where her new life would lead her when she made a decision to enroll in college. She recalls that there were so many things that entered her mind that week before classes began. "Would I be able to handle the stress of raising three children alone and going to school, since I had been out for so many years? How would I be able to focus on studying and being able to maintain the grades I want?" Furthermore, many members of Kelley's family could not understand why she would want to go back to school after so many years and were not supportive of her decision. They felt that she "should not waste her time with it because she would only end up either quitting or neglecting her children." However, there was one person who understood Kelley's need to return to school and she kept her focused on what it was she wanted to accomplish for herself. Even though Kelley still felt very little support from her family when she began college, she was determined to prove to them that she was able to handle her family and school responsibilities at the same time.

After the first week of classes, Kelley knew that she was not going to give up. She admits that it was very difficult for her to get back into the stream of school, but once her "insecurities lifted," she "loved being in that academic atmosphere." Another difficult task that Kelley had to face was dealing with a learning disability, which made it difficult to stay focused in classes. In spite of that, she discovered so many talents that she never knew she possessed. She also recalls receiving a lot of assistance from her professors, the tutors in the writing center, and the learning specialists in the center for developmental education who helped her to stay focused on why she was in college. Consequently, her learning disability did not weaken her determination to succeed in college, which was an element that she noticed many of the traditional aged students in her classes that first semester lacked.

Kelley first learned of the writing center from her English professor who indicated that she "wrote very well but did not have enough confidence." She went to the writing center so often to have the tutors assist her with her writing, it became her "second home" and her "haven." Towards the end of that first semester, a peer tutor who worked with Kelley on many of her papers asked if she would consider becoming a peer tutor. She encouraged Kelley to speak with the director of the writing center, who had also assisted her with her papers. The director indicated that he really enjoyed reading Kelley's papers and thought that she would be of benefit to many of the students who needed the assistance of a writing tutor. Kelley thought it over and decided that she did love writing and she also enjoyed helping others. So, she became a tutor during the following fall semester.

Kelley attended a two-week training seminar with other peer and faculty tutors at which different techniques of tutoring were discussed. The students and the professors also made suggestions about how to make tutoring easier. Despite the training, Kelley said that she was still "very terrified" until after tutoring that first student. Then she felt that she had nothing to worry about because "tutoring came easily" for her. She has been tutoring now for five semesters. Subsequently, Kelley has fulfilled all of the requirements for peer tutors including attending ongoing training, completing a specified amount of hours tutoring, and completing a required course on how to tutor. Kelley said that she found this course to be very helpful because the peer tutors who were in it shared their different perspectives on their tutoring experiences. They also discussed the different types of learning styles many students have and how to handle tutoring students with specific types of assignments that professors require their students to complete.

As a result of her tutoring experiences, Kelley found that she enjoyed helping others who have similar needs to her own. She has now been asked to become a Coach Mentor for students with learning disabilities. Kelley said that she was not too sure about this at first since it would be a different type of experience in assisting students. Once she met with the specialists in the Office of Disability Services and they explained the responsibilities of a Coach Mentor, however, Kelley made the decision that it would be beneficial for her to do it. She decided that she would be able to help those who really need the help as she herself had been helped. Kelley said she has had a coach mentor since beginning her life at college and she has been a tremendous help to her. "Funny thing is, she has been trying to talk me into becoming a coach mentor since my second semester on campus. I finally decided that I would and she was thrilled. However, I still have her by my side when I need her help. It helps me to know that there is someone there for me who will help guide me in the right direction."

Kelley's present goal is to be one of those individuals who helps students with special needs stay in school and succeed. Kelley intends to graduate from the community college with her Associate's Degree and plans to go on for her Baccalaureate Degree. She eventually wants to become a speech pathologist. Her tutoring and coach mentoring training and work experience will be valuable assets for her as she advances toward her career goals.

Explore Possible Career Paths, Related Salaries, and Working Conditions

Once you identify a general career area or vocational field of interest in which you will be able to use your talents and do work you love, begin to explore all the possible career options in that field and weigh the pros and cons of pursuing each one. Begin by examining your beliefs about the suitability of various careers for women and men to make sure that you are not basing your career decisions on outmoded gender role stereotypes. In the past, for example, many women avoided careers in math, science, engineering, and computer science and had low self-efficacy for them because these areas were gender role stereotyped as male domains. Instead, they selected college majors in elementary school teaching or humanities and social science areas such as literature, psychology, and sociology. Since the majority of entry level jobs available to college graduates with a math, science, engineering, or computer science background pay much more than the jobs in elementary education, the humanities, or social science, many women college graduates found themselves in lower paying jobs than male college graduates.

Beginning in the 1970s, women started selecting traditionally "male" college majors and professions in medicine, law, engineering, computer science, and university teaching (U.S. Department of Labor, 1991; 1993). Today, these women who are working in traditionally "male" careers earn more money than those who are in traditionally "female" occupations. This difference in salary can really add up over a lifetime career. "However, women are still underrepresented in science, math, and engineering (SME) fields, holding only 9% of engineering positions, 22% of physical science positions, and about 20% of all SME positions combined" (National Science Board, 2000, as cited in Nauta & Epperson, 2003, p. 448). Do not eliminate yourself from high paying careers in science and engineering because you did not take enough math and science courses in college. By taking math and science courses you are opening up many rewarding career opportunities.

Before making a final decision about a possible career path and college major, get detailed information about projected opportunities in your field of interest that will be available in the future. You can find a great deal of information about college majors, related careers, job outlook, salaries, employers, and professional associations on the website of the National Association of Colleges and Employers (NACE) at http://www.jobweb.com. Average salaries for "top jobs" and "top paid" college majors for 2004–2005 reported by NACE are shown in Tables 6a and 6b below. The data in Table 7 below is from 'hottest jobs' list on the *2004–*

2005 Occupational Outlook Handbook, which is published by the United States Government, available on the Internet at http://stats.bls.gov/emp/emptab3.htm.

Table 6a.
Entry Level Salaries for "Top Jobs" for 2005 Graduates with Bachelor's Degrees

Job Function	Average Salary Offer
Management Trainee	$36,491
Sales	$37,269
Consulting	$48,098
Teaching	$30,793
Accounting (Private)	$43,003
Accounting (Public)	$42,366
Financial/Treasury Analysis	$44,501
Design/Construction Engineering	$45,734
Software Design & Development	$52,471
Project Engineering	$47,827
Registered Nurse	$41,156

Table 6b.
Entry Level Salaries for 2005 Graduates with Bachelor's Degrees for "Top Paid" College Majors

Major	Average Salary
Chemical Engineering	$53,813
Computer Engineering	$52,464
Electrical/Electronics & Communications Engineering	$51,888
Aerospace/Aeronautical/Astronautical Engineering	$50,993
Systems Engineering	$50,887
Computer Science	$50,820
Mechanical Engineering	$50,236
Industrial/Manufacturing Engineering	$49,567
Engineering Technology	$45,234
Information Sciences & Systems	$44,775

Source: Summer 2005 Salary Survey, National Association of Colleges and Employers (NACE). Retrieved August 27, 2005 from http://www.jobweb.com/

Table 7.
Fastest Growing Occupations Projected for 2002–2012

Occupation	Degree Required	% Employment Increase Projected	2002 Median Annual Earnings
Network systems and data communications analysts	Bachelor's	57	$41,820 +
Physician assistants	Bachelor's	49	$41,820 +
Computer software engineers, applications	Bachelor's	46	$41,820 +
Computer software engineers, systems software	Bachelor's	45	$41,820 +
Physical therapist assistants	Associate's	45	$27,500 to $41,780
Database administrators	Bachelor's	44	$41,820 +
Veterinary technologists and technicians	Associate's	44	$19,710 to $27,380
Dental hygienists	Associate's	43	$41,820 +
Computer systems analysts	Bachelor's	39	$41,820 +
Occupational therapist assistants	Associate's	39	$27,500 to $41,780
Environmental engineers	Bachelor's	38	$41,820 +
Postsecondary teachers	Doctor's	38	$41,820 +
Network and computer systems administrators	Bachelor's	37	$41,820 +
Environmental science and protection technicians, including health	Associate's	37	$27,500 to $41,780

Source: U. S. Department of Labor, Bureau of Statistics (2005). *The 2004–05 Occupational Outlook Handbook*. Retrieved August 27, 2005, from http://stats.bls.gov/emp/emptab3/htm.

Table 7 above presents the educational requirements, percent projected increase in employment, and median annual salaries for some of the fast growing future careers. These salary amounts can vary widely across different regions of the country. Therefore, they might not be accurate for the location in which you desire to live and work.

"The Career Key" is a useful career exploration website that is available at http://www.ncsu.edu/career/students/major.htm. This site was developed by Lawrence K. Jones, Professor Emeritus in the College of Education, North Carolina State University, Raleigh, North Carolina, USA. This site has a free career interest inventory that is instantly scored on the Internet. The results of the career interest inventory are linked to *The Occupational Outlook Handbook.*

Consider interviewing a person who is already doing the kind of work you'd like to do in order to find out more information about it. You can find the name and contact information for a professional person in your area that might be willing to talk to you on a membership list of a professional organization for a career in which you are interested. Tell the person you contact that you are asking for an interview as part of your career exploration process and will meet at his or her workplace. State that you have just a few well-organized questions and will limit the interview to five minutes. Under these circumstances, most professionals you call will agree to meet with you for a five-minute interview at their workplace.

Once you identify the level of education required to pursue your desired career, investigate the cost of such an education and your options for financing it. You want to make sure that you can finance your education and that the salary you will make will enable you to live the life style you envision. Don't worry if the required education sounds expensive. Many colleges offer scholarships and teaching and research assistantships for graduate students in master's and doctoral degree programs that provide free tuition plus a salary. You can get expert advice and help figuring out how to pay for your education from the financial aid office at your college as well as from others who have financed their own.

You can also get a great deal of additional information about a variety of careers and scholarships from your college's library and from career and job placement counselors at your college's counseling center. Many colleges have interactive career exploration computer programs and testing services available. Be sure to find out about and take advantage of these free career and job placement services available at your college.

Be Open to Experience and Happenstance in Your Career Decision Making

Chance plays an important role in the careers of many people. To avail yourself of the opportunities surrounding you, it is necessary to be open to new experiences and possibilities. The first author saw a position opening posted on the bulletin board outside of the Department Chair's office when she was completing the coursework for her Master's degree. Although most of her coursework was in experimental and physiological psychology, the position opening was in survey research. She was open to exploring this opportunity because she had worked on a research project as an undergraduate doing a survey related to housing in the community surrounding her college. She applied and did not get this job. A few months later the company posted another position one level below the one for which she first applied, and she got a job as Assistant Survey Director for a corporation conducting marketing and survey research on a national level. As a result of the interest generated in social psychology by her having worked in a related applied field, a few years later, she pursued a doctorate in social psychology.

In recent years, career counselors are beginning to teach clients to engage in exploratory activities to increase the probability that unplanned events can become opportunities for learning and careers. Work world shifts occur at an ever accelerating rate in the modern world, and people need to be prepared, responding to career uncertainties by being open to possibilities in their environment (Mitchell, Levin, & Krumboltz, 1999).

Different forms of career indecision exist (Lucas & Epperson, 1990). In a study with 196 undecided college students, some students were more anxious, have a lower self-esteem, and perceived barriers in the pursuit of their career goals, while others scored higher on self-esteem and higher on leisure orientation and lower in anxiety. Other students, mainly women, showed a high interest in relationship, work, and leisure activities. Some students showed anxiety in trying to juggle these diverse interests, whereas others had less anxiety over it. Some students no longer have faith that one right career exists. This view can lead to an openness to experience to the opportunities that may be available to them from diverse sources (networking, career counseling office, position announcements, etc.).

Proactively Evaluate the Demands
of Possible Career Options

It is important for you to identify the pros and cons of various careers and consider the trade-offs involved before making a final decision. What is your life vision? Do you plan to combine a high-powered, high paying career and family life? Do you plan to work when you have small children? Do you plan to share work inside the home and child care equitably with your partner? Is it easier for women and men to balance marriage, family, child-care, and career while employed in some types of occupations than in others?

Researchers find that it is somewhat easier for women to combine career and marriage in a female-dominated profession than in a male-dominated profession. A comparison of women librarians with MLS degrees and women managers with MBA degrees found that it was somewhat easier for librarians to combine career and marriage than it was for business managers. This is because of the greater availability of part-time work in those professions and the lesser negative effect of job interruptions on later salaries (Olson, Frieze, & Detlefesen, 1990).

Researchers have found, however, that there are a number of other factors that you should seriously consider before making a career decision based simply on the opportunity for readily available, part-time work. For example, the literature investigating factors involved with paid work that influence women's mental health (e.g., Lennon, 1987; Barnett, Marshall, Raudenbush, & Brennan, 1993) indicates that job complexity and amount of reward are important to women's psychological well-being. Researchers have found that women with paid jobs of higher complexity who get high rewards for it have higher levels of psychological well-being than women with dead end paid jobs of low complexity who get low rewards for it. In contrast, women who experience work overload, low rewards, and no opportunity for advancement experience work stress, which in turn affects the quality of both their work life and their family life.

Now that dual-career couples are the norm rather than the exception, many companies who formerly imposed rigid time schedules and work demands on their employees are developing more family friendly work schedule policies. They are changing in order to attract and retain young professional women and men who want to perform high quality work outside the home without sacrificing the quality of their family life. This action is consistent with research indicating an increasing tendency for both women and men to trade career advancement to remain in satisfying professional jobs that also provide them with time away from work in which they can enjoy a high quality family life (Shapiro, 1997). Researchers have found that flextime policies are beneficial for both employees and employers. "Workers who have more control over their time have fewer incidences of reported stress, miss fewer days of work, and are more committed to their employers" (Diane Halpern as cited in Crawford, 2003, p.20).

If you are a woman who is contemplating having it all by successfully combining marriage, raising children, and having a career outside the home in a high-powered, non-traditional area, do not change your mind or become disheartened by the research results reported in this section. We are not trying to discourage you from pursuing a non-traditional career in which the job complexity and financial rewards are greater than they are in female dominated professions. Rather, we are attempting to help you become cognizant of the fact that if that is your career choice you will need to proactively plan strategies for managing the competing demands of your professional life and personal life. For example, you will need to make arrangements for sharing the work in the home including child-care with your husband or partner, family members, friends, and/or paid help. Similarly, if you are a man who is contemplating having it all by successfully combining marriage and raising children, with a high-powered traditional career, we encourage you to consider how you will balance your work life and personal life. We also encourage you to consider selecting an employer with family friendly policies so that you will be able to spend quality time with your family without jeopardizing your career success.

Develop Skills that Potential Employers Value

Contrary to what many people think, a college degree does not automatically guarantee a high paying job in one's field of interest. In fact, it may not even guarantee any job in vocational areas in which there are more graduates than jobs available (Mittelhauser, 1998). What are the skills and experiences potential employers are looking for in the college graduates they hire?

Labor market researchers have found that the labor market success of college graduates is highly correlated with the skills college graduates possess. The higher paying college-level jobs require a high level of functional literacy—the ability to read, interpret documents, and perform quantitative calculations in real-life situations (Pryor & Schaffer, as cited in Mittelhauser, 1998). College-educated workers with low functional literacy were more likely to be employed in lower paying jobs requiring a high school education. Since the skills contributing to functional literacy can be learned in various college courses, Pryor and Schaffer point out that success in the labor market is definitely influenced by the efforts of each college student to learn the skills that are needed in the workplace of the future. What other skills are needed to land a high paying job? In our technological society, recent college graduates with computer literacy and information management skills are finding employment easier and more lucrative than graduates without such skills.

According to Sharon Crum Mazyck, Director of the Career Development Office at Rhode Island College, "… when you find out what employers are looking for, you'll find out that they're not only looking at the degree. There are many people out there with degrees. What else have you got? Did you do an internship, volunteer work, paid employment? These are the things they look for." (as cited in Brown, 2001, p.7). While in college, be sure to gain the functional literacy and technical skills and career related experiences that will help your application for a job after graduation stand out from the crowd of other recent college graduates.

Most of our students work in paid employment as well as attend college. One of the suggestions we make to them is to get a job that has relevance to their future career plans. For example, psychology majors should quit the job at the local supermarket and get a part-time job at a mental hospital or outpatient mental health clinic, or in a psychology research program in order to see if they have the interests, skills, and personality to work in the mental health field. Chemistry majors should seek a job in a research laboratory either on campus or at a chemical company. Having worked in a job related to your major will provide you with valuable experience for either graduate school or a career position when you receive your Bachelor's degree.

Photo Courtesy of Rhode Island College.

Be Active in Your College Community

You will attain many very important benefits from becoming an active member of your college community, especially if you choose the activities in which you participate wisely. The first and foremost benefit you will attain is that you'll begin to identify with your college. As you get involved in college activities and meet people, you'll feel that you belong and are accepted there. Researchers have found that students at both two-year and four-year colleges who identify with their college and feel as if they are accepted members of their college community are more likely to graduate from college than those who attend classes and remain socially isolated from faculty members and fellow students.

Researchers who examined long-term persistence of two-year college students found that academic and social integration consistently had positive effects on persistence and completion of a degree. (Pascarella, Smart, & Ethington, 1986, as cited in Johnson, 1997). The researchers concluded that, "Other things being equal, the greater the individual student's level of integration into the social and academic systems of the college, the greater his or her subsequent commitment to the college and the goal of college graduation respectively" (p. 49).

A longitudinal study that surveyed 171 mainly undergraduate commuter students investigated factors that discriminate between students who persist and those who drop out of college. The students were surveyed a number of times during the six years. "Faculty-and staff-student interaction and connection was found to be the most important characteristic distinguishing the retained from the dropout students" (Johnson, 1997, p. 323)

If you participate in college clubs and activities that interest you, a second benefit you will attain from being active in your college community is that you will meet and have the opportunity to network with many people who share your interests. A third benefit is that you will be in a position to network with a club advisor or others you meet in conjunction with college activities, such as a guest speaker, who may become valuable mentors for you.

A fourth benefit you will attain from being active in your college community is that your experiences will help you grow as a person and improve your interpersonal communication, social, and leadership skills. A fifth benefit is that you will be able to demonstrate that you are a well-rounded person who possesses communication, social, and leadership skills and that you are a person who contributes to his or her community. In addition to the many personal rewards, your history of service will be recognized when you send your résumé or portfolio to honors award and scholarship review committees, prospective employers, and graduate school entrance committees.

Bob was a non-traditional student who enrolled at a community college after a decade of working in a restaurant management position. Even though Bob earned a good salary at that job, he left it because he felt that he wanted a job in which he could contribute to the well-being of others. He enjoyed college and became an active and well liked member of the college community, serving in a leadership position on the student senate as well as being a member of the ecology and science clubs. After finishing a psychology of child development course, Bob said that he decided that he wanted to work with children with special needs. He felt that he was particularly well suited for such a job since he had diabetes as a child. When he told his new career plan to an influential person whom he met through his position as student senator, that person told Bob of an available job managing a camp program for children with diabetes, for which he offered to write him a letter of recommendation. Bob landed the job, which has an employee education program that he will rely on to help finance his continuing education.

Don't be like students we know who thought that achieving a high GPA was the only criteria that they needed to achieve their future life goals. Every academic year professors hear many complaints from students who find out the hard way that even having a 4.0 average is not enough to be selected as class valedictorian, to earn prestigious awards and scholarships, or to land their dream job. In addition to having a high GPA, the people selected for honors and other special opportunities invariably have a long history of service within the community in which they live as well as in the college community.

What kind of clubs and activities do colleges offer? The options, which are numerous and varied, typically include clubs for members who share a(n):

- Ethnic group affiliation;
- Professional interest or hobby (e.g., art, computers, education, law, math, medicine, music, photography, psychology, science, theatre);
- Religious affiliation;
- Social concern (e.g., AIDS, gay and lesbian issues, ecology and environmental pollution, women's or men's issues); and
- Student government and services (e.g., student senate, tutoring club).

Look in your college catalog and identify the types of college clubs and activities available. Select one or two groups that you might be interested in joining and make arrangements to find out more about them. If you need more information, contact the specific club advisor or student officers of the club, or your student government office. Once you identify clubs and activities that interest you, consider attending a few activities to see if you feel comfortable with the people involved and then contact the person in charge to find out how to join if you still want to do so. Even if you have many competing home and work obligations, try to make time to become a contributing member of at least one group in your college community. This is a great way to maximize the benefits you gain from college in a way that enhances your personal growth, demonstrates your interest in community activities, and provides an enjoyable social outlet for you.

Create a Mentoring Network

Researchers have found that having a mentor early in one's career is an important secret of success. People who achieve financial success and rise to leadership positions often have had at least one *mentor* or person who acted as a role model, guide, coach, or teacher to them when they first started their career (e.g., Levinson, D. J., 1978; Erinakes, 1980; Sheehy, 1981; Dreher & Ash, 1990). A mentoring relationship with a knowledgeable, skilled master can be very useful to a person learning a new craft or skill or starting a new career because one can learn a great deal of knowledge and skill by serving as an apprentice or protégé to such a person. The apprentice or protégé is in a great position to benefit from lessons learned by the mentor. For example, the protégé can learn invaluable lessons from watching the mentor work, gain supervision from a successful expert in her or his field, and be introduced to other successful people who can also help him or her to achieve success at work. Additionally, the apprentice or protégé typically receives emotional support, encouragement, and glowing, personalized letters of recommendation from a good mentor.

As research exposing the powerful relationship between mentoring and student success is becoming more well known, many colleges and universities are establishing formal mentoring programs that link an incoming student with a successful upper class student with the same interests or college major (Murray, 1998b). If your college or university has such a mentoring program in place, participate fully in it. As an entering or reentering college student, you can learn from the experiences of another student who has been successful in the college program in which you want to be accepted. When you are an upper class student yourself, you can benefit from acting as a mentor and role model to entering students who share your interests.

If you are lucky, you will have several mentors who provide you with support, guidance, and opportunities for personal and professional development. These mentors and your relationships with them might be very different. Nevertheless, each will teach you how to profit from a mentoring relationship and how to become a successful mentor to others. You might even be able to form a mentoring network in which each of your mentors and their protégés are in a mutually supportive relationship (Zahm, 1998).

Create your own mutually supportive mentoring network and receive guidance and support from others while offering it to others in return. How might these mentoring relationships begin? How might they evolve? Begin by establishing a relationship with professors who teach classes you love or people you trust at college or work who seem interested in establishing a mentoring relationship with you, as did Karla who is featured in our student success profile in Chapter 3. Establish relationships with peers who are enrolled in the same courses you are taking with whom you can form a study group. Join college, community, and professional organizations that will give you the opportunity to meet and work with more advanced students and faculty members who share your interests and have a wealth of information about interesting college courses and future career opportunities to share with you.

Joan H. Rollins, Ph.D. and Mary Zahm, Ph.D.

Photo courtesy of Rhode Island College.

Reach out to professionals in your field of interest who are in a position to offer career guidance and advice to you, as Karla did. Participate in a service-learning program in your field of interest so that you might be able to meet a mentor in your community who has the career you desire (McGoldrick, 1998). Join professional groups that share your interest as a student member. Participate in their conferences. Join a mentoring and support group sponsored by a recognized professional organization in your field of career interest to gain access to career related information.

It is becoming easier to contact professionals anywhere in the world now that professional organizations are establishing mentoring and support groups on the Internet. This trend will surely continue to grow in the future. For example, the American Psychological Association's Division 35 (Psychology of Women) members have an online forum called POWR-L, which affords an opportunity for professionals and students to discuss current topics of interest to them and to ask questions about resources in the field. A similar mentoring network was established by the Asian American Psychological Association for it's members (Murray, 1998a). Find addresses for professional organizations and online support groups of interest to you by going to the reference section at your college's library or conducting an online search. You can find addresses for professional organizations and online support groups of interest to you by surfing on the wide world web using http://www.google.com or http://www.ask.com and entering the name of your career area of interest (e.g., computers, education, engineering, law, nursing, psychology) and "professional organization" as keywords. Then go to the site and find out more details about the organizations. If student memberships are offered, consider joining one that interests you. Be sure to note your membership on your résumé or vita.

Complete Internships to Develop Practical Intelligence (Common Sense) for Career Success

Robert J. Sternberg (1997) has developed a *Triarchic Theory of Human Intelligence* that distinguishes among academic-analytical, synthetic-creative, and practical-contextual aspects of human abilities. *Academic-analytical intelligence* is measured by the standard tests of intelligence and is used when one has to compare and contrast, evaluate, or critique material. *Synthetic-creative* abilities are used when one hypothesizes, discovers, or invents as noted in a previous chapter. *Practical-contextual* abilities are applications of one's knowledge to the world (Sternberg, 1988).

Important to success in college and life, particularly in the world of work, is practical intelligence or common sense. What is common sense? Psychologists who study practical intelligence describe it as tacit knowledge, which is characterized by an action-orientation that is procedural (Sternberg, Wagner, Williams, & Horvath, 1995). It is relevant to attaining valued goals. It is also acquired with little help from others. Common sense may be automatic and people may not be conscious of the process they are using. For this reason and the fact that it may be difficult to articulate, people may know more than they can tell. Although there are large individual differences in the extent that people have practical intelligence or common sense, it is independent of intelligence as measured by traditional IQ tests. Some examples of situations that require using practical intelligence would be:

- Deciding what to do in everyday problem situations such as when a landlord won't make repairs;
- Figuring out how to acquire the information needed to fill out a complicated form;
- Deciding how to respond to criticism from a parent or child;
- Figuring out how to get a friend to visit you more often; or
- Deciding what to do when you are passed over for promotion.

Practical intelligence has been related to both successful job interview performance (Fox & Spector, 2000) and management success (Williams & Sternberg as cited in Sternberg et al., 1995). For example, in samples of business managers, their scores on a test of tacit or practical knowledge were related to higher salary, working for a company at the top of the Fortune 500 list, and years of management experience (Wagner & Sternberg, 1985). Among insurance sales persons, those who scored higher on measures of tacit or practical knowledge had higher sales and received more sales awards (Wagner, Rashotte, & Sternberg, 1992, as cited in Sternberg et al., 1995).

People can be trained in tacit or practical knowledge by making explicit "rules of thumb." That is the goal of this book, to help you understand some of the methods for processing information and learning, managing your emotions, identifying and achieving goals, and managing all of the activities you have scheduled with less stress. Discovering these "rules of thumb" could take you many years to develop through common sense, if at all, but our making explicit this body of practical intelligence gained from the research and our years of experience as college professors can greatly increase your tacit or practical intelligence. We highly recommend that you complete internships or service-learning opportunities to help you learn the practical aspects of a career that you might consider entering. When working in your chosen field, pay attention to the advice given by people with years of experience. These are the "rules of thumb" they have developed by coping with many different situations on the job.

Develop a Résumé or Vita to Demonstrate Your Marketability

A résumé or vita is a self-marketing tool that lists your educational, work, and life experiences. You should include information about your internships as well as your career objectives. You should also include other accomplishments such as extracurricular activities and conferences in which you participated, honors and awards you have won, publications or products you produced, professional organizations of which you are a student member, and work skills you have mastered.

It is a good idea to begin to create a résumé early in your college career and to update it frequently as you make progress toward graduation and starting your career. This living document will not only show your progress toward graduation but will also motivate you to gain the skills and experiences you need to set your job application apart from the crowd at graduation time. In your senior year, send your résumé to the career development center at your college so that it can be made available to prospective employers who recruit college graduates on your campus.

Do you know how to create a professional looking résumé that outlines your skills and experiences in a manner that sets you apart from the crowd? If not, get help preparing one that highlights all your capabilities to the best advantage from the people working at your college's writing or career counseling centers, as needed, when applying for scholarships, graduate programs, or jobs. Would you like more tips on how to make yourself more marketable to employers, scholarship committees, or graduate schools? If yes, go to http:// www.ncsu.edu/career/students/major.htm in order to gain access the "The Career Key." This career exploration website was developed for public use by Lawrence K. Jones, Professor Emeritus in the College of Education, North Carolina State University, Raleigh, North Carolina, USA.

Save Samples of Your "Personal Best" Work for Your Job Portfolios

What is a portfolio? Originating in the world of work, a portfolio is a collection of one's work designed to show the array of a seller's products or services. Portfolios are also recognized as a measure of educational gain and can demonstrate student accomplishment in basic academic skills, as noted in a previous chapter (MacKillop, 1994, as cited in Aderman & Choi, 1997; Paris, 1994). Even if you do not intend to apply for course credit for life experiences, develop a portfolio file or treasure trove that you can use to assess your progress and create job portfolios in the future.

Create a portfolio treasure trove using a sturdy protective container and fill it with artifacts and samples of your personal best college work and other important materials and documents that you need to keep for future reference. Store it in a safe place from which you can gain quick access to its contents for creating portfolios for specific purposes, as needed.

When should you start? What should you put in your portfolio treasure trove? Right from the start of your college career, store samples of your *best* work in your portfolio treasure trove. Replace these original samples with better ones as you progress in college. Include samples of your college work and special projects, such as

- essays,
- research papers and reports,
- scientific reports,
- journals,
- collages,
- portfolios,
- computer programs,
- videos,
- multimedia projects, and

- articles written for the school newspaper.

Also include any other artifacts that you might need to retrieve in the future to demonstrate your progress toward your degree and your proficiency in areas in which you might be interested in working, including copies of:

- evidence of any credits granted for previous educational or work experiences;
- the college catalog listing the requirements for graduation as of the year you were accepted into your specific degree program;
- letters documenting any changes to your program of study that were approved by your advisor;
- evidence of clubs and other college activities in which you have participated;
- posters and paper presentations you make at college or professional meetings;
- papers documenting scholarships and awards you win;
- letters of recommendation written about you, if you can access a copy of them; and
- data files you may need to recreate any of your papers or products if you ever need to do so.

How will your portfolio treasure trove and the specific portfolios you create benefit you? The artifacts that you store in your portfolio treasure trove and the specific portfolios you create are invaluable because they are "…a repository of information for you to review and check your progress." (Aderman and Choi, 1997, p. 28). Portfolios also facilitate your job search directly when you construct and use them during a job interview.

Are there guidelines you should follow when constructing your portfolios for prospective employers? In a focus group, Aderman and Choi (1997) solicited suggestions for creating portfolios from prospective employers about the portfolios that college students had brought with them to the interview.

Regarding design, employers suggested:

- Make most of the material reproducible so that applicants can leave copies with the interviewer and keep the original.
- Show selected samples of student work.
- Consider including a photograph of the student "at work."
- Make sure that the portfolio is well organized so that the employer can get an immediate good impression of the applicant's training, credentials, and personal attributes.
- Individualize the portfolio content with some material that shows the student's ideas and creative expression.
- Include a personal essay by the student that addresses common interviewer questions and explains why the applicant will be a good employee. (p. 28)

After interviewing students who brought a portfolio to the interview employers commented:

- Portfolios help the applicant stand out in a crowded field.
- They show that the applicant is well prepared for the interview.

- They stimulate and focus communication during the interview for both the applicant and interviewer (Aderman & Choi, 1997, p. 29).

The results of this research imply that you can demonstrate your proficiencies by creating a portfolio treasure trove and using the materials in it to construct portfolios when you are applying for particular scholarships or jobs. It also illustrates that these treasures are invaluable for helping you document, evaluate, and appreciate your own progress and accomplishments.

A former community college student, Jennifer, developed the habit of creating portfolios highlighting her best work when she was a student teacher in an elementary school classroom. While working as a teacher in a day care center during the past year, she has continued to build her portfolio by including positive evaluations and letters she has received from supervisors, coworkers, and parents. She also has filled a portable file case with examples of successful student projects she has designed and implemented in the day care setting. When she went on a spur of the moment interview for a head teacher position at another center recently, she was able to bring her portfolio and student project file to demonstrate her competence and areas of special expertise. She got the job!

Be an Effective Leader

Take advantage of leadership training programs and opportunities for leadership positions in organizations and activities of interest to you at your college and in your community. Having good leadership skills will be a valuable asset to you when you graduate from college and enter the professional world of work.

A good leader is someone who is able to help the group achieve its goals. So, for example, if you are coach of a basketball team and have a winning season, you are a good leader. If you are sales manager of a company, and the sales of the company keep rising, you are a good leader. Surprisingly, personality and other characteristics of the individual have only a small relationship to whether he or she will be a good leader. Leaders are more likely than non leaders to talk more early in the group process, to be somewhat more intelligent, to be taller, more socially skilled, and more adaptable and flexible than the others in their group (Albright & Forziati, 1995; Malloy & Janowski, 1992; Mann, 1959).

To understand who is likely to be a good leader, we must take aspects of the situation into account as well as personal characteristics. Several theories of leadership say that the effectiveness of the leader results from an interaction of the leader's characteristics and the situation. Fiedler's *Contingency Model of Leadership* (1967; 1978) divides leaders into task-oriented or relationship-oriented depending on their style of interaction with their followers.

- *Task-oriented leaders*—are primarily concerned with getting the job done
- *Relationship-oriented leader*—are concerned with relationships between the workers and want to resolve conflicts that arise and maintain harmony in the group.

The type of leader that is more effective is contingent on the situation in which he or she is leading. According to Fiedler, there are three situational factors that also have to be taken into account in determining which type of leader will be more effective:

- *Positional power* —the degree of power the leader has by virtue of the position (i.e., an army captain has high power, but the President of the PTA has a low power position);
- *Popularity of leader*—how well the leader is liked by the followers; and
- *Task structure*—how well-structured the task is (thinking up creative ideas in a group is unstructured, whereas building a house from blueprints is structured).

When the leader has high power, is well liked, and the task is highly structured, the leader is said to have *high control* in the situation. The leader has *low control* when the leader has low power, is not well liked, and the task is highly unstructured. Fiedler's research studying hundreds of leaders in many different types of groups finds that task-oriented leaders are most effective in situations of either very high (everything is going well), or very low control (things are chaotic). In these situations someone who takes charge and focuses on the task will get the most done. Relationship-oriented leaders, on the other hand, are most effective in situations that are moderate in control. In this case things are going fairly smoothly, and all that is needed is some attention to relationships, conflict, and hurt feelings in the group. Other researchers argue that some leaders deal effectively as both task and relationship leaders, changing their style as the situation requires it. A leader who is capable of exhibiting both styles, as appropriate, is overall a more effective leader (Misumi, 1985).

Analyses of large numbers of studies of gender differences in leadership style indicate that men are more likely to emerge as task-oriented leaders (Eagly & Karau, 1991). Women are more likely to emerge as relationship-oriented leaders and to be more democratic in leadership style (Eagly & Johnson, 1991). Keep in mind, however, that these are average differences and many men have a relationship style and similarly many women have a task oriented style. When women take a more task-oriented, "masculine" approach, however, they are more likely to be evaluated negatively. Women and men, across situations, nevertheless, do not differ in leadership effectiveness (Eagly, Karau, & Makhijani, 1995).

What type of a leader do you tend to be? You are a Relationship-Oriented Leader if you tend to want to find acceptance within your group and have a group in which there is harmony. You are a Task-Oriented Leader if you are motivated to get the task accomplished.

People have to be true to their own personality style when playing a leadership role. However, this research reveals that you should learn to pay attention to situational factors and modify your leadership style, as needed, in order to be effective in a given leadership situation. Perhaps, women and men who have a task-oriented, autocratic style, however, should also make an effort to be democratic by asking for member input in decision making, particularly when the situation is intermediate in favorableness for the leader. Women and men with a relationship style should try to be more task-oriented in very favorable or unfavorable situations. Develop and practice these leadership skills while in college so that you will be ready and able to assume a professional leadership position after graduation.

Success Recommendations

This section contains a summary of the main points in this chapter to help you reflect on and recall what you have learned.

- **Understand How Ability, Past Performance, Self-Efficacy, Outcome Expectations and Performance Attainment Levels Affect Your Career Development Process.** If you are able to master a particular subject area, you are more likely to develop a sense of self-efficacy for that area and to develop the interest and intentions to go into a related career field.

- **Take the Myers-Briggs Type Indicator and Identify Your Psychological and Temperament Types and Careers that are Compatible with Them.** The MBTI is popular among industrial organizational psychologists and career counselors who use it as a tool for predicting people's suitability for various types of jobs, careers, and leadership positions. It is also very popular among college students as a tool for selecting a tentative career and a college major.

- **Take David Keirsey's Temperament Sorter Type II Online and Discover your Possible Career Options.** Keirsey's scale simplifies the 16 Myers-Briggs Psychological Types by specifying only four temperament types: Rational, Idealist, Artisan, and Guardian. You can take Keirsey's scale online at http://ww.keirsey.com and read about what occupations would be suitable for your personality type.

- **Identify Your Personality Type, Strengths, and Work Preferences on the Strong Interest Inventory.** Consider going to your college's career counseling center and asking to have the Strong Interest Inventory (SII) to learn more about your personality type and strengths. You will also gain access to a list of careers that people with your personality type enjoy. Use the results as one of many sources of input when making decisions about your ideal future life career path.

- **Explore Possible Career Paths, Salaries, and Working Conditions.** Do your own checking to get more accurate information for your desired career and geographic area. Look up and reflect on information such as degree and training requirements, typical salaries, and types of workplaces for specific careers in which you are interested.

- **Be Open to Experience and Happenstance in Your Career Decision Making.** Luck plays a role in all of our lives. Take advantage of chance opportunities that arise even if it means a new direction that you never contemplated. Happenstance can lead to exciting career choices.

- **Proactively Evaluate the Demands of Possible Career Options.** Identify the pros and cons of various careers and consider the trade-offs involved before making a final decision. Make sure that the demands of the career (e.g., commuting time, required travel for business, working hours) are compatible with your life vision and values.

- **Develop Skills Employers Value.** Develop the functional literacy and technical skills needed to land a high paying job in the highly competitive job market.

- **Be Active in Your College Community.** Look through your college catalog for a list of clubs and activities. Select several of them that seem most compatible with your talents, interests, abilities, or future career plans and investigate these further. Join at least one club or activity and be a contributing member and leader of your college community.

- **Create a Mentoring Network.** Join student and professional organizations in which you will have an opportunity to meet more advanced students, faculty members, and other professionals who share your interest and might be potential mentors and colleagues. If your college or university has a formal mentoring program in which students are matched with professors or members of the community who have volunteered to be a mentor to someone like you, join it. In time, become a mentor yourself.

- **Develop Practical Intelligence (Common Sense) for Career Success.** In college and life, you will encounter many situations that will require using practical intelligence or common sense to solve personal and professional problems and, thereby, achieve your goals and have your needs and desires satisfied. You can greatly increase your tacit or practical intelligence by developing "rules of thumb" from the results of scholarly research, from listening to "lessons learned through life experience" offered by successful people, and from completing internships or service-learning opportunities for a career that you might consider entering.

- **Create a Dynamic Résumé.** Construct a résumé on the computer so that you can easily add your educational accomplishments and life experiences to it. Seek opportunities to learn skills related to your career interests as well as leadership opportunities so your résumé will stand out from those of the crowd.

- **Start a Portfolio File.** Start a portfolio treasure trove. Fill it with samples of your personal best work. Store it in a safe place where you will be able to gain quick access to your work, as needed, for creating customized portfolios for specific purposes, such as honors awards, scholarship, and job applications.

- **Be an Effective Leader.** Develop the habit of assessing your leadership style (relationship oriented–democratic or task oriented–autocratic) and situational factors (positional power, popularity, task structure) in order to have the ability to modify your leadership style, as needed, to be effective in a variety of leadership positions.

References

ACT, Inc. (2002, November 15). College graduation rates steady despite increase in enrollment. Retrieved April 2, 2003, from http://www.act.org/2002/11–15–02.html

Aderman, B., & Choi, J. (1997) Job portfolio: It's the door opener. *Adult Learning, 8*(4), 26–28.

Albright, L. & Forziati, C. (1995). Cross-situational consistency and perceptual accuracy in leadership. *Personality and Social Psychology Bulletin, 21*, 1269–1276.

Alexander, P. A., Jetton, T. L., & Kulkowich, J. M. (1995). Interrelationship of Knowledge, Interest, and Recall: Assessing a Model of Domain Learning. *Journal of Educational Psychology, 87,* 559–575.

Amabile, T. M. (2001). Beyond talent: John Irving and the Passionate Craft of Creativity. *American Psychologist, 56,* 333–336.

American College Testing Program (1981). *Technical report for the unisex edition of the ACT Interest Inventory (UNIACT).* Iowa City, IA: Author.

American Psychological Association (2003). Guidelines on multicultural education, training, research, practice, and organizational change for psychologists. *American Psychologist, 58,* 377–402.

American Psychological Association (2001). *Publication manual of the American Psychological Association* (5th ed.). Washington, D.C. Author.

Ames, C., & Archer, J. (1988). Achievement in the classroom: Student learning strategies and motivational responses. *Journal of Educational Psychology, 80,* 260–267.

Anaya, G., & Cole, D. G. (1001). Latina/o student achievement: Exploring the influence of student-faculty interactions on college grades. *Journal of College Student Development, 42,* 3–14.

Anderson, M. J., Petros, T. V., Beckwith, B. E., Mitchell, W. W., & Fritz, S. (1991). Individual differences in the effect of time of day on long-term memory access. *American Journal of Psychology, 104,* 241–255.

Arkin, R. M., & Baumgardner, A. H. (1985). Self-handicapping. In J. H. Harvey & G. Weary (Eds)., *Attributions: Basic issues and applications* (pp. 169–202). New York: Academic Press.

Arenson, K. W. (2000, April 13,). Columbia lesson: No lying to professor. *The New York Times*, p. B3.

Aspinwall, L. G., & Taylor, S. E. (1997). A stitch in time: Self-regulation and proactive coping. *Psychological Bulletin*, 121, 417–436.

Astin, A. W. (1993). *What matters in college? Four critical years revisited.* San Francisco: Jossey-Bass.

Atkinson & Shiffrin (1968). Human memory: A control system and its control processes. In K. Spence, (Ed.), *The psychology of learning and motivation* (Vol. 2). New York: Academic Press.

Baddeley, A. D. (1992). The magical number seven: Still magic after all these years? *Psychologcal Review, 101,* 353–356.

Baddeley, A. D. (2002). Is working memory still working? *European Psychologist, 7*(2), 85–97.

Baddeley, A. D., & Longman, D. J. (1978). The influence of length and frequency of training session on the rate of learning to type. *Ergonomics, 2,* 627–635.

Bandalos, D. L., Yates, K., & Thorndike-Christ, T. (1995). Effects of math self-concept, perceived self-efficacy, and attributions for failure and success on test anxiety. *Journal of Educational Psychology, 87,* 611–623.

Bandura, A. (1997). *Self-efficacy: The exercise of control.* New York: W.H. Freeman & Company.

Barnett, R. C., Marshall, N. L., Raudenbush, S. W., & Brennan, R. T. (1993). Gender and the relationship between job experiences and psychological distress: A study of dual-earner couples. *Journal of Personality and Social Psychology, 64,* 794–806.

Barrett, L. F., & Pietromonaco, P. R. (1997). Accuracy of the Five-Factor Model in predicting perceptions of daily social interactions. *Personality and Social Psychology Bulletin, 23,* 1173–1187.

Bartlett, R. L. (1996, Spring). Discovering diversity in introductory economics. *Journal of Economic Perspectives, 10,* 141–153.

Baum, A., & Davis, G. E. (1980). Reducing the stress of high-density living: An architectural intervention. *Journal of Personality and Social Psychology, 38,* 471–481.

Baum, A., Harpin, R. E., & Valins, S. (1975). The role of group phenomena in the experience of crowding. *Environment and Behavior, 7,* 185–198.

Baum, A., & Valins, S. (1979) Architecture and social behavior: Psychological studies of social density. Hillsdale, NJ: Erlbaum.

Baumeister, R. F. (Ed.). (1993). *Self-esteem: The puzzle of low self-regard.* New York: Plenum.

Baumeister, R. F. (Ed.) (1999). *The self in social psychology: Essential readings.* Philadelphia: Psychology Press.

Baumeister, R. F., Bratslavsky, E., Muraven, M., & Tice, D. M. (1998). Ego depletion: Is the active self a limited resource? *Journal of Personality and Social Psychology, 74,* 1252–1265.

Baumgardner, A. H. (1990). To know oneself is to like oneself: Self-certainty and self-affect. *Journal of Personality and Social Psychology, 58,* 1062–1072.

Beck, A. T. (1988). *Love is never enough.* New York: HarperCollins.

Bednar, R. L., Wells, M. G., & Peterson, S. R. (1995). *Self-esteem* (2nd ed.). Washington, DC: American Psychological Association.

Bens, S., & Danielson, J. (2001, July). Retention—The sequel: The development of a first-year experience seminar program at a Canadian university. Paper presented at The Fourteenth International Conference on The First Year experience, in conjunction with the Fifth Pacific Rim First Year in Higher Education Conference. Honolulu, Hawaii.

Bliming, G. S. (1999). A meta-analysis of the influence of college residence halls on academic performance. *Journal of College Student Development, 40,* 551–561.

Bliss, T. V., & Collingridge, G. L. (1993). A synaptic model of memory: long-term potentiation in the hippocampus. *Nature, 361*(6407), 31–39.

Bloom, B. S., Englehart, N. D., Furst, E. J., Hill, W. H., & Krathwohl, D. R. (1956). *Taxonomy of educational objectives. Handbook I: Cognitive domain.* New York: McKay.

Bloom, K. C., & Shuell, T. J. (1981). Effects of massed and distributed practice on the learning and retention of second-language vocabulary. *Journal of Educational Research, 74,* 245–248.

Bornstein, B. H., & Chapman, G. B. (1995). Learning lessons from sunk costs. *Journal of Experimental Psychology: Applied, 1,* 251–269.

Bost, J. M. (1984). Retaining students on academic probation: Effects of time management peer counseling on student's grades. *Journal of Learning Skills. 3*(2), 38–43.

Boulmetis, J., & Sabula, A. M. (1996). Achievement gains via instruction that matches learning style perceptual preferences. *The Journal of Continuing Higher Education, Fall,* 15–24.

Bower, G. H. (1970). Organizational factors in memory. *Cognitive Memory, 1,* 18–46.

Britton, B. K., & Tesser, A. (1991). Effects of time-management practices on college grades. *Journal of Educational Psychology, 83,* 405–410.

Brody, J. E. (1987, March 11). Personal health. *New York Times,* p. C10.

Brody, J. E. (2000, July 30). *The Providence Sunday Journal, Health & Fitness Monthly,* M2.

Broocks, A., Bandelow, B., Pekrun, G., Annette, G., Meyer, T., Bartmann, U., Hillmen-Voger, U.., & Ruether, E. (1998). Comparison of aerobic exercise, clomipramine, and placebo in the treatment of panic disorder. *American Journal of Psychiatry, 155,* 603–609.

Brown, G. (2001, March). Career development in generation X: An interview with Sharon Crum Mazyck. The PSA @ RIC Report. Providence, RI: The Professional Staff Assoc. at Rhode Island College.

Brown, J. D. (1991). Staying fit and staying well: Physical fitness as a moderator of life stress. *Journal of Personality and Social Psychology, 60,* 555–561.

Busato, V. V., Prins, F. J. Elshout, J. J., & Hamaker, C. (2000). Intellectual ability, learning style, personality, achievement motivation and academic success of psychology students in higher education. *Personality & Individual Differences, 29,* 1057–1068.

Butler, D. L. (1998). The Strategic Content Learning approach to promoting self-regulated learning: A report of three studies. *Journal of Educational Psychology, 90*(4), 682–697.

Campbell, J. D. (1990). Self-esteem and clarity of the self-concept. *Journal of Personality and Social Psychology, 59,* 538–549.

Campbell, J. D., Chew, B., & Scratchley, L. S. (1991). Cognitive and emotional reactions to daily events: The effects of self-esteem and self-complexity. *Journal of Personality, 59*(3), 473–505.

Cano-Garcia, F., & Hughes, E. (2000). Learning and thinking styles: An analysis of their interrelationship and influence on academic achievement. *Educational Psychology, 20,* 413–430.

Carver, C. S., Reynolds, S. L., & Scheier, M. F. (1994). The possible selves of optimists and pessimists. *Journal of Research in Personality, 28,* 133–141.

Ciarrochi, J., Chan, A., Caputi, P., & Roberts, R. (2001). Measuring emotional intelligence. In J. Ciarrochi, J. P. Forgas, & Mayer, J. D. (Eds.), *Emotional intelligence in everyday life: A scientific inquiry* (pp. 25–45). Philadelphia: Psychology Press.

Cisero, C. A., Royer, J. M., Marchant, H. G., & Jackson, S. J. (1997). Can the Computer-Based Academic Assessment System (CAAS) be used to diagnose reading disability in college students? *Journal of Educational Psychology, 89*(4), 599–620.

Cohn, E., Cohn, S., & Bradley Jr, J. (1995). Notetaking, working memory, and learning in principles of economics. *Journal of Economic Education, 26*(4), 291–207.

Collins, J. M., & Gleaves, D. H. (1998). Race, job applicants, and the Five-Factor model of personality: Implications for Black psychology, industrial/organizational psychology, and the Five-Factor theory. *Journal of Applied Psychology, 83,* 531–544.

Cooley, C. H. (1902). *Human nature and social order.* New York: Scribner's.

Coopersmith, S. (1967). *The antecedents of self-esteem.* San Francisco: W. H. Freeman.

Covey, S. R. (1989). *The 7 habits of highly effective people: Restoring the character ethic.* New York: Simon & Schuster.

Covey, S. R. (1999). *Living the 7 habits*. New York: Simon & Schuster.

Crawford, N. (2003, May). Conference examined healthy workplace issues. *Monitor on Psychology*, p. 20.

Crowder, R. G. (1993). Short-term memory: Where do we stand? *Memory and Cognition, 21,* 142–145.

Csikszentmihalyi, M. (1990). *Flow: The psychology of optimal experience*. New York: HarperCollins.

Csikszentmihalyi, M. (1999). If we are so rich, why aren't we happy? *American Psychologist, 54,* 821–827.

Curry, L. A., Snyder, C. R., Cook, D. L., Ruby, B. C., & Rehm, M. (1997). Role of hope in academic and sport achievement. *Journal of Personality and Social Psychology, 73,* 1257–1267.

D'Esposito, M., Detre, J. A., Alsop, D. C., Shin, R. K., Atlas, S., & Grossman, M (1995). The neural basis for the central executive system of working memory. *Nature, 378,* 279–281.

Dickinson, D. J., O'Connell, D. Q., & Dunn, J. S. (1996). Distributed study, cognitive study strategies and aptitude on student learning. *Psychology: A Journal of Human Behavior,* (33), 31–39.

Digman, J. M. (1997). Higher-order factors of the Big Five. *Journal of Personality and Social Psychology, 73,* 1246–1256.

Diehl, M., & Stroebe, W. (1987). Productivity loss in brainstorming groups: Toward the solution of a riddle. *Journal of Personality & Social Psychology, 53,* 497–509.

Dreher, G. F., & Ash, R. A. (1990). A comparative study of mentoring among men and women in managerial, professional, and technical positions. *Journal of Applied Psychology, 75,* 539–546.

Dreher, M. J. & Brown, R. F. (1993) Planning prompts and indexed terms in textbook search tasks. *Journal of Educational Psychology, 85,* 662–669.

Dreher, M. J. & Guthrie, J. T. (1990). Cognitive processes in textbook chapter search tasks. *Reading Research Quarterly, 25,* 323–339.

Diehll, M., Driskell, J. E., Willis, R. P., & Copper, C. (1992). Effect of overlearning on retention. *Journal of Applied Psychology, 77,* 615–622.

Dugosh, K. L., Paulus, P. B., Roland, E. J., & Yang, H-C. (2000). Cognitive simulation in brainstorming. *Journal of Personality and Social Psychology, 79, 722–735.*

Dunifon, R., & Duncan, G. J. (1998). Long-run effects of motivation on labor-market success. *Social Psychology Quarterly, 61,* 33–48.

Dweck, C. S. (1986). Motivational processes affecting learning. *American Psychologist, 41,* 1040–1048.

Dweck, C. S. (1999). *Self-Theories: Their role in motivation, personality, and development*. New York: Psychology Press.

Dweck, C. S., & Leggett, E. L. (1988). A social-cognitive approach to motivation and personality. *Psychological Review, 25,* 109–116.

Eagly, A. H., & Johnson, B. J. (1991). Gender and leadership style: A meta-anlaysis. *Journal of Personality and Social Psychology, 60,* 685–710.

Eagly, A. H., & Karau, S. J., (1991). Gender and the emergence of leaders: A meta-analysis *Journal of Personality and Social Psychology, 60,* 685–710.

Eagly, A. H., Karau, S. J., & Makhijani, M. G. (1995). Gender and the effectiveness of leaders: A meta-analysis. *Psychological Bulletin, 117,* 125–145.

Ebbinghaus, H. (1885/1964). *Memory: A contribution to experimental psychology* (H. A. Ruger & E. R. Bussemius, Trans.). New York: Appleton-Century Crofts. (Original work published, 1885).

Eccles, J. S. (1987). Gender roles and women's achievement-related decisions. *Psychology of Women Quarterly, 11,* 135–172.

Ehrlich, M. F., & Tardieu, H. (1991). Slow and fast adult readers in text comprehension. *European Journal of Psychology of Education, 6,* 337–349.

Eichenbaum, H. (1997). Declarative memory: Insights from cognitive neurobiology. *Annual Review of Psychology, 48,* 547–572.

Elias, M. J., Hunter, L., & Kress, J. S. (2001). Emotional intelligence and education. In J. Ciarrochi, J. P. Forgas, & J. D. Mayer (Eds.), *Emotional intelligence in everyday life: A scientific inquiry* (pp. 133–149). Philadelphia: Psychology Press.

Elliot, E. S., & Dweck, C. S. (1988). An approach to motivation and achievement. *Journal of Personality and Social Psychology, 54,* 5–12.

Elliot, A. J., McGregor, H. A., & Gable, S. (1999). Achievement goals, study strategies, and exam performance: A mediational analysis. *Journal of Educational Psychology, 91,* 549–563.

Elliot, A. J., & Sheldon, K. M. (1997). Avoidance achievement motivation: A personal goals analysis. *Journal of Personality and Social Psychology, 73,* 171–185.

Entwistle, N. (1983). Learning and teaching in universities: The challenge of the part-time adult student. In R. Bourne (Ed.), *Part-time first degrees in universities.* London: Goldsmiths' College. (Available from ISEM, 10429 Barnes Way, St. Paul, MN 5507)

Epstein, S., & Meier P. (1989). Constructive thinking: A broad coping variable with specific components. *Journal of Personality and Social Psychology,* 57, 332–350.

Epstein, S., Pacini, R., Denes-Raj, & Heier, H. (1996). Individual differences in intuitive-experiential and analytical-rational thinking styles. *Journal of Personality and Social Psychology, 71,* 390–405.

Erinakes, D. M. (1980). An analysis of women elementary school principals and long term women teachers in relation to selected psychological and situational variable. (Doctoral Dissertation, University of Connecticut, 1980).

Erwin-Grabner, T., Goodill, S. W., Hill, E. S., & Von Neida, K. (1999). Effectiveness of dance/movement therapy on reducing test anxiety. *American Journal of Dance Therapy, 23*(1), 19–34.

Etnier, J. L., Salazar, W., Landers, D. M., Petruzzello, S. J., Han, M., & Nowell, P. (1997). The influence of physical fitness and exercise upon cognitive functioning: A meta-analysis. *Journal of Exercise Psychology, 19,* 249–277.

Feist, G. J. (1998). A meta-analysis of personality in scientific and artistic creativity. *Personality and Social Psychology Review, 2,* 290–309.

Ferrari, M., Bouffard, T, Rainville, L. (1998). What makes a good writer? Differences in good and poor writers' self-regulation of writing. *Instructional Science, 26,* 473–488.

Fiedler, F. E. (1971). *Leadership.* Morristown, NJ: General Learning Press.

Fiedler, F. E. (1981). Leadership effectiveness. *American Behavioral Scientist, 24,* 619–632.

Fiedler, F. E. (1993). The leadership situation and the black box in contingency theories. In M. M. Chemers & R. Ayman (Eds.), *Leadership theory and research: Perspectives and directions* (pp. 1–28). San Diego: Academic Press.

Fouad, N. A., Smith, P. L., & Zao, K. E. (2002). Across academic domains: Extensions of the social-cognitive career model. *Journal of Counseling Psychology, 49,* 164–171.

Fox, S., & Spector, P. E. (2000). Relations of emotional intelligence, practical intelligence, general intelligence, and trait affectivity with interview outcomes: It's not all just 'G'. *Journal of Organizational Behavior, 21,* 203–220.

Friend, R. (Dec. 2000/ Jan. 2001). Teaching summarization as a content area reading strategy. *Journal of Adolescent and Adult Literacy, 44,* 320–329.

Friend, R. (2001). Effects of strategy instruction on summary writing of college students. *Contemporary Educational Psychology, 26,* 3–24.

Fromm, E. (1965). *Escape from freedom.* New York: Avon Books.

Gandara, P., & Lopez, E. (1998). Latino students and college entrance exams: How much do they really matter? *Hispanic Journal of Behavioral Sciences, 20,* 17–38.

Gardner, H. (1993). *Frames of mind: The theory of multiple intelligences.* New York: Basic Books.

Gardner, H. (1999). *Intelligence reframed: Multiple intelligences for the 21st century.* New York, NY: Basic Books.

George, J. M., & Zhou, J. (2001). When openness to experience and conscientiousness are related to creative behavior: An interactional approach. *Journal of Applied Psychology, 86,* 513–524.

Gilbert, D. T., Krull, D. S., & Malone, P. S. (Oct, 1990). *Journal of Personality and Social Psychology.* Unbelieving the unbelievable: Some problems in the rejection of false information, *59*(4), 601–613.

Gilbert, D. T., Tafarodi, R. W., & Malone, P. S. (1993). You can't not believe everything you read. *Journal of Personality and Social Psychology, 65,* 221–233.

Gobet, F., & Simon, H. A. (1996). Recall of random and distorted chess positions: Implications for the theory of expertise. *Memory and Cognition, 24,* 493–503.

Goodwin, D. W. (1969). Alcohol and recall: State-dependent effects in man. *Science, 163,* 1358–1360.

Gose, B. (1996). Minority students were 24% of college enrollment in 1994. *The Chronicle of Higher Education, 42,* A32.

Grant, H., & Dweck, C. S. (2003). Clarifying achievement goals and their impact. *Journal of Personality and Social Psychology, 85*(3), 541–553.

Habley, W. (2001, April). "More first-year college students return for second year; Fewer students graduate." ACT, Inc.. Retrieved May 19, 2001, from http://www.act.org/news/)

Haffner, K. (2001, June 28). Lessons in the school of cut and paste. *The New York Times,* pp. E1, E6.

Halpern, D. F. (1997). Sex differences in intelligence implications for education. *American Psychologist, 52*(10), 1091–1102.

Halpern, D. F. (1998). Teaching critical thinking for transfer across domains. *American Psychologist, 53,* 449–455.

Harackiewicz, J. M., Barron, K. E., Carter, S. M., Lehto, A. T., & Elliot, A. J. (1997). Predictors and consequences of achievement goals in the college classroom: Maintaining interest and making the grade. *Journal of Personality and Social Psychology, 73,* 1284–1295.

Hatcher, R. R., & Pond, B. N. (1998). Standardizing organizational skills for student success. *Phi Delta Kappan, 79*(9), 715–717.

Heatherton, T. F., & Polivy, J. (1991). Development and validation of a scale for measuring state self-esteem. *Journal of Personality and Social Psychology, 60*, 895–910.

Hebel, S. (2000, June 14). U.S. workers value general skills over specific ones, survey on education finds. *Chronicle of Higher Education, 45*(42), p. A4.

Heishman, S. J., Arasteh, K., Stitzer, M. L. (1997). *Pharmacology, Biochemistry & Behavior, 58,* 93–101.

Higher Education and National Affairs Council on Education (HENA) (2002, December, 9). "Facts in brief: Community college attrition related to first-year attendance status." Retrieved April 2, 2003, from http://www.acenet.edu/hena/facts in brief/.

Hoff–Macan, T., Sahani, C., Dipboye, R. L., & Phillips, A. P. (1990). College students time management: Correlations with academic performance and stress. *Journal of Educational Psychology, 82*, 760–768.

Holland, J. L. (1985). *Making vocational choices: A theory of careers.* Englewood Cliffs, NJ: Prentice-Hall.

Holland, J. L. (1997). *Making vocational choices: A theory of vocational personalities and work environments* (3rd ed.). Odessa, FL: Psychological Assessment Resources.

Hong, Y., Chiu, C., Dweck, C. S., Lin, D. M. S., & Wan, W. (1999). Implicit theories, attributions, and coping: A meaning system approach. *Journal of Personality and Social Psychology, 77,* 588–599.

Hull, R. F. C. (1971). *The portable Jung.* New York: Viking.

Individuals With Disabilities Education Act of 1990 (1990). *Federal Register*, Pub. L., No. 94–142.

Inzlicht, M., & Ben-Zeev, T. (2000). A threatening intellectual environment: Why females are susceptible to experiencing problem-solving deficits in the presence of males. *Psychological Science, 11,* 365–371.

Jakubowski, P., & Lange, A. J. (1978*). The assertive option: Your rights and responsibilities.* Champaign, Il: Research Press.

Janis, I. L. (1982). *Victims of groupthink (2nd ed.).* Boston, MA: Houghton Mifflin.

Johnson, J. L. (1997). Commuter college students: What factors determine who will persist or who will drop out? *College Student Journal, 31*(3), p. 323–332.

Kavale, K. A., & Forness, S. R. (1987). Substance over style: Assessing the efficacy of modality testing and teaching. *Exceptional Children, 54,* 228–239.

Keppel, G., & Underwood, B. J. (1962). Retroactive inhibition of R-S associations. *Journal of Experimental Psychology, 64,* 400–404.

Kidwell, B., & Turrisi, R. (2000). A cognitive analysis of credit card acquisition and college student financial development. *Journal of College Student Development, 41,* 589–598.

Keirsey, D. (1998). *Please understand me II: Temperament, character, intelligence.* Del Mar, CA: Prometheus Nemesis Book Co.

Kiewra, K. A. (1991). Aids to lecture learning. *Educational Psychologist, 26,* 37–53.

King, L. A. (2001). The health benefits of writing about life goals. *Personality and Social Psychology Bulletin, 27,* 799–807.

Kirschenbaum, D. S., Malett, S. D., & Humphrey, L. (1982). Specificity of planning and maintenance of self–control: A one year follow-up of a study improvement program. *Behavior Therapy, 13,* 232–242.

Klaczynski, P. A., Gordon, D. H., & Fauth, J. (1997). Goal-oriented critical reasoning biases. *Journal of Educational Psychology, 89*, 470–485.

Klein, S. B., & Loftus, J. (1988). The nature of self-referent encoding: The contributions of elaborative and organizational processes. *Journal of Personality and Social Psychology, 55*, 5–11.

Kolb, D. (1984). *Experiential learning: Experience as a source of learning and development.* Englewood Cliffs, NJ: Prentice-Hall.

Kolb, D. A., Osland, J. S., & Rubin, I. M. (1995). *Organizational behavior: An experiential approach* (6th ed.). Englewood Cliffs, NJ: Prentice-Hall.

Korsgaard, M. A., Roberson, L., & Rymph, R. D. (1998). What motivates fairness? The role of subordinate assertive behavior on managers' interactional fairness. *Journal of Applied Psychology, 83*(5), 731–744.

Koss, M. P., & Burkhart, B. R. (1989). A conceptual analysis of rape victimization: Long-term effects and implications for treatment. *Psychology of Women Quarterly, 13*, 27–40.

Kosslyn, S., Seger, C., Pani, J. R., & Hillger, L. A. (1990). *Journal of Mental Imagery, 14*(3–4), 131–152.

Krug, D., Davis, T. B., & Glover, J. A. (1990). Massed versus distributed repeated reading: A case of forgetting helping recall? *Journal of Educational Psychology, 82*, 366–371.

Lakein, A. (1973). *How to get control of your time and your life.* New York: Signet.

Landman, J., Vandewater, A. A., Stewart, A. J., & Malley, J. E. (1995). Missed opportunities: Psychological ramifications of counterfactual thinking in midlife women. *Journal of Adult Development, 2*, 87–97.

Lattimore, R. R., & Borgen, F. H. (1999). Validity of the 1994 Strong Interest Inventory with racial and ethnic minority groups in the United States. *Journal of Counseling Psychology, 46*(2), 185–195.

Lee, F. K., Sheldon, K. M., & Turban, D. B., (2003). Personality and the goal-striving process: The influence of achievement goal patterns, goal level, and mental focus on performance and enjoyment. *Journal of Applied Psychology, 88*, 256–265.

Leith, K. P., & Baumeister, R. F. (1996). Why do bad moods increase self-defeating behavior? Emotions, risk taking, and self-regulation. *Journal of Personality and Social Psychology, 71*, 1250–1267.

Lennon, M. C. (1987). Sex differences in distress: The impact of gender and work roles. *Journal of Health and Social Behavior, 28*, 290–305.

Lindgren, H. C. (1969). *The dynamics of college success: A dynamic approach.* New York: Wiley.

Linville, P. W. (1987). Self-complexity and affective extremity: Don't put all your eggs in one cognitive basket. *Social Cognition, 3*, 94–120.

Locke, E. A., & Latham, G. P. (1990). Work motivation and satisfaction: Light at the end of the tunnel, *Psychological Science, 1*, 240–246.

Logie, R. H., Cocchini, G., Della Sala, S. & Baddeley, A. D. (2004). Is There a Specific Executive Capacity for Dual Task Coordination? Evidence From Alzheimer's Disease. *Neuropsychology, 18*(3), 504–513.

Loftus, E. F., Loftus, G. R., & Messo, J. (1987). Some facts about "weapon focus." *Law and Human Behavior, 11*, 55–62.

Lorentz, S. C., Maton, K. L., & Greene, M. L. (2001). Definitions of success, reasons for lack of success, and messages of encouragement for peers: Views of academically successful African-American women. Poster presented at the annual meeting of the Eastern Psychological Association.

Lucas, M. S. & Epperson, D. L. (1990). Types of vocational undecidedness: A replication and refinement. *Journal of Counseling Psychology, 37,* 382–388.

Luzzo, D. A., Hasper, P., Albert, K. A., Bibby, M. A., & Martinelli, E. A., Jr. (1999). Effects of self-efficacy interventions on the math/science self-efficacy and career interests, goals, and actions of career undecided college students. *Journal of Counseling Psychology, 46*(2), 233–243.

Lynn, R., & Mau, W. C. (2001). Ethnic and sex differences in the predictive validity of the Scholastic Achievement Test for college grades. *Psychological Reports, 88,* 1099–1104.

Maas, A., Colombo, A., Sherman, S. J., & Colombo A. (2001). Inferring traits from behaviors versus behaviors from traits: The induction-deduction asymmetry. *Journal of Personality and Social Psychology, 81,* 391–404.

Maddux, J. E. (1991). Self-efficacy. In C. R. Snyder & D. R. Forsyth (Eds.) *Handbook of social and clinical psychology: The health perspective* (pp. 57–78). New York: Pergamon Press.

Makin, D. J., & Hoyle, P. J. (1993). The Premack Principle: Professional engineers. *Leadership and Organization Development Journal, 14,* 16–21.

Malloy, T. E., & Janowski, C. L. (1992). Perceptions and metaperceptions of leadership: Components, accuracy, and dispositional correlates. *Personality and Social Psychology Bulletin, 18,* 700–708.

Mann, R. D. (1959). A review of the relationships between personality and performance in small groups. *Psychological Bulletin, 56,* 241–270.

Martin, G. L., & Osborne, J. G. (1989). *Psychology: Adjustment and everyday living.* Englewood Cliffs, NJ: Prentice Hall.

Martinez-Pons, M. (1997). The relation of emotional intelligence with selected areas of personal functioning. *Imagination, Cognition and Personality, 17*(3), 3–13.

Maton, Hrabowski, F. A., III , & Grief, (1998). Preparing the way: A qualitative study of high-achieving African American males and the role of the family. *American Journal of Community Psychology, 26,* 639–668.

Mayer, J. D., & Salovey, P. (1993). The intelligence of emotional intelligence. *Intelligence, 17,* 433–442.

McClanaghan, M. E. (2000). A strategy for helping students learn how to learn. *Education, 120*(3), 479–486.

McCrae, R. R., & Costa, P. T. (1994). The stability of personality: Observation and evaluations. *Current Directions in Psychological Science, 3,* 173–175.

McCaulley, M. H. (2000). Myers-Briggs Type Indicator: A bridge between counseling and consulting. *Consulting Psychology Journal: Practice and Research, 52*(2), 117–132.

McCutchen, D., Francis, M. & Kerr, S. (1997). Revising for meaning: Effects of knowledge and strategy. *Journal of Educational Psychology, 89,* 667–676.

McEntee, D. J. , & Halgin, R. P. (1999). Cognitive group therapy and aerobic exercise in the treatment of anxiety. *Journal of College Student Psychotherapy, 13,* 37–55.

McGregor, I., & Little, B. R. (1998). Personal projects, happiness, and meaning: On doing well and being yourself. *Journal of Personality and Social Psychology, 74,* 494–512.

Meece, J. L., Blumenfeld, P. C., & Hoyle, R. H. (1988). Students' goal orientations and cognitive engagement in classroom activities. *Journal of Educational Psychology, 80,* 514–523.

Mehrabian, A. Beyond IQ: Broad-based measurement of individual success potential or "Emotional intelligence." *Genetic, Social, and General Psychology Monographs, 126*(2), 133–239.

Miller, G. A. (1956). The magical number seven plus or minus two: Some limits on our capacity for processing information. *Psychological Review, 63,* 81–97.

Mishel, W., Ebbeson, E. B., & Zeiss, A. (1972). Cognitive and attentional mechanisms in delay of gratification. *Journal of Personality and Social Psychology, 21,* 204–218.

Mistlberger, R. E., & Rusak, B. (1989). Mechanisms and models of the circadian timekeeping system. In M. H. Kryger, T. Roth, & W. C. Dement (Eds.), *Principles and practice of sleep medicine* (pp. 141–152). Philadelphia: W. B. Saunders.

Misumi, J. (1985). *The behavioral science of leadership.* Ann Arbor: University of Michigan Press.

Mitchell, K. E., Levin, A. S., & Krumboltz, J. D. (2003). Planned happenstance: Constructing unexpected career opportunities. *Journal of Counseling & Development, 77,* 115–124.

Mittelhauser, M. (1998, Summer). The outlook for college graduates, 1996–2006: Prepare yourself. Number of college graduates exceeds college-level jobs. *Occupational Outlook Quarterly, 42*(2), 3–9.

Morgan, H. J., & Janoff-Bulman, R. (1994). Positive and negative self-complexity: Patterns of adjustment following traumatic versus non-traumatic life experiences. *Journal of Clinical Psychology, 13,* 16–85.

Morgan, C., Isaac, J. D., & Sansone, C. (2001). The role of interest in understanding the career choices of female and male college students. *Sex Roles, 44,* 295–320.

Moyers, B. (1988; Audio taped in 1990). *Joseph Campbell's The Power of Myth, Volume 3: The First Storytellers.* St Paul, MN: High Bridge Company.

Muraven, M., & Baumeister, R. F. (2000). Self-Regulation and Depletion of Limited Resources: Does Self-Control Resemble a Muscle? *Psychological Bulletin, 126*(2), 247–259.

Muraven, M., Tice, D. M., & Baumeister, R. F. (1998). Self-control as limited resource: Regulatory depletion patterns. *Journal of Personality and Social Psychology, 74,* 774–789.

Murray, B. (1998a, November). Mentoring via the Internet is thriving. *Monitor on Psychology.* Washington, DC: American Psychological Association, p. 34.

Murray, B. (1998b, December). Peer mentoring gives rookies 'inside advice'. *Monitor on Psychology.* Washington, DC: American Psychological Association, p. 30.

Myers, I. B. (1992). *Introduction to type.* Palo Alto, CA: Consulting Psychologists Press.

Myers, I. B., & McCaulley, M. H. (1985). *Manual: A guide to the development and use of the Myers-Briggs Type Indicator.* Palo Alto, CA: Consulting Psychologists Press.

National Center for Education Statistics (NCES) (1998, March). *Gender differences in earnings among young adults entering the labor market.* U.S. Department of Education, Office of Educational Research and Improvement.

Nauta, M. M., & Epperson, D. L. (2003). A longitudinal examination of the social-cognitive model applied to high school girls' choices of nontraditional college majors and aspirations. *Journal of Counseling Psychology, 50,* 448–457.

Neck, C. P., & Manz, C. C. (1992). Thought self-leadership: The influence of self-talk and mental imagery on performance. *Journal of Organizational Behavior. 13,* 681–699.

Nelson, W. L. (1994). Receptivity to institutional assistance: An important variable for African-American and Mexican-American student achievement. *Journal of College Student Development, 35,* 378–383.

Neufeldt, V., & Guralnik, D. B. (Eds.) (1994). *Webster's New World Dictionary of American English* (3rd College ed*.).* New York: Macmillan.

Norvell, N. , & Belles, D. (1993). Psychological and physical health benefits of circuit weight training in law enforcement personnel. *Journal of Consulting and Clinical Psychology, 61,* 520–527.

Orange, C. (1997). Gifted students and perfectionism. *Roeper Review*, *20*(1), p. 39 (3p, 2 charts). Item Number: 9710254859.

Paris, S.G. (1994*). Becoming reflective students and teachers with portfolios and authentic assessment.* Washington, DC: American Psychological Association.

Park, C. L., Moore, P. J., Turner, R. A., & Adler, N. E. (1997). The roles of constructive thinking and optimism in psychological and behavioral adjustment during pregnancy. *Journal of Personality and Social Psychology, 73,* 584–592.

Pascarella, E. T. , Palmer, B., Moye, M., & Pierson, C. T. (2001). Do diversity experiences influence the development of critical thinking? *Journal of College Student Development, 42*(3), 257–271.

Pauk, W. (2000). *How to Study in college,* 7th ed. Boston, MA: Houghton Mifflin Company.

Pauk, W., & Fiore, J. P. (2000). *Succeed in college,* 5th ed. Boston, MA: Houghton Mifflin Company.

Paul, R. W. (1995). *Critical thinking: How to prepare students for a rapidly changing world.* Santa Rosa, CA: Foundation for Critical Thinking.

Peterson, L. R., & Peterson, M. J. (1959). Short-term retention of individual verbal items. *Journal of Experimental Psychology, 58,* 193–198.

Pham, L. B., & Taylor, S. E. (1999). From thought to action: Effects of process-versus outcome-based mental simulations on performance. *Personality and Social Psychology Bulletin, 25,* 250–260.

Philbin, M., Meier, E., Huffman, S. & Boverie, P. (1995). A survey of gender and learning styles. *Sex Roles, 32,* 485–494.

Pike, G. (1999). The effects of residential learning communities and traditional living arrangements on educational gains during the first year of college. *Journal of College Student Development, 40,* 269–284.

Pinto, M. B., Parente, D. H., & Palmer, T. S. (2001). College student performance and credit card usage. *Journal of College Student Development, 42*, 49–58.

Pokay, P., & Blumenfeld, P. C. (1990). Predicting achievement early and late in the semester: The role of motivation and use of learning strategies. *Journal of Educational Psychology, 82*, 41–51.

Pugh, S. L., & Pawan, F.. (1991). Reading, writing and academic literacy (pp. 1–27). In R. F. Flippo and D. C. Caverly. *College reading & study strategy programs.* Newark, DE: International Reading Association.

Reed, J. L. H., & Shallert, D. L. (1993). The nature of involvement in academic discourse tasks. *Journal of Educational Psychology, 85*, 253–266.

Reisberg, D. (1997). *Cognition: Exploring the science of the mind.* New York: Norton.

Reisberg, L. (1999, June 25). For new graduates, road to riches is paved with computer skills. *The Chronicle of Higher Education, 45*(42), p. A51.

Reisberg, L. (2000, June 16). 10% of Students May Spend Too Much Time Online. *The Chronicle of Higher Education, 46*(41), p. A43.

Rideout, B. E., & Taylor, J. (1997). Enhanced spatial performance following 10 minutes exposure to music: A replication. *Perceptual & Motor Skills, 85,* 112–113.

Robbins, R. W., & Pals, J. L. (2002). Implicit self-thories in the academic domain:Implications for goal orientation, attributions, affect, and self-esteem. *Self and Identity, 1*, 313–336.

Roese, N. J. (1997). Counterfactual thinking. *Psychological Bulletin, 121*(1), 133–148.

Rogers, C. R. (1961). *On becoming a person: A therapist's view of psychotherapy.* Boston, MA: Houghton Mifflin Company.

Rollins, J. H. (2003, November). *Beyond SATs: Strategies for College Success.* Presidential Address presented at the 43rd annual meeting of the New England Psychological Association: Salem, MA.

Rollins, J. H., Zahm, M., Merenda, P. F., & Burkholder, G. (2002). Development of the Student Success Scale to predict non-intellectual factors related to student retention and achievement. *Issues in Teaching and Learning, 1*(1), Providence, RI: Rhode Island College.

Roney, C., Higgins, E. T., & Shah, J. (1995). Goals and framing: How outcome focus influences motivation and emotion. *Personality and Social Psychology Bulletin, 21*, 1151–1160.

Russell, R. J. H., & Wells, P. A. (1994). Predictors of happiness in married couples. *Personality and Individual Differences. 17,* 313–321.

Sadler-Smith, E. (2001) The relationship between learning style and cognitive style. *Personality and Individual Differences, 30,* 609–616.

Salovey, P. (2001). Applied emotional intelligence: Regulating emotions to become healthy, wealthy, and wise. In J. Ciarrochi, J. P. Forgas, & J. D. Mayer (Eds.). *Emotional intelligence in everyday life: A scientific inquiry* (pp. 168–204). Philadelphia: Psychology Press.

Sanday, P. R. (1990). *Fraternity gang rape: Sex, brotherhood and privilege on campus.* New York: New York University Press.

Sandelands, L. E., Brockner, J., & Glynn, M. A. (1988). If at first you don't succeed, try, try again. Effects of persistence performance contingencies, ego involvement and self esteem on task persistence. *Journal of Applied Psychology, 73,* 208–218.

Sax, L. J., Astin, A.W. , Korn, W.S., & Mahoney, K. M. (2000). *The American freshman national norms for fall 2000.* The Higher Education Research Institute, UCLA Graduate School of Education & Information Studies, 3005 Moore Hall, Box 951521, Los Angeles, CA 90095–1521.

Schacter, D. L. (2001). *The seven sins of memory: How the mind forgets and remembers.* New York: Houghton Mifflin Company.

Schacter, D. L. (1996). *Searching for memory: The brain, the mind, and the past.* New York: Basic Books.

Schacter, D. L. (1992). Understanding implicit memory: A cognitive neuroscience approach. *American Psychologist, 47,* 559–569.

Schacter, D. L. (1987). Implicit memory: History and current status. *Journal of Experimental Psychology: Learning, Memory, and Cognition, 13,* 501–518.

Schaefers, K. G., Epperson, D. L., & Nauta, M. M. (1997). Women's career development: Can theoretically derived variables predict persistence in engineering majors? *Journal of Counseling Psychology, 44*(2), 173–183.

Schmeck, R. R. (1988). *Learning strategies and learning styles.* New York: Plenum Press.

Schmeichel, B. J., Vohs, K. D., & Baumeister, R. F., (2003). Intellectual Performance and Ego Depletion: Role of the Self in Logical Reasoning and Other Information Processing. *Journal of Personality and Social Psychology, 85*(1), 33–46.

Schowers, C. J., & Ryff, C. D. (1996). Self-differentiation and well-being in a life transition. *Personality and Social Psychology Bulletin, 22,* 448–460.

Schutte, N. S., Malouff, J. M., Hall, L. E., Haggarty, D. J., Cooper, J. T., Golden, C. J., & Dornheim, L. (1998). Development and validation of a measure of emotional intelligence. *Personality and Individual Difference, 25,* 167–177.

Schwartz, P. (1994). *Love between equals: How peer marriage really works.* New York: The Free Press.

Semb, G. B., Ellis, J. A., & Araujo, J. (1993). Long-term memory for knowledge learned in school. *Journal of Educational Psychology, 85, 305–316.*

Schaefers, K. G., Epperson, D. L., & Nauta, M. M. (1997). Women's career development: Can theoretically derived variables predict persistence in engineering majors? *Journal of Counseling Psychology, 44*(2), 173–183.

Shapiro, L. (1997). The myth of quality time: Working parents spend too little time with their children. *Newsweek, 129*(19), pp. 62–69.

Sheehy, G. (1981). *Pathfinders.* New York: Morrow.

Sheldon, K. M., & Elliot, A. J. (1998). Not all personal goals are personal: Comparing autonomous and controlled reasons for goals as predictors of effort and attainment. *Personality and Social Psychology Bulletin. 24*(5), 546–557.

Sheldon, K. M., Ryan, R. M., Rawsthorne, L. J., & Ilardi, B. (1997). Trait self and true self: Cross-role variation in the Big-Five personality traits and its relation with psychological authenticity and subjective well-being. *Journal of Personality and Social Psychology, 73,* 1380–1393.

Shell, D. F, Murphy, & Bruning (1989). Self-efficacy and outcome expectancy mechanisms in reading and writing achievement. *Journal of Educational Psychology, 81,* 91–100.

Shiffrin, R. M., & Atkinson, R. C. (1969). Storage and retrieval processes in long term memory. *Psychological Review, 76,* 179–193.

Shoda, Y., Mishel, W., & Peake, P. K. (1990). Predicting adolescent cognitive and self-regulatory competencies from preschool delay of gratification. *Developmental Psychology, 26,* 978–986.

Simonton, D. K. (2000). Creativity: Cognitive, personal, developmental, and social aspects. *American Psychologist, 55,* 151–158.

Sinetar, M. (1989). *Do what you love, the money will follow.* New York, New York: Dell.

Smith, E. E. (2000). Neural bases of human working memory. *Current Directions in Psychological Science, 9,* 45–49.

Smith, R. J., Arnkoff, D. B., & Wright, T. L. (1990). Test anxiety and academic competence: A comparison of alternative models. *Journal of Counseling Psychology, 37,* 313–321

Snyder, C. R. (1994). *The psychology of hope: You can get there from here.* New York: Free Press.

Snyder, C. R., Shorey, H. S., Cheavens, J., Pulvers, K. M., Adams, V. H., & Wiklund, C. (2002). Hope and academic success in college. *Journal of Educational Psychology, 94,* 820–826.

Snyder, C. R., Sympson, S. C., Ybasco, F. C., Borders, T. F., Babyak, M. A., & Higgins, R. L. (1996). Development and validation of the State Hope Scale. *Journal of Personality and Social Psychology, 70,* 321–335.

Spires, H. A., & Donley, J. (1998). Prior knowledge activation: Inducing engagement with informational texts. *Journal of Educational Psychology, 90,* 249–260.

Sperling, G. (1960). The information available in brief visual presentations. *Psychological Monograhs, 74,* 1–29.

Squire, L. R., Knowlton, B., & Musen, G. (1993). The sructure and organization of memory. *Annual Review of Psychology, 44,* 453–495.

Steblay, N. M. (1992). A meta-analytic review of the weapon-focus effect. *Law and Human Behavior, 16,* 413–424.

Steele, C. M. (1997). A threat in the air: How stereotypes shape intellectual identity and performance, *American Psychologist, 52*(6), 613–629.

Steele, C. M. (2003, August). Contingencies of social identity: Their implications for achievement and intergroup relations. Invited address presented at the annual meeting of the American Psychological Association. Toronto.

Steele, C. M., & Aronson, J. (1995). Stereotype threat and the intellectual test performance of African Americans. *Journal of Personality and Social Psychology, 69,* 797–811.

Steinberg, L., Dornbusch, S. M., & Brown, B. B. (1992). Ethnic differences in adolescent achievement: An ecological persepective. *American Psychologist, 47,* 723–729.

Sternberg, R. J. (1988). *The triarchic mind: A new theory of human intelligence.* New York: Viking Press.

Sternberg, R. J. (1996). *Successful intelligence.* New York: Simon & Schuster.

Sternberg, R. J. (1997). The concept of intelligence and its role in lifelong learning and success. *American Psychologist, 52*(10), 1030–1037.

Sternberg, R. J. (1997). *Successful Intelligence: How Practical and Creative Intelligence Determine Success in Life.* New York: Plume, Penguin Books.

Sternberg, R. J. (1998). *In search of the human mind (2nd ed.).* Ft. Worth, TX: Harcourt Brace.

Sternberg, R. J (Ed.). (1999). *Handbook of creativity.* Cambridge, UK: New York: Cambridge University Press.

Sternberg, R. J. (1999). A propulsion model of types of creative contributions. *American Psychologist, 3,* 83–100.

Sternberg, R. J. (2001). What is the common thread of creativity? Its dialectical relation to intelligence and wisdom. *American Psychologist, 56,* 360–362.

Sternberg, R. J., & Grigorenko, E. L. (1997). Are cognitive styles still in style? *American Psychologist, 52*(7), 700–712.

Sternberg, R. J., Wagner, R. K., Williams, W. M., & Horvath, J. A. (1995). Testing common Sense. *American Psychologist, 50,* 912–927.

Stich, F. A. (1995, Feb.). A meta-analysis of physical exercise as a treatment for symptoms of anxiety and depression. *Dissertation Abstracts International. Section B. The Sciences and Engineering. 59*(8–B). pp. 4487.

Stratton, V. N., & Zalanowski, A. H. (1989). The effects of music and paintings on mood. *Journal of Music Therapy, 26,* 30–41.

Strober, M., & McGoldrick, K. M. (1998, Fall). Service learning in economics: A detailed application. *The Journal of Economic Education, 29*(4), 365–376.

Strunk, W. & White, E. B. (1979). *The elements of style* (3rd Ed.) Boston, MA: Allyn and Bacon.

Student Retention and Graduation Rates. (1998, April). Rhode Island College: Providence, RI: Office of Institutional Research.

Symons, C. S., & Johnson, B. T. (1997). The self-reference effect in memory: A meta-analysis. *Psychological Bulletin, 121,* 371–394.

Taylor, D. W., Berry, P. C., & Block, C. H. (1958). Does group participation when using brainstorming facilitate or inhibit creative thinking? *Administrative Science Quarterly, 3,* 23–47.

Taylor, G. J. (2001). Low emotional intelligence and mental illness. In J. Ciarrochi, J. P. Forgas, & J. D. Mayer (Eds.), *Emotional intelligence in everyday life: A scientific inquiry* (pp. 67–81). Philadelphia: Psychology Press.

Taylor, S. E. (1999). *Health Psychology.* Boston: McGraw-Hill.

Taylor, S. E., Pham, L. B., Rivkin, I. D., & Armor, D. A. (1998). Harnessing the imagination: Mental simulation, self-regulation, and coping. *American Psychologist, 53,* 429–439.

Thompson, W. F., Schellenberg, E. G., Husain, G. (2001). Arousal, mood, and the Mozart effect. *Psychological Science, 12,* 248–251.

"Three Providence players are expelled for fighting." (2000, May 18) *The New York Times*, pp. C26 & D7(L).

Timberlake, W., & Farmer-Dougan, V. A. , (1991). Reinforcement in applied settings. Figuring out ahead of time what will work. *Psychological Bulletin, 110,* 379–391.

Toffler, A. (1991). *Future shock.* New York: Bantam Books.

Townsend, M. A. R., Hicks, L., Thompson, J. D. M., Wilton, K. M., Tuck, B. F., & Moore, D. W. (1993). Effects of introductions and conclusions in assessment of student essays. *Journal of Educational Psychology, 85,* 670–678.

Tucker, A., & Bushman, B. J. (1991). Effects of rock and roll music on mathematical, verbal, and reading comprehension performance. *Perceptual and Motor Skills, 72,* 942.

Tulving, (1993). What is episodic memory? *Current Directions in Psychological Science, 2*(3), 67–70.

Turner, M. E., Pratkanis, A. R., Probasco, P., & Leve, C. (1992). Threat, cohesion, and group effectiveness: Testing a social identity maintenance perspective on groupthink. *Journal of Personality and Social Psychology, 63,* 781–796.

Ungerleider, L. G. (1995). Functional brain imaging studies of cortical mechanisms for memory. *Science, 270,* 769–775.

U.S. Census Bureau (2004). Current Population Survey, 2004 Annual Social and Economic Supplement, as reported by the U.S. Census Bureau (2004). Retrieved July 16, 2005, from http://pubdb3.census.gov/macro/032004/perinc/new03_010.htm

U.S. Department of Labor (1991, March). Office of employment and public affairs. The employment situation: February 1991. *Women & work.* Washington, DC: U.S. Government Printing Office.

U.S. Department of Labor (1993, May). Office of employment and public affairs. *The employment situation: February 1991. Women & work.* Washington, DC: U.S. Government Printing Office.

Van Boxtel, M. P. J., Paas, F. G. W. C., Houx, P. J., Adam, J. J., Teeken, J. C., & Jolles, J. (1997). Aerobic capacity and cognitive performance in a cross-sectional aging study. *Medicine & Science in Sports & Exercise, 29,* 1357–1365.

Van Zile-Tamsen, C. & Livingston, J. A. (1999). The differential impact of motivation on the self-regulated strategy use of high-and low-achieving college students. *Journal of College Student Development, 40,* 54–60.

Vermetten, Y. J., Lodewijks, H. G., & Vermunt, J. D. (2001). The role of personality traits and goal orientations in strategy use. *Contemporary Educational Psychology, 26,* 149–170.

von Oech, R. (1983). *A whack on the side of the head: How to unlock your mind for innovation.* New York: Warner Books.

Wade, S. E., & Trathen, W. (1989). Effect of self-selected study methods on learning. *Journal of Educational Psychology, 81,* 40–47.

Wagner, R. K., & Sternberg, R. J. (1985). Practical intelligence in real-world pursuits: The role of tacit knowledge. *Journal of Personality and Social Psychology, 49,* 436–458.

Wainer, H., Saka, T., & Donoghue, J. R. (1993). The validity of the SAT at the University of Hawaii: A riddle wrapped in an enigma. *Educational Evaluation and Policy Analysis, 15,* 91–98.

Wallace, D. L., Hayes, J. H., Hatch, J. A., Miller, W., Moser, G., & Silk, C. M. (1996). Better revision in eight minutes? Prompting first-year college writers to revise globally. *Journal of Educational Psychology, 88,* 682–688.

Waskal, S. A., & Owens, R. (1991). Frequency distribution of trigger events identified by people ages 30 through 60. *College Student Journal, 25*(2), 235–239.

Welsh, D. H., Bernstein, D. J., & Luthans, F. (1992). Application of the Premack principle of reinforcement to the quality performance of service employees. *Journal of Organizational Behavior Management. 13,* 9–32.

Willingham, D. T. (2005). How we learn: Ask the cognitive scientist. Do visual, auditory and kinesthetic learners need visual, auditory, and kinesthetic instruction. *American Educator, 29*(2), 28–35, 44.

Willoughby, T, Wood, E., & Khan, M. (1994). Isolating variables that impact on or detract from the effectiveness of elaboration strategies. *Journal of Educational Psychology, 86,* 279–289.

Wilson, T. L., & Brown, T. L. (1997). Reexamination of the effect of Mozart's music on spatial-task performance. *Journal of Psychology, 131,* 365–370.

Zahm, M. (1996). *Create your ideal life: Applied psychology of personal adjustment and growth.* Dubuque, IA: McGraw-Hill Course Works.

Zahm, M. (1998). Creating a feminist mentoring network. In Collins, L. H., Chrisler, J. C., & Quina, K. (Eds.). *Arming Athena: Career strategies for women in academe* (pp. 239–241). Thousand Oaks, CA: Sage Publications.

Zajonc, R. B. (1965). Social facilitation. *Science, 149,* 269–274.

Zuber, J. A., Crott, H. W., & Werner, J. (1992) Choice shift and group polarization: An analysis of the status of arguments and social decision schemes. *Journal of Personality and Social Psychology, 62,* 50–61.

Zuckerman, M., Kieffer, S. C., & Knee, R. C. (1998). Consequences of self-handicapping: Effects on coping, academic performance, and adjustment. *Journal of Personality and Social Psychology, 74,* 1619–1628.

Zuckerman, M., Ulrich, R. S., & McLaughlin, J. (1993). Sensation seeking and reactions to nature paintings. *Personality and Individual Differences, 15,* 563–57.

Index

Livingston, J. A. 92, 93, 226
Locke, E. A. 30, 31, 166, 218
Lodewijks, H. G. 79, 226
Loftus, E. F. 96, 218
Loftus, G. R. 96, 218
Loftus, J. 104, 218
Logie, R. H. 89, 218
Longman, D. J. 102, 211
Lopez, E. 1, 216
Lorentz, S. C. 16, 219
Lucas, M. S. 195, 219
Luthans, F. 33, 226
Luzzo, D. A. 62, 219
Lynn, R. 1, 219

M

Maas, A. 145, 146, 219
Maddux, J. E. 55, 219
Madeline 7
Mahoney, K. M. 2, 222
Makhijani, M. G. 208, 215
Makin, D. J. 33, 219
Malett, S. D. 32, 217
Malley, J. E. 173, 218
Malloy, T. E. 207, 219
Malone, P. S. 137, 138, 216
Malouff, J. M. 60, 223
Mann, R. D. 207, 219
Manz, C. C. 175, 220
Marchant, H. G. 82, 213
Marcy 83
Marshall, N. L. 195, 212
Martin, G. L. 30, 219
Martinelli, E. A. 62, 219
Martinez-Pons, M. 58, 219
Maton, K. L. 16, 17, 219
Mau, W. C. 1, 219
Mayer, J. D. 58, 219
McCaulley, M. H. 184, 219, 220
McClanaghan, M. E. 69, 219
McCrae, R. R. 51, 219
McCutchen, D. 118, 219
McEntee, D. J. 39, 219
McGoldrick, K. M. 75, 203, 224
McGregor, H. A. 79, 215
McGregor, I. 165, 219
McLaughlin, J. 132, 226
Meece, J. L. 127, 220
Mehrabian, A. 58, 59, 220
Meier, E. 76, 221
Meier, P. 143, 144, 215
Memory
    sensory stores:perceptual data

inpputs 88
short-term store:proactive inter-
    ference 101
short-term store:serial position
    effect, recall 102
Memory,working
    executive control system:main-
        tenance rehearsal 89
    short-term stores:executive con-
        trols attention 89
Memory, long-term
    declarative:episodic 90
    declarative:explicit 90
    declarative:semantic 90
    permanent stores 90
    procedural:actions, skills, opera-
        tions 91
    procedural:implicit 91
Memory, working
    episodic buffer:integration of
        coded data for use 89
    executive control system: atten-
        tion 89
    phonological rehearsal loop:sub-
        vocal articulation rehearsal
        89
    short-term stores:links to sen-
        sory stores, LTM 88
    visuospatial sketchpad:solving
        visuospatial problems 89
    visuospatial sketchpad:visual,
        spatial spatial data 89
Memory Strategies
    knowledge acquisition 104
Memory strategies
    chunking 100, 101
    elaborative information process-
        ing 103
    mnemonic devices:acronyms
        100
    mnemonic devices:acrostics
        100
    mnemonic devices:categorical
        clustering 100
    mnemonic devices:interactive
        images 101
    overlearning 103
    recall 101
    rehearsing 102
    relearning 103
    self-reference effect 100
    spaced, distributed practice 103
Merenda, P. F. 25, 92, 222, 239
Messo, J. 96, 218

Meyer, T. 213
Miller, G. A. 89, 100, 220
Miller, W. 226
Mishel, W. 172, 220, 223
Mistlberger, R. E. 41, 220
Misumi, J. 208, 220
Mitchell, K. E. 195, 220
Mitchell, W. W. 41, 211
Mittelhauser, M. 91, 196, 220
Money management
    budget 42
    cooperative education program
        43
    credit cards 41
    debit card 42
    Financial:Aid Officer 42
    long term goals 44
    scholarships 42
    tuiton 42
    work 44
Monster.com, Inc. 63
Moore, D. W. 225
Moore, P. J. 143, 221
Morgan, C. 189, 220
Morgan, H. J. 55, 220
Moser, G. 226
Moye, M. 141, 221
Moyers, B. 181, 220
Multiple intelligences
    bodily-kinesthetic 68
    interpersonal 68
    intrapersonal 68
    logical-mathematical 68
    musical-rhythmic 68
    naturalist 68
    verbal-linguistic 68
    visual-spatial 68
Muraven, M. 94, 95, 212, 220
Murphy, C. C. 118, 223
Murray, B. 201, 203, 220
Musen, G. 90, 224
Mussen, G. 91
Myers, I. B. 184, 220

N

National Association of Colleges
    and Employers (NACE)
    192
National Center for Education
    Statistics (NCES) 19, 220
Nauta, M. M. 55, 56, 191, 220,
    222, 223
Neck, C. P. 175, 220

About the Authors

Joan H. Rollins, Ph.D. is Professor and Chair of the Psychology Department at Rhode Island College, Providence, Rhode Island. Currently, she is a member of the Rhode Island Board of Examiners for Psychology. Previously, she served as President of the Rhode Island Psychological Association, and President of the New England Psychological Association, and as a member of the Council of Representatives of the American Psychological Association. Dr. Rollins is the author of Women's Mind's/Women's Bodies (Prentice Hall, 1996), a textbook for Psychology of Women classes, and editor of Hidden Minorities (University Press of America, 1981), an interdisciplinary book about several ethnic groups in southern New England.

Mary Zahm, Ph.D. is Professor and former Chair of the Psychology and Sociology Department at Bristol Community College, Fall River, Massachusetts where she has received awards for outstanding teaching. She is also an Adjunct Professor at the University of Rhode Island. Currently, Dr. Zahm is President of the New England Psychological Association. She is the author of *Create Your Ideal Life* (McGraw-Hill Course Works, 1996), a textbook for Psychology of Personal Adjustment classes. She also brings a practical bent to the book based on her 13 years as a Human Factors Engineer for Raytheon Company.

Drs. Rollins and Zahm are currently developing the Academic Self-Regulation scale, with their colleagues Dr. Gary Burkholder and Dr. Peter F. Merenda, which is highly correlated with grade point average and graduation rates of college students. They are available for the presentation of workshops on strategies for college student success.

Printed in the United States
92671LV00006B/11/A